T0244108

My Darling Boys

A Family at War, 1941–1947

Fred H. Allison

Number 23 in the North Texas Military Biography
and Memoir Series

University of North Texas Press
Denton, Texas

10 9 8 7 6 5 4 3 2 1

Permissions:
University of North Texas Press
1155 Union Circle #311336
Denton, TX 76203-5017

The paper used in this book meets the minimum requirements of the
American National Standard for Permanence of Paper for Printed Library
Materials, z39.48.1984. Binding materials have been chosen for durability.

Library of Congress Cataloging-in-Publication Data

Names: Allison, Fred H., 1950- author.
Title: My darling boys : a family at war, 1941-1947 / Fred H. Allison.
Other titles: North Texas military biography and memoir series ; no. 23.
Description: Denton, Texas : University of North Texas Press, [2023] |
    Series: Number 23 in the North Texas military biography and memoir
    series | Text of collective biography incorporates a memoir written by
    Oscar Allison in 1972. | Includes bibliographical references and index.
Identifiers: LCCN 2023038999 (print) | LCCN 2023039000 (ebook) |
    ISBN 9781574419061 (cloth) | ISBN 9781574419184 (ebook)
Subjects: LCSH: Allison, Harold, 1917-1991. | Allison, Oscar, 1919-1982. |
    Grizzle, Wiley, Jr., 1924-1945. | Allison family. | United States.
    Army Air Forces--Airmen--Biography. | Air pilots, Military--United
    States--Biography. | Farmers--Pecos River Valley (N.M. and Tex.)--
    Biography. | War and families--Pecos River Valley (N.M. and Tex.) |
    World War, 1939-1945--Aerial operations, American. | World War,
    1939-1945--Personal narratives, American. | BISAC: HISTORY / Wars &
    Conflicts / World War II / General | HISTORY / Military / Aviation &
    Space | LCGFT: Biographies.
Classification: LCC D790.2 .A45 2023 (print) | LCC D790.2 (ebook) |
    DDC 940.5449730922--dc23/eng/20230909
    LC record available at https://lccn.loc.gov/2023038999
    LC ebook record available at https://lccn.loc.gov/2023039000

My Darling Boys is Number 23 in the North Texas Military Biography
and Memoir Series.

The electronic edition of this book was made possible by the support of
the Vick Family Foundation. Typeset by vPrompt eServices.

Contents

Preface

Three sons of the Wiley Grizzle family went to war. Harold Allison, Oscar Allison, and Wiley Grizzle Jr., or simply Junior. (They have different last names because of the early death of the Allison boys' father, Oscar Allison Sr. Their mother, Ollie, later remarried to Wiley Grizzle.) Harold joined the Army Air Forces (AAF) and became a fully trained copilot on North American B-25 Mitchell bombers. On a physical before deploying to the Pacific war theater, he was found to have a hernia. He was replaced as copilot and his crew went to war without him. He later retrained as a B-17 copilot, but the war ended before he could deploy to combat. He was devastated. His two younger brothers, though, did see war—the good and the bad.

Oscar became a flight engineer and top turret gunner on a Consolidated B-24 Liberator bomber. His crew deployed to Italy and flew in combat with the 716th Bomb Squadron, 449th Bomb Group, Fifteenth Air Force. Wiley Grizzle Jr. became a fighter pilot flying the North American P-51 Mustang aircraft. In combat he was assigned to the Eighth Air Force, 350th Fighter Squadron, 353rd Fighter Group.

In about 1973 my uncle Oscar Allison approached me and asked if I would like to record his memoirs of World War II. I was excited to hear about his war experiences. I grew up in close proximity to Oscar and his family because he partnered with my father, Harold, in farming in West Texas. I was well aware that he was a B-24 crewman in the war and had been shot down and captured. I always wished that he would relate more details. He had previously offered only snippets of information, anecdotes, and quick flashes into his World War II life, so I looked forward to hearing more. We met and he began telling me about joining the army and training. It was very interesting, but we never got together again. I do not know why. Perhaps he did not want to bring up old and dark memories and tell them to his young nephew who would not understand.

I was delighted when at Christmas 1984, Aunt Sammy, Oscar's wife, gave to my wife, Martha, and me Oscar's handwritten memoir about his

World War II experiences. He had written it in 1973. That was the year that his bomber crew, led by pilot Bob Bird, had a reunion in Kansas City. It had been forty years since the crew had come together and deployed to Italy and to war. The reunion probably spurred Oscar to write his story. It was in him, and he considered it significant. I, for one, am grateful. His memoir is central to this story, mainly because it is well written and tells his story beginning to end in an engaging and compelling manner. It is quoted at length and verbatim in appropriate chapters as the book moves chronologically from 1941 to the end of the war, and beyond. Context is applied around Oscar's narrative to help the reader understand the time, place, and events transpiring. Another key primary resource are family letters that span the war years. Fortunately, the three boys' mother, father, and siblings (Gerald, Ollie Mae, Mary, and Jim) retained the war letters and passed them down to the children of the siblings, my cousins. They loaned them to me as I undertook writing this book. For this I am most grateful. There is a large stock of them. Seventy are used as I tell the story of the three sons and the Grizzle family in World War II.

Many of the letters are from Junior to his mother. These are the main source for telling of Junior's war experiences. Junior was an uncle I never knew but whom I had heard a lot about. As noted, he flew a P-51 Mustang fighter and was killed in combat over Germany.

In the mid-1990s I was visiting my parents at their farm home outside of Muleshoe, Texas. One afternoon my mother, Jean, jumped up and said, "Let's go open Junior's trunk." I did not even know there was a "Junior's trunk." In our garage was a big trunk that I had seen for quite some time, but I never knew what it contained. As the lid came open, a musty smell spilled out. Inside were file folders of documents, military insignia, and uniforms. This was material that had been hastily gathered up by an army officer from Junior's living area at his base in England after he did not return from his last flight. Water had damaged the contents, and while the documents were stained and starting to crumble, they were still readable. Many of the documents were his official military records, administrative forms, flight training and combat records, and statistics, and I used them as primary resources for this book. There was also a blue-striped Army Air Corps towel and uniforms that were in a serious state of decay. His uniform patches were in good shape, and these, along with the metal insignias and badges, which also were in good condition, are now treasured family heirlooms. The contents of this trunk helped to introduce me to Junior. Through the family letters, I became much more acquainted with him.

The letters, besides being the main source of primary information for Junior's story, also introduce other family members and tell us of their life on the home front, which, for the Grizzles, was a farm in eastern New Mexico, near Roswell.[1] Understandably, few Americans today can relate to farm life. However, in the years before and during World War II, the 1930s and 1940s, one-third of all Americans lived on and operated farms. By 1981 this number had fallen to only three percent, and today it is even less.[2] World War II strongly stimulated the trend toward urbanization in American society. Events on the Grizzle farm bore witness to this dramatic change.

A note on the letters: I use selected passages from the letters, but only those parts that are appropriate for the story. The parts of letters included are as written, verbatim, including punctuation and spelling. The letter writers used a family kind of slang that makes them sound a bit "hickish." Be assured this was just family lingo. They were well-educated, having completed high school and some college.

Additionally, the reader needs to understand that the sons in the army were careful when writing the letters to protect the readers, especially their mother and their younger siblings. They sanitized the letters and left out anything that might cause the readers to take alarm or worry any more than they already did. That is why I have made comments to give context and further illumination to the time and place, because there was so much unsaid that the boys were experiencing. Also, recall that in most instances there was a considerable time gap between mailing the letter and receiving it, so the dates on the letters often do not correspond to the date on which the letter was read. This is especially the case with Oscar when he was in the Stalags. In his case there could be months between when the letter was written and when the recipient read it.

Reading the memoir and the letters drew me back to World War II. They personalized the war and the influences that shaped society in those days. I also became much more familiar with my uncles and aunts. Most apparent in the letters are the powerful emotional bonds of the family— the love, care, and concern they had for one another, and especially for the boys who were in harm's way. Mother Ollie is a central figure. All three sons had an amazingly close relationship with her. Her compassionate and loving presence expressed in the letters was a lifeline to the boys as they dealt with life-and-death issues on a daily basis. She often refers to her sons as "darling," from which comes this book's title. Finally, one comes to realize the emotional turmoil, torment, and trauma that families suffered and still suffer as loved ones go into a combat zone.

These three boys were not war heroes; there were no Medals of Honor among them. Their story is the story of thousands of other "average" Americans who fought in World War II. Sometimes it was not pretty; war is vicious, cruel, and at times incredibly terrifying. Nevertheless, they manned their aircraft and fought honorably and bravely. Like others at war, they suffered and sacrificed, some even to the last full measure. World War II was a dramatically important time for the nation, and it was that also for the Grizzle family of New Mexico. But for them, like thousands of other families, the consequences of war were the darkest of times.

Acknowledgments

I t is a daunting task to try to recognize everyone who has helped on this work. First and foremost are family members who were so kind as to dig through old photographs, folders, and files to find letters and other documents. Oscar's sons, Sam and Mack Allison, besides being great encouragers also provided essential documents and photos regarding their father. Mack sent me authoritative books on Oscar's bomb group and helped with commentary about his family. Sam read the manuscript multiple times and made valuable suggestions. Larry Allison, Gerald and Ethel's third son, was super encouraging and helpful. Always responsive, he provided pictures, read and meticulously critiqued drafts, and provided good insight about his family. Cindy Pennington and Jo Johnson, the daughters of the Grizzles' youngest, Jim, were of immense help. Cindy provided a large collection of letters and photographs. She and Jo read and commented on the manuscript, Cindy more than once. Georga Mae Didlake Collins (now deceased), the oldest daughter of Ollie Mae (Grizzle) and George Didlake, provided a large collection of letters, and her younger brother, Tom, provided photographs and commentary. Pat Andreas (the younger son of Mary Grizzle Andreas and her husband, Floyd "Andy"), is guilty of starting the whole thing. He planted the idea of finding out what really happened to Wiley Grizzle Jr. during the war. Pat's older brother, Mike, along with Pat, provided photographs, letters, and commentary on their family. Others who contributed, encouraged, and generally supported me were older sister Veta Skogland and my younger brother, Jim Allison. Jim was especially helpful on agricultural matters. He has remained involved with farming throughout his life. Susan Black, second daughter of Sammy from her first marriage, provided valuable comments and context regarding the early days of Oscar and Sammy's marriage.

Some of the grandchildren of the "Darling Sons" were most helpful. A key player was the family historian (and a professional archivist in his own right) my nephew Austin Allison, son of Harold's youngest, Jim. He provided help with period newspapers, supplied a superb collection of pictures, and was a great reference on family history. My eldest daughter, Olivia, a published author herself, provided wonderful advice and direction for the manuscript, as well as being a powerful encourager, as were my other kids, Daniel, Stuart and Marissa. Christy Allison Wylie, daughter of Robert Allison, Gerald's youngest, was of great assistance by providing letters from Gerald and Ethel's early days. One can see that the book is a family project.

Outside the family, a number of agencies and individuals provided help. Two are foremost. The first is Dr. Graham Cross, senior lecturer at Manchester Municipal University (UK), an authority on the Eighth Air Force, and in particular the 353rd Fighter Group. His books *Jonah's Feet Are Dry* (Thunderbolt, 2002) and *Slybirds* (Fighting High, 2017) are the absolute last authority on the 353rd. Besides being great reading, these are archives in book form. Graham also opened his photo archive of the 353rd to me and read and commented on pertinent parts of the manuscript.

The second, Austrian Christian Arzberger, was uniquely helpful in regards to the experiences of Oscar's B-24 crew after they bailed out and landed in Austria. Christian actually grew up within a few miles of the crash site of Oscar's bomber. From an early age, he has been fascinated with the air war over Austria. His perspectives were invaluable regarding the Austrian view of the air war. He also personally took photos of the region to illustrate where Oscar's bomber crashed and where the crew was captured. Of note, Christian has led an effort in Austria to honor, through commemorative monuments, the Allied airmen who were killed in Austria. He was also most helped in locating Wiley Jr.'s crash site in Germany.

Dr. Forrest L. Marion, Col. USAF (Ret.) and Kara Newcomer of the United States Air Force Historical Research Agency were particularly helpful with official records and official USAF photos. The Historical Society for Southeast New Mexico, and in particular volunteer Heidi Huckabee, assisted with information on Roswell, Hagerman, and farming history. Dr. Colin Colbourne, lead historian with Project Recover, and Annette Amerman, DOD POW/MIA Accounting Agency, were instrumental in tracking down Wiley Jr.'s burial records.

I thank the 449th Bomb Group Association and their historian, Mark Coffee, for their assistance and kind permission for using their photos.

Both the 449th Bomb Group Association and the 353rd Fighter Group have great Facebook sites that are useful not only for connecting with the descendants of veterans of 449th or 353rd but also as a means of research. For instance, I met R. J. Gustke, son of Wiley's best friend, Richard "Gus" Gustke, through the 353rd's Facebook site. They were often together in combat, including on Wiley's last mission. R. J. provided information and a compelling letter about this mission. Katy Carter, another descendant of a 353rd pilot (Gordon B. Compton), voluntarily provided valuable research materials and photographs regarding Wiley Jr. Donna Trapp, daughter of Loyd Lewis, a 449th veteran, was quite helpful in my research and provided the introduction to Christian Arzberger for me.

I could not have done this project without the loving support of my wife of forty-four years, Martha. Her talent as an English grammar expert was essential. She reviewed and corrected each draft—and there were many. She also does genealogical research on the family, which was a big help. She patiently supported and encouraged me throughout while keeping our "home front" in good order, even during our rapid move from Virginia back to the promised land (i.e., Texas) at the height of the COVID-19 pandemic.

I am extremely grateful to the University of North Texas Press. The director, Ronald Chrisman, was extremely professional and patient. His guidance was essential and his encouragement for this project was a great motivator. I thank the staff for their expertise in producing attractive, influential, and relevant books.

I hope that by telling the war story of the Darling Boys, it will honor them and, actually, all World War II veterans who selflessly served their nation. Like so many others, they were not great war heroes. They served, did their duty, and, when it came time to fight, they did so with great courage and lethality, with little regard for their own welfare. Finally, and most importantly, I credit my Lord and Savior Jesus Christ for the opportunity, resources, desire, and will to write this story.

Prologue

Oscar Allison, February 22, 1944, an excerpt from his memoir:

As I fell out the bomb bay door backward, I thought my helmet was going to blow away. I grabbed it with my left hand to hold it on. As I lay there on nothing, it was the softest thing ever, and I had no sensation of falling. A ME-109 passed slowly above me just a few feet away traveling in the direction we'd been going. I clearly saw the pilot's face as he leaned over to his left slightly and seemed to look me right in the eye. He was gone in a split second, but I'll never forget it.

I was still above the overcast and my right hand pulled the D-ring. I was still lying on my back, on that soft bed of nothing, not tumbling. The ring, with about a foot-long piece of small steel cable, came out of the pack and separated completely from the pack. I didn't remember if this was normal or not but since nothing happened, I dropped the ring and hung onto my helmet thinking I'd have to dig the chute out by hand. This was my first experience with a parachute, and I thought when you pulled the old ripcord you got jerked out of your shoes. I started to go into the pack with my right hand (it seemed everything was in slow motion, and the sound of silence was deafening) when out popped the little "pilot" chute, then the main canopy blossomed slowly. I was gently pulled upright and started floating down. Just as Pistol Packin' Mama [B-24] disappeared into the overcast, I saw a chute open. I guessed it was Deane or Jackson, but it could have been someone from the rear section. I hoped everyone could get out in time. I don't know what our altitude was, but I had no trouble breathing.

All the things I'd heard about bailing out didn't happen to me. I never thought I'd have to jump, but after the peaceful feeling of the softness and the quietness of free fall and the gentleness of floating down under that beautiful white nylon canopy that was like a huge, inverted magnolia blossom, I can see how one could easily become addicted to skydiving.

Everything disappeared for a minute as I went through the overcast. Then I could see Mother Earth coming up to meet me. Beautiful rolling hills and mountains covered with some kind of evergreen forest with small clearings here and there, and soon I could distinguish houses widely separated and some of the clearings. The slow-motion effect stopped, and one house started to come up just directly under me.

I landed in the middle of a steep rooftop covered with about six inches of snow, slid down the side, and landed softly in a deep drift of snow beside the house. I couldn't think and still, to this day, I don't know what I was thinking. I guess I wasn't. It's more puzzling to me as I write this than it has ever been. This is the first time I've seriously tried to bring the thing back to mind, and I find it a bit disturbing. I have an odd feeling that I'd rather just go on trying to forget it.

I remember wondering if anyone was in the house. I heard nothing. I hadn't heard a thing since the 109 roared above me just after I bailed out.

My ears were still covered by the earphones built into my helmet, but sounds were very loud in the plane before I jumped. I thought I might be deaf.

Chapter 1

Farming and Families in the Pecos River Valley

To set the stage, the Grizzle-Allison family farms, where the three sons grew up, were situated in eastern New Mexico, near Hagerman, which is about thirty miles south of Roswell, which in the 1940s was a city of about forty thousand people. About one thousand people lived in Hagerman at the time and many more on the farms surrounding the town. Hagerman was named after a prosperous businessman, J. J. Hagerman, who undertook the development of this part of New Mexico. The people who lived there, especially the older citizens, could be considered pioneers. This region was lately settled, beginning in the last decades of the nineteenth century. The Pecos River, which begins in the Santa Fe Mountains of north-central New Mexico, runs south and east through eastern New Mexico into West Texas, where it meets the Rio Grande. Before US citizens, mostly whites, migrated into the Pecos River Valley here, Native Americans of Apache tribes inhabited the region. They were nomadic hunter-gatherers. Although the Apaches continued to fight against Anglo colonization in Arizona into the 1880s, by the 1860s they had been entirely subdued in eastern New Mexico, where Hagerman was situated.

The first whites were ranchers. In the 1860s and 1870s, they drove herds of cattle north to New Mexico frontier army forts, Fort Sumner and

Fort Bascum. The Pecos River Valley was a natural highway that provided grass and water for the cattle. Some herds were driven farther to railheads, shipping points to move cattle by rail to slaughterhouses in cities up north. The famous rancher-pioneer John Chisum ranched nearby with a headquarters about six miles south of Roswell.[1]

Settlement followed the railroads. Farmers seeking cheap or even free land began arriving in the late 1800s as railroads arrived. The Hagerman area sat oasis-like in the midst of a great expanse of desert. J. T. West, an early pioneer, came by train to Hagerman in 1904. He recalled, "The country between Amarillo and Roswell discouraged me to the point that I decided that I would only be in Hagerman one week. After leaving Roswell the scenery began to get better and I was completely overcome by the difference. . . . The closer I got to Hagerman, the better I liked the country. I have never been sorry that I decided to make my home in Hagerman."[2] The fertile and watered Pecos River Valley attracted farmers and ranchers alike. Apple orchards, grain crops, cotton, and alfalfa became the principal commodities produced. The alfalfa grown there was reputedly of the highest quality. The dry climate was also a draw for many who sought a healthy environment to ward off the scourges of tuberculosis and influenza, serious health threats at the time. New immigrants, mostly Europeans, also arrived, many by "immigrant trains."[3]

The Grizzles and Allisons were early settlers. The boys' mother, Ollie (her maiden name was Ingle), was born in 1892. She had come as a teenager with her family to New Mexico in 1907–1908 from Oklahoma. The draw was free land. The government offered it to citizens if they settled on it, remained at least five years, and made improvements.[4] In this austere and waterless area, that was quite a challenge, but free land was a mighty magnet, and they were determined to try.

They made the trip via covered wagon and settled on desert land about fifty miles north of Roswell. With other families they established Ingleville, named after Ollie's father, James. Roswell was the closest town of any size and they traveled there for supplies. It took them two days by wagon to make the trip.[5] Ingleville is a ghost town today. Without water it was impossible to turn the desert into a farm, but when they first arrived, the settlers built a schoolhouse and invited a young man to teach there. His name was Oscar Allison Sr.

Oscar, a native of Eastland County, Texas, about 360 miles east of Roswell, was the sixth of eight children. He had declined farming or the lure of well-paying jobs in business and industry that a rapidly industrializing America offered to young men. He instead set out to teach. He studied education at a new college in San Marcos, Texas: Southwest Texas Normal School (now Texas State University).

The Ingleville school was not his first paid teaching position. He had taught for a year at a country school in Crowell, Texas. We are not sure why, but he moved to New Mexico and taught at Ingleville in the 1907–1908 school year. He married one of his students, Ollie Ingle, in 1909. He was 25 and she was 17. She, being underage, had to obtain permission from her parents to marry. At some point Ollie and Oscar moved to Roswell. They bought an apple orchard and got into the apple-growing business. At this time apples were the main crop for the area. Oscar also began work as a mailman for the US Postal Service, probably because teaching, which paid only about fifty dollars a month, did not provide the income needed to support his growing family. Three sons were born to Ollie and Oscar: Gerald in 1913; Harold in 1917; and Oscar in 1919. It is not clear why they named their third son after his father, but this Oscar, the son, was destined to become a gunner and flight engineer on a B-24, and his memoirs are the main part of this story.

Oscar Sr. developed spinal tuberculosis and died a painful death in 1920. Family lore says this was caused by carrying a heavy mail sack.[6] Ollie was left with the three boys to raise and an apple orchard to maintain and hopefully provide the means to support her family. When she needed a new water well, the young man Wiley Grizzle drilled it for her. A romance developed between the two, and they were married on March 19, 1923. Ollie remarked later that Wiley was a "godsend." He provided for the family and helped raise the three sons.

Wiley was a native of Tennessee and had come to New Mexico with his family in 1900. He was 5 years old. We do not know a lot about his family or boyhood. He served in the navy in World War I aboard a minesweeper. Family lore says that after the war he rode a bicycle from New York to get back to New Mexico. He returned to Roswell, where he met and married Ollie. They raised and marketed apples and might have operated an apple cider mill.[7]

Five years after their marriage, in 1928, Wiley, Ollie, and their now six children moved south to Hagerman. Wiley was hardworking and ambitious. He purchased acres of native grassland northwest of Hagerman and turned it into a farm. He plowed up the grass and planted crops that were watered by a well he drilled himself. The three Allison sons—Gerald, now 15; Harold, 11; and Oscar, 9—were an important labor source for Wiley's farming, live-stock raising, and well drilling. Wiley and his Allison sons always worked. The boys had started doing menial jobs at young ages. As they matured they were given more responsibility and more sophisticated work, such as manag-ing and driving mule or horse teams that pulled farm equipment, irrigating crops, and completing the myriad of other tasks associated with working a farm. When tractors were acquired (we are not sure when this was), the boys drove them too, using them to pull more modern farm implements.

Wiley had discovered there was money to be made in drilling water wells. The Roswell and Hagerman region of eastern New Mexico sits over an underground reservoir of water, the four-thousand-square-mile Artesian-Roswell Basin.[8] The water, while shallow, is also brackish—not so tasty when drunk but fine for irrigating crops. Engine-driven wells brought massive quantities to the surface. They irrigated large fields of cotton, alfalfa (a very thirsty crop), and grain crops. Water, as is said, made the desert bloom, and in blooming it was profitable. Wiley seemed to have a sixth sense for finding underground water. Over his life he bought arid desert land, brought in the water, then sold the land at a nice profit. He died a millionaire. But that was much later. In the prewar years, farming and well drilling was hard and demanding work, and the Grizzles were far from being wealthy.

While Wiley was a hard-driving man, he was not a tyrant. He was a quiet man who rarely engaged in small talk. He was also a good neighbor. Before Hagerman had school buses, he drove his own children and neighbor kids to school and back. He also drilled water wells for needy neighbors at no charge.[9]

At the time of the move to Hagerman, the Grizzle family had expanded. A fourth son, Wiley Grizzle Jr., was born in 1924. This was

"Junior," and he would become a fighter pilot and go fight in Europe during World War II flying a P-51 Mustang. The Grizzles finally had a daughter, Ollie Mae, born in 1926, followed by another daughter, Mary, in 1928. Another son, Jim, arrived in 1929. Two years later, at the age of 39, Ollie had twin daughters. Named Edith and Elizabeth, they both died within days of their birth. Ollie was brokenhearted and bore no more children after this tragedy.

While Wiley might have been the hardest working man around, Ollie had to be the hardest working woman. She managed a household and seven children during the 1920s and 1930s. It was hard work with a family of nine to cook, clean, wash, and sew for. Their home was, at first, a small frame structure, but Wiley and the boys, on two occasions, built additions to accommodate the growing family and at some point installed indoor plumbing—a rarity for farm homes in those days. Cooking was done from scratch on a woodburning stove. The stove also heated the house in cold weather. Clothes washing was done manually with a wringer washing machine and hung dry on a clothesline. Ollie made biscuits from scratch daily. They were the "best ever," her kids raved about them. But once the kids were out of the house, she never made them again. She could not stand the thought of it. Gardening was a lifelong passion. Her carrots took top prize at the 1938 Hagerman fair. Her 9-year-old son, Jim's, took second place. Her flower gardens were magnificent.

She was thin and petite, efficient and work driven, and pretty, with long braided hair. She raised her children to respect and love one another. Their well-being was paramount. No sacrifice was too great to make on their behalf.

In 1928, at the time of the move to Hagerman and while establishing the new farm, trouble brewed in the family. Oldest son Gerald, now 15 years old, developed a respiratory illness that inhibited his ability to work. Without really understanding what was wrong with Gerald, Wiley assumed he was lazy and just avoiding work. This ignited a conflict between the two. Tension might have already been building between them. After all, Gerald had been the man of the house previously. He felt a strong sense of responsibility for his younger siblings and might have resented Wiley taking over.

The issue came to a head when Wiley laid down the law: if you don't work, you don't eat. At this impasse no doubt Ollie intervened with a solution. Gerald would go live with Allison relatives, at his biological father's family home in Carbon, Texas, a small farm community near Eastland, Texas. Annie and Ed Allison, his natural father's younger sister and brother, lived on and worked the family farm there. Ollie had remained close to Annie and Ed after husband Oscar's death and for years afterward. She corresponded regularly by letter with them.[10]

The Allisons' loving care restored Gerald's health. Part of the treatment was to have Gerald sit shirtless on their porch soaking up sunlight. Gerald was healed, almost. As it turned out, he had tuberculosis. Later it was discovered that he had lost the use of one lung, and by the time he reached middle age, this one lung had entirely withered away. This, of course, impaired his stamina for the remainder of his life. The bad feelings incurred by this falling-out remained, however. As a teenager and into early adulthood, he was largely on his own. He had to grow up fast and did not return to the family farm until World War II.[11] That story will be told later.

When the family moved to the Hagerman farm in 1928, Harold, 11 years old, and Oscar, 9, were in their late boyhood years and moving into their teens. Wiley was trying to gain a foothold and get the farm and family secure, not easy in the hard years of the Depression. Work was the lifeline.

Harold and Oscar worked alongside Wiley farming and drilling wells. Work was done every day—before school and after, during holidays and summer vacation, even on Sundays. Weather was no deterrent if wells were to be drilled. A neighbor girl, Jean McKinstry (this family we will hear much more about), a schoolmate and friend of the Allison boys, recalled riding to church one frigid winter day. She saw Wiley, Harold, and Oscar out operating a drilling rig. She felt sorry for the teenage boys laboring in the freezing cold. Only one day was a holiday for the Grizzle family: the Fourth of July. That day was usually spent in Ruidoso, New Mexico, where they enjoyed the cool and refreshing mountain air.

The boys did not complain, resent, or resist Wiley. They willingly and heartily worked. Maybe it was the hard times of the Depression that impressed upon them the need to work. It was survival. Plenty of farmers had lost everything. One could see farm families on the roads, their Model Ts loaded up. They were heading out to find work somewhere else. It boosted the boys' self-worth to be an integral and important part of the family's success, and they developed a strong work ethic. The boys also acquired mechanical skills that would serve them well in later life. Wiley was incredibly resourceful and innovative. He built his first well-drilling rig himself.[12] This spirit of make-do and mechanical ingenuity rubbed off on the boys. Oscar especially had a fascination for and understanding of mechanics. This was exactly what was required when he became a B-24 engineer.

Jean McKinstry's family were nearby neighbors of the Grizzle family. Sam and Loveta McKinstry had three beautiful daughters: Sammy, born in 1920; Jean, in 1922; and Mildred, in 1927. They are an important part of the story, as we will see, because two of them would marry Allison boys. Sammy, between Harold and Oscar in age, was especially close with them. Sammy, Oscar, and Harold, along with other neighbor kids and cousins, were a "gang" and ran together. From the earliest school days they rode the bus together, were in class together, and played together. Loveta McKinstry did not like it that the Allison boys often arrived late to pick up Sammy. The girls' father, Sam, knew they were good boys and were late only because they had been working. He overrode Loveta and let Sammy go out with them.

Jean was too young to join with Sammy's bunch. Jean became much closer socially with Junior, who was around the same age. Indeed, they became sort of boyfriend and girlfriend during junior high and early high school. Jean recalled the first meeting with Junior in the fourth grade: "Junior Grizzle was in my class and was very smart [Junior was a year ahead in school, having started four months before his sixth birthday]. I liked him the first time I saw him. He had thick unruly, almost red hair, and big feet."[13] While they were considered boyfriend/girlfriend, Jean was prone to flirt with other boys, which kept him upset.[14] The youngest McKinstry daughter, Mildred, and Mary Grizzle were the same age in school and were friends.

Whereas the Grizzles, like so many farm families, were working hard to pull themselves up and clear the economic slog of the Depression, the McKinstrys had money and position. Sam McKinstry was part of the large McKinstry family that had settled in the area, one of ten children.

Sam's parents, James and Sarah, were natives of Northern Ireland and had migrated to the United States in 1888. They settled initially in Illinois, but the health of daughter Adeline, who had contracted tuberculosis, brought on the move to New Mexico. They bought a good-sized tract of land northwest of Hagerman from J. J. Hagerman in 1905 and began farming.

The McKinstrys were big people. Three of their sons were over six feet and the others approached it.[15] The sons who remained in Hagerman served on community boards, and Sam was a longtime member of the school board, most of this time as its president.

The McKinstrys did not work on Sundays but dutifully went to the Presbyterian Church in Hagerman. The Grizzles also attended the Presbyterian Church, but not on a regular basis. Work came first. When weather prevented working, Harold drove his younger siblings to church.[16] The McKinstry house was nicer, and Sam's farm did well. He was a sharp cowman, too. Actually, he preferred stock raising to farming. He held off switching from animal power to tractors; he preferred doing his plowing and planting with horses and mules.[17] But during the Depression he fell on hard times. One especially hard year, the bank refused to loan Sam the money to continue to operate his farm, so he found work in a local butcher shop, dressing beef for the market. He got free groceries for the family, which included the less desirable parts of cattle. His family was nourished on cow hearts, brains, livers, and other delicacies during those years, and he was able to keep his farm.[18]

In 1938 Wiley bought a farm near East Grand Plains, New Mexico, twenty miles north of Hagerman and only about ten miles southeast of Roswell. The family moved and, with his sons, he built a three-bedroom house on the farm. It was modern with indoor plumbing. The move to East Grand Plains ended Junior and Jean's relationship. Junior was 14 and Jean 15. Junior wrote Jean a letter apologizing for being jealous of her "looking around." He acknowledged that they were too young to get serious.[19]

By 1935 the oldest son, Gerald, returned to the Roswell area. He was tall, slender, and handsome, shy and introspective. Having missed out on a lot of normal teen activities, he seemed to lack direction until he met his future wife, the dark-haired, dark-eyed beauty Ethel Lenore Wells of Roswell. Deeply in love, Gerald was determined to stay and marry Ethel. He sought work in the oil boomtown of Hobbs, New Mexico, which lay 115 miles southeast of Roswell. Oil had been discovered there in 1928. It turned the tiny little desert town, windblown and desolate, into a thriving but rough and rowdy boomtown.[20]

The country was in the depth of the Depression, and Gerald discovered that, even in a boomtown, work was hard to find. He daily went out and made the rounds of companies servicing the oilfields, seeking work, any kind of work. Sometimes he found a temporary job, usually paying less than a dollar an hour, sometimes only forty cents. Whatever it paid, he took it. Often, however, he heard, "No, nothing today." At one point he was down to sleeping in his car on frigid winter nights. Such situations were not unusual at that time. The Depression spread misery comprehensively throughout society.

Like his younger brothers, farming was in his blood and in his future. He sought to gain a foothold and return to farming. He tried working again with Wiley farming, but this did not last. There were still hard feelings.

He landed a good job in 1936 working on a ranch near Hope, New Mexico. Hope was about seventy miles southwest of Roswell. Actually, Ethel had previously gone to work there as a live-in cook for the ranch family. The family offered Gerald a good-paying job as a ranch hand. Now, with a good income assured, he married Ethel. The next year they had their first child, Jimmy. Gerald later found steady and good-paying work in Hobbs. They settled there until a farming partnership was formed with Harold and Oscar.[21]

Harold and Oscar would hardly be recognized as brothers—Harold had a ruddy complexion and light brown hair, whereas Oscar was dark complected with jet-black hair—but as teenagers and young men, they were inseparable. They were both short and wiry thin, Harold about five feet, eight inches tall, and Oscar slightly shorter. Years of hard work made them muscular.

Harold was probably the most socially inclined of the boys. He never met a stranger. He was athletic and played basketball for the Hagerman high school team. He was also a bit of a daredevil. One memorable antic was him doing handstands on the balcony rail that overlooked the lower floor in the school auditorium.

Wiley Jr., like Harold, was a good basketball player. The Grizzle kids were bigger than the Allisons. Junior was five feet, nine inches in height. He was light complected with sandy-brown hair and was outgoing, friendly, and enjoyed a risk. On a date with Jean McKinstry, he discovered that the wheels of the car in which they rode would fit perfectly on the inside of railroad tracks, above the ties. So they drove merrily along the railroad. That Jean was petrified made it all the more enjoyable for Junior. He and Jean graduated in 1941, albeit from different high schools. Jean's older sister, Sammy, had already graduated and was attending college. After graduation Junior began college at New Mexico A&M. The Grizzle girls—Ollie Mae, 15, and Mary, 13—were growing into cute and happy teens. They were good students, consistently making the school honor roll. They worked at home helping Mother Ollie manage the home.[22]

Both Harold and Oscar graduated from Hagerman High School before the move to East Grand Plains. Harold began college at New Mexico Agricultural and Mechanical College (now New Mexico State University) in Las Cruces after graduation in 1935. He later transferred to the University of New Mexico. He studied mechanical engineering but never graduated.

Oscar was more intellectual. He had done extremely well in school and graduated in 1936—one of nine hundred New Mexico seniors recognized by the state for scholarly achievement. During high school he had also acted in school plays and, along with Harold, had participated in competitive agricultural events. He was an excellent writer, articulate and expressive (perhaps one will agree with this when reading his memoirs below). After graduation he explored the country and worked at odd jobs, one of which was operating a motion picture projector. He spent some time with relatives in Carbon, Texas. He also worked in the oil field near Hobbs, New Mexico. But by 1940 he was back home and entered into a farming venture with older brother Harold. The war in Europe was a year old. Many Americans hoped to steer clear of that gathering storm while the United States, led by President Franklin Roosevelt, geared for the worst.

It is not clear why Harold and Oscar decided to start farming on their own except the natural inclination of young men to be independent.

Farming was what they knew, so it was almost a foregone conclusion that they would be farmers. It is a bit ironic, however, that they would want to farm. The previous decade, the 1930s, had been a travail for farmers in the Great Plains (of which eastern New Mexico is considered a part). The vicious economic downturn of the Depression had settled over the land and, indeed, the world. Farm commodity prices were low. Farmers had no money, and many had lost their farms. It was a decade of drought. Despite the availability of underground water in the Hagerman area, relatively few farmers had yet tapped it. This led to the Dust Bowl and black blizzards, or "dusters," that periodically swept over parts of the Great Plains, including eastern New Mexico.[23] With the severe difficulties farmers faced, it is a wonder that Harold and Oscar would voluntarily stake their future on farming.

Their timing was good, though. With war beginning the year before in Europe, farmers anticipated an increased demand for textiles and food from Allied nations, which equated to higher prices for farm commodities. But farmers were also wary that if they produced too much and the war ended too soon, as fortuitous as that might be, there could be a collapse in agricultural prices. A farm depression might follow such as had occurred after World War I twenty years before. By mid-1941 farm income was already escalating upward, with a 25 percent increase in purchasing power.[24] It continued to increase during the war years.

Farms were modernizing at the time. Mechanization made for greater efficiency and higher production with less need for laborers. Before the 1920s tractors were available but were a rarity because they were too heavy, too slow, and too costly. Instead, farmers used horses and mules to pull farm implements.[25]

In the 1930s things really changed. Tractors became modernized and affordable to the average farmer. They were much better also. Important inventions that went into making the modern tractor included diesel engines and a "power take-off." This transferred tractor engine power to the pulled implement so that a separate engine was not required to operate an implement such as a hay baler or threshing machine. Hydraulic-driven power lifts allowed a farmer to simply pull a lever and the implement being pulled could be raised or lowered. This was much easier than stopping at the end of a row, getting off the tractor, and manually raising the plow before turning into the next row. Low-pressure rubber tires kept tractors from sinking into soft soil or mud and thus did not leave deep tracks in the field.

Finally, mass production had lowered the price of tractors to a level that the average farmer could now afford to buy one. Naturally, Ford led the way here when, in 1917, Ford Motor Company began mass producing tractors. Called Fordsons, they were small, lightweight, and inexpensive, only four hundred to seven hundred dollars per tractor. Ford dominated the market until the mid-1920s. International Harvester, Ford's chief competitor, matched Ford's low price. Most importantly, in 1928, Ford shut down its tractor assembly lines to make way for Model A automobile production. With this opening, International Harvester took over the market with its tractors, called Farmalls. They introduced the letter series of tractors by 1939. It is likely that the tractor Harold and Oscar obtained to start off farming was one of the lettered Farmalls, a B, H, or M. They possessed all these models on their farm through the 1950s. By 1938 tractor technology had reached "dominant design." Tractors remained basically the same for the next thirty years.[26] By 1940, when Harold and Oscar began farming, a Farmall cost about $1,000.[27]

Wiley had probably started using tractors early on. He was a forward thinker and bent on efficiency. But even as Wiley might have obtained tractors, there was probably a need for draft animals for niche type work. Youngest son Jim, born in 1929, was tasked as a child with tending the farm animals, including draft horses and mules. He had to hook them to a plow or some type of implement to work in the fields all day long in all weather, driving the animals up and down long rows of cotton or grain. This indicates that he was doing serious farmwork at a very young age, which would certainly have been the case for his older brothers, too. Jim so disliked working with horses and mules while a youngster that he refused to own them when he had a farm and family. His children begged for a pony, but he would not relent.[28]

Once war commenced for the United States, tractors and farm equipment became virtually unobtainable as manufacturers shifted to war production (tanks, airplanes, jeeps, etc.). Harold and Oscar, therefore, were fortunate to start farming before the war when land was cheaper and agricultural equipment was readily available. The outbreak of war however, changed the boys' plans in regards to farming and just about everything else. Involvement with the military became a very real possibility. Oscar, Harold and Junior were fascinated by aviation, and it is apparent that they welcomed, indeed sought, a chance to fly in the military, as we will see.

Chapter 2

Aviation, a Budding Interest, and Oscar into the Army Air Corps: 1940–1942

While farming was in their blood, it was not hard for Harold, Oscar, and later Junior to get interested in aviation. Barnstormers[1] had visited Roswell, and the boys watched them fly and perform aerobatics. Then there was the thrilling flight of Charles Lindbergh across the Atlantic in 1927; Harold and Oscar were 12 and 10 years old, respectively. Lindbergh and Eddie Rickenbacker, the most prominent of World War I American aviators, captured the attention of Depression-era boys. Airmen broke flight records. The introduction of airlines and advances in military aviation made the 1920s and 1930s the Golden Age of Aviation. Roswell itself had an aviation/space pioneer, Robert Goddard. He was a local celebrity, famous for his research and experiments in rocketry.

With a strong desire to fly, Oscar's and Harold's first step toward accomplishing that dream was enrolling in the Civilian Pilot Training Program (CPTP), which was started in 1938, three years before the United States entered the war. Its purpose was to train civilians to become pilots and have ready a pool that could move quickly into military flight training. Over 435,000 were trained from 1938 to 1944, and all were required to go into the military. The forward-thinking CPTP also allowed flight instruction for African Americans and women; to wit, one of Oscar's classmates was female. It was evident that US leaders anticipated the important role aviation would play in any future conflict.[2]

Oscar's memoir starts with background on his personal situation: a young man looking to make a start in life with nothing but memories of the hard times of the Depression as a frame of reference. Now war was threatening—a worrisome specter indeed. How was one ever to get ahead in life when things seemed so bleak and unpromising? One thing he could rely on was his family. His mother and stepfather and his siblings (Gerald, Harold, Wiley Jr., Ollie Mae, Mary, and Jim) were a stabilizing force. They were close, loving, and supportive.

Oscar's memoir begins:

> In 1940, World War II was just bad news to me. I, like most other Americans, had no thought of becoming personally involved. A few adventurous, brave flyers took an active part flying for the RAF [Royal Air Force], as some had taken sides in China by flying against the Japanese with General [Claire L.] Chennault's Flying Tigers.[3] But it really wasn't my problem. The things happening in Europe were very bad, of course, but I had problems of my own. Prosperity hadn't been achieved through FDR's [President Franklin Delano Roosevelt] "New Deal," and I had the military draft hanging over my 1-A head.[4] Already draftees were promising they'd go "over the hill in October," or OHIO, when their year of service was finished.

Oscar is referring to opposition to an extension of drafted service that arose after the first peacetime draft in the United States had been implemented by the Burke-Wadsworth Act of 1940. Initially this law called for draftees to serve only a year, but in 1941 President Roosevelt asked Congress to extend the term of service beyond a year, which Congress did. Soldiers who had come in under the one-year agreement threatened to desert after their year of service, which had begun in October 1940, was completed, thus OHIO—"over the hill in October." In some instances, *OHIO* was painted on the draftees' barracks walls.[5]

> We were sympathetic toward France, Britain, and the other countries being taken over by Hitler, the "Mad Dictator" of Germany, and shocked by the atrocities committed in Poland by both Adolph Hitler

and Josef Stalin of Russia.[6] We had practically forgotten [Benito] Mussolini's having taken over Ethiopia by force in Africa. Nothing was really happening to us.

I was busy trying to live and acquire a few material things. I was 21 years old, four years out of high school, and had found nothing profitable in the outside world. Like the prodigal son, I had come back home and had worked two years toward setting up a farming partnership with my brother just older than I [Harold]. We had just gone into business in 1940 starting actual operations about February 15 [1941] on 180 acres of irrigated land in the Pecos Valley of New Mexico. At that time, one could get started with much less money than now. In fact, the down payment on land, a nearly new International Harvester tractor, plow, and other necessary equipment was only about $4,000.

In the summer of 1940, we [Harold and Oscar] had read about a program called Civil Pilot Training and we both made immediate application for this program at Roswell, New Mexico. We were both accepted for the program and started about twenty weeks of classroom study. We learned the history of aviation, theory of flight, meteorology, navigation, aircraft engines and [airframe] structures, and other topics about flying. About 40 were in the class and we were greatly honored by getting lectures and various demonstrations on the action of gyroscopes in relation to their use in aircraft engines by Dr. Robert Goddard, the father of rocketry, who was at that time conducting experiments near Roswell without government aid or grants. Several times Colonel Charles A. Lindbergh flew into Roswell to consult with him, usually in the latest, fastest fighter of the Army Air Corps. I never met Colonel Lindbergh, but both of them I admired very much, and they were both great men of science. They were misunderstood by many. Some high government officials were suspicious of Lindbergh's politics, and many thought that Dr. Goddard was just a "crazy old man." Time has proven that they were at least ten years ahead of others in the rocket field, and Colonel Lindbergh's war record, though not much publicized, showed him to be a loyal American flyer of great skill and courage. He flew more than his share of combat missions in World War II. In my opinion these two men, without much financial or physical aid, could have put an American satellite into orbit before December 7, 1941.

Dr. Robert H. Goddard (1882–1945) is now recognized as the pioneer of rocket research that underlies the technology required for space flight. This earned him the title Father of Modern Rocketry.[7] Through his research and experimentation, he pioneered the use of liquid fuel for rockets.[8] Although he was a PhD physicist, he was considered by many at the time as foolish and delusional. Most famously, the *New York Times* wrote a scathing attack on Goddard's work in 1920. The Times retracted and apologized for this writing in 1969 on the occasion of Apollo 11's moon flight.[9]

In 1930 Goddard had moved to Roswell, New Mexico, to work and experiment in seclusion; it was also a good climate for both work and health. He had suffered a serious bout with tuberculosis earlier in life.[10] Oscar mentioned that they were honored to have Goddard speak to his CPTP class about gyroscopes despite Goddard being the subject of negative publicity. In the Roswell area, though, he was a celebrity and well regarded. Gyroscopes were a big part of Goddard's rocket research as a means to ballistically steer rockets. Germany was especially interested in Goddard's gyroscopic research, and German scientists later used his research and experiments as they developed their V-2 rockets, which terrorized England during the war, flying unmanned and loaded with explosives to hit targets in England.[11] Goddard was finally recognized and honored for his work when, in 1959, a major space laboratory in Greenbelt, Maryland, was named the Goddard Space Flight Center.[12]

Goddard, despite the negative publicity, was admired and respected by the famous aviator Charles A. Lindbergh, who had gained heroic status in the country and indeed worldwide upon his successful nonstop flight across the Atlantic in 1927. Lindbergh, who was impressed with Goddard's work and saw its value, consulted Goddard on several occasions about aeronautical technology. Goddard obtained grants starting in 1930 from the Guggenheim Foundation for the promotion of aeronautics. These grants financed Goddard's move to Roswell and his work there.[13] Goddard had also obtained funding from the Smithsonian Institute, so Oscar's statement that he received no government assistance is only partially true. By coming from the Smithsonian, government assistance came in a roundabout manner.[14]

Charles Lindbergh was promoted from captain to colonel in the Army Air Service Reserve by President Calvin Coolidge after his successful Atlantic-crossing flight. Lindbergh fell from political favor after visiting Germany in the 1930s to learn about the German air force, the Luftwaffe.

He wrote about the Luftwaffe in an admiring tone and then, as war became ever more likely, advocated staying out of the war, thus promoting isolationism. He also had anti-Semitic views and opposed aid to the British. He was widely perceived as being sympathetic to Naziism. He was publicly rebuked by President Franklin D. Roosevelt for his positions, and in response Lindbergh, in April 1941, resigned his army commission. Once the United States was officially at war, Lindbergh tried to be reinstated in the army, but President Roosevelt would not allow it. Lindbergh nevertheless supported the war effort by working as an aircraft consultant for United Aircraft. In this assignment he toured combat aviation units in the Pacific, both army and marine, to investigate ways to enhance aircraft performance, specifically for P-38s and F4Us. In so doing he flew a number of combat missions, reportedly fifty, and even obtained an aerial kill of a Japanese aircraft.[15]

Oscar continues describing his time in CPTP:

I completed the classroom and paperwork. This was all done at night after working hours, although I did a lot of studying while running irrigation water on the family farm.[16] I was one of five students with a score high enough in the final examination to qualify for the actual flight training. Four men and one girl were in this group.

We started flight training in about October 1940 in a two-place, side-by-side Porterfield high-winged monoplane powered with a five-cylinder fifty horsepower radial air-cooled engine. This plane belonged to a local rancher and was used only until our instructor, Cal Barnett, a World War I flyer about 40 years old, could get his own plane. He bought a new Piper Cub J-3 tandem trainer powered with a four-cylinder opposed, air-cooled engine of fifty horsepower. This cute little yellow creature was also a high-wing monoplane weighing 590 pounds dry and unloaded. It was horribly expensive. Cal said it cost more than $1,000 delivered to Roswell.

Cal proceeded to show us how to put into practice the things we had learned in theory. We were to solo in eight hours or less, or out we went. Washed out! This plus thirty-five hours more of dual and solo would qualify us to take the written and flight test to become a private pilot licensed by the Civil Aeronautics Authority.

I was not a natural flyer, but I liked it and was determined not to fail. I worked hard at it. My brothers and my dad were very cooperative, and I could always get time off to go fly, which I did about two hours at a time, twice a week. Finally, all five of us passed all the tests, got our wings which I still have and of which I am still proud. My certificate making me a private pilot has long since expired, and I have no idea where the original might be. I never knew how many pilots were licensed under this program, but we five are all of which I ever heard.

Harold and I had started our farming operation in February 1941. We were both unmarried and classified 1-A. The draft board was breathing down our necks. I had passed quite a thorough examination and physical, to qualify for civil pilot training so I had no doubt that I could qualify for aviation cadet training in the Army Air Corps.

The local draft board called me in, and the head man told me that in his opinion either one of us would have to go into military service. Well, I took the bull by the horns and without consulting anyone, I joined the Army Air Corps and applied for appointment to the aviation cadets.

Oscar enlisted on June 29, 1941—the peacetime army, supposedly. Harold was left to manage their farm on his own, although Wiley and Wiley Jr., and actually even young Jim, now 12 years old, were close by to help. The family was pleased to see this new direction for Oscar. The military, however, was an entirely new proposition. It was an unknown, an altogether different undertaking. They warily watched the world situation. In 1941 war had engulfed all of Europe. The United States seemed to be dancing around the flames, and the likelihood of involvement was a forbidding possibility.

The Battle of Britain had been fought and won by the British the year before, 1940. Britain was the only country in Europe that Hitler had not conquered. Belgium, the Netherlands, France, Denmark, Norway, Luxembourg, and Romania had all fallen in 1940. Germany, Italy, and Japan had signed a joint military and economic agreement. In Asia Japan had invaded China and moved steadily toward subduing that large nation. The world situation was ominous indeed.

Popular opinion in the United States opposed getting involved and favored isolationism. Despite this, President Roosevelt led the nation toward preparing for war. Airpower had obtained a favorable position as a key factor for national defense. While all the services were ramping up for war, the growth of the US Army Air Corps (soon to be renamed the Army Air Forces, or AAF) was especially dramatic. The air corps had grown from 2,546 aircraft and 20,196 service personnel in 1938–1939 to a whopping 72,726 aircraft and 2,372,292 people at its wartime peak in 1944. Its proportionate size grew from 11 percent of the total army strength to 31 percent.[17] Oscar, Harold, and Junior were a part of this massive mobilization.

The air corps's growth was not just about building planes and adding troops. Military aviation was a new endeavor, barely forty years old, whereas the traditional military, the army and navy, had decades, indeed centuries, of tradition and experience on which to draw. Aviation technology, weaponry, and aerial tactics had to be considered, absorbed, and taught. Only recently, in World War I, had men begun to fight in the air; now, with rapidly advancing technology, they fought in the air but at much higher altitudes and faster speeds, in extremes of cold, obscured visibility, raging storms, and wind. Training to fly, fight, and maintain the new high-speed and sophisticated aircraft had to be done on a massive scale. Having only 17 air bases in 1939, the AAF grew to 783 bases by 1945.[18] The growth and development of a premier aviation fighting force during World War II is one of the greatest achievements of the American military.

Having joined well before the onset of war, Oscar was in the leading wave of this massive buildup. The air corps was thoroughly swamped with recruits in 1941 as the nation geared for war. The AAF was just not ready to train such a surge of manpower. Oscar and his fellow recruits probably lived in tents because Jefferson Barracks, an old army fort, had just recently been pressed into service as a basic training center. There were shortages of training staff, equipment, and facilities.[19] The basic training centers "for thousands of recruits . . . were primarily reception centers where they were processed, given only the most superficial kind of training, and then shipped off to technical schools."[20] As a result, the men of the AAF were truly "citizen-soldiers."

After basic training Oscar went to technical training at Chanute Field near Rantoul, Illinois. Aircraft of various types were based at Chanute. This appealed to Oscar's essential interest in machines and mechanics. Others were not so impressed with Chanute. Air force historians had this to say about Chanute: "Chanute [was] overcrowded and run-down because of the long indecision on its fate, and was a post which personnel avoided when they could. 'Don't shoot 'em, Chanute 'em,' had become a popularly conceived punishment in the air corps."[21]

From Chanute Oscar was ordered to Shaw Army Airfield in South Carolina. There he worked as an aircraft mechanic on an assortment of aircraft. He was also given responsibility for training raw recruits. The flood of new recruits had overwhelmed AAF basic training centers, which resulted in recruits beginning their military service at operational commands. Oscar's lax attitude about giving recent inductees basic military training is understandable. He probably was not comfortable with it because he had gotten very little military training himself at Jefferson Barracks. His focus was on aircraft and mechanics. He considered this the priority for himself and the men he trained. This matched the AAF's top priority: keeping aircraft flying. There was little likelihood its enlisted mechanics would be required to engage in infantry combat. But at Shaw Oscar began doing what he had come into the AAF for: flying!

Oscar continues:

I enlisted and was very disappointed when I failed the physical exam with a minor defect in my right ear. At that time, they were very particular. I then applied for aircraft mechanics training and was accepted with no complications. I had to go to Jefferson Barracks, Missouri for six weeks of basic training, then I was transferred to Chanute Field, Illinois. After weeks of both theoretical and practical training, eight hours a day, six days a week, I graduated with the classification of Aircraft and Engine Mechanic.

For the first three months I was paid $21 a month. After three months we were so rich that a friend and I pooled our money and bought a 1931 Model A Ford two-door sedan. On Sundays, we'd take short trips around that part of Illinois which is in the very good corn producing part of the United States. I couldn't believe that such corn could be grown without irrigation.

Army life in peacetime 1941 wasn't all bad. A dollar would buy a dollar's worth, and I was able to occasionally rent a J-3 Piper Cub to keep my logbook and license in order. Some of my friends were brave enough to ride with me. It was expensive, though, about $5 per hour, so I didn't do too much flying.

Chanute Field was a fascinating place. In the hangars there were aircraft of which I'd never heard. Some of the experimental planes were one of a kind, and many models and types of operational aircraft existed in numbers of ten or less. There was one XP37 and two YFM1s, two or three PB2As, etc. I think every plane ever used by the Army was there, from the tiny Boeing P-26s to their latest Boeing B-17s, with all shapes and sizes in between. I wonder if they are still there.

The Army Air Corps had been created in 1907 with three men. Their equipment was not specified, but it couldn't have been more than a hydrogen filled balloon for observation purposes, since heavier aircraft had not yet been flown by the Army. By 1941, much change had been made and now the changes were hard to follow. New tech orders and manuals came like the daily paper, with extras.[22]

I was proud to be a member of this elite corps, and there was much for us to learn. Army aircraft were generally much more complex than our J-3 Cub. Here we had air-cooled radial engines with as many as eighteen cylinders, producing as much as 2,000 horsepower and liquid-cooled V-12 engines of more than 1500 horsepower. This was quite different than the little four cylinder, fifty horsepower engine on the Cub. This was incredible equipment then, but now it is as obsolete as an ox cart.

I was asleep Sunday afternoon, December 7, 1941. It was a cold, snowy day at Chanute Field, and I was enjoying just doing nothing when word came about the bombing of Pearl Harbor in Hawaii. It was hard to believe. But by night, extra guards were at all gates, and passes and ID cards were being checked very carefully. We were at war, and my days in the peacetime Army were over. War was formally declared the next day, December 8, 1941, against Japan and, soon after, on the Rome-Berlin-Tokyo axis. We were allied with Britain and her crown colonies, with the Free French and I suppose with Russia, which formally was considered part of the "Free World."

For the Grizzle family back home in New Mexico, like all Americans, the Pearl Harbor attack was a bolt out of the blue. It was a day no one ever forgot. The world as they knew it was about to change. Evidence of coming war had already arrived in Roswell when earlier that year (1941) construction began on a big army airfield. It lay only three miles south of the town's center. This would have direct implications for Jean McKinstry, the middle daughter of Sam and Loveta McKinstry. Jean had attended business college after high school. After Pearl Harbor she wanted to go to go to England and serve in some capacity there assisting the British people who had endured aerial bombing. Her father resisted that idea, as he had already "lost" one daughter, Sammy.

Sammy had eloped with a Roswell young man, Aubrey Hewatt, in 1939, who immediately after Pearl Harbor joined the AAF. Jean acquiesced to her father's wish and instead of going to England landed a job as a secretary in the transportation office at the new Roswell base.

Both Jean and, later, Mary Grizzle worked at the base. This marked another significant aspect of the World War II home front: Women worked out of the home much more than before, which helped them foster a spirit of independence. They obtained skills that supported their independence after the war, met people from distant places, and became more self-sufficient. They also met their future spouses at the base. This was the case with Mary, who met a soldier, Floyd "Andy" Andreas, from Washington State who served in the medical field. They met at a dance in Roswell, possibly a USO (United Service Organization) dance, dated, fell in love, and were married in 1946.

Working for the government paid a fantastic salary for the time. This allowed for more discretionary spending. Jean and Mary lived frugally. Mary lived with her parents, while Jean rented a room from an older widow woman in Roswell. She rode a city bus to work and otherwise walked to where she needed to go. The federal government, through the War Production Board, mobilized industry toward producing war materials. This agency also introduced a system of rationing that limited access to various goods needed for the military such as rubber, sugar, butter, and gasoline.[23] So although Jean and Mary made a good salary, there were not a lot of consumer goods on which to spend it. Jean, Mary, and millions of others bought war bonds and saved instead. When the war was over, their savings and pent-up demand spurred an era of solid economic growth well into the 1950s. The citizens of Hagerman and Roswell, like the vast majority of Americans, understood what was at stake and willingly abided by the government rationing decrees. The war had to be won not only in combat but also on the home front.

Oscar continues:

> The sneak attack on Pearl Harbor changed public opinion overnight. America was united with a purpose now. It must save the world from the crushing heels of the Nazi fascists and Japanese dictators—the

villains of all time. Hitler of Germany, Mussolini of Italy and Hirohito of Japan (considered to be a god by the Japanese) held the fate of the world in their grasping selfish hands. They must be stopped.

I completed my training at Chanute Field in January 1942 and was sent to a basic training field [Shaw Airfield] of the Southeast Air Training command, in South Carolina. I had again applied for appointment to be a flying cadet, but still my right ear wasn't quite right. The examining officer advised me to try again soon as he thought standards for appointment would soon be lowered now that we were at war.

I was soon promoted to corporal and now wore four stripes, two on each arm. I stayed in South Carolina until about April 1943, trying a third time to pass the test for flight training but failed for the same reason. Incidentally, I never felt that anything was wrong with my right ear until about five or six years ago [1967–1968] when it really has given me trouble.

[While at Shaw Airfield] I worked on the maintenance line of the 77th Air Base Squadron. We maintained all base aircraft not used in training. We did have three BT-13As in the squadron that base officers used for practice flying. The BT-13A was a heavy tandem, two-place, single engine trainer built by Vultee Aircraft and powered with a 450 horsepower Pratt and Whitney nine-cylinder engine of radial design, the R-985-AN-1. The school squadrons who trained cadets had these and also the BT-15 which was identical except for its being powered with a nine-cylinder Wright radial engine of 450 horsepower designated as R-975-A. They looked identical and were all called "Vultee Vibrators," being very noisy with their two position propellers. In our squadron we also had two twin-engine AT-8s built by Cessna and powered with two 350 horsepower Jacobs radial air-cooled engines. These were used by base headquarters personnel for transportation among the various bases in the Southeast Training Command. This area included all the South Atlantic states and Alabama, Tennessee, Mississippi, and Kentucky. For some reason, all our civilian depot maintenance was done at Middletown, Pennsylvania which I guess was the only air depot in the East.[24]

We also had two L-4s (actually J-3 Piper Cubs) used to locate downed, lost training planes and men. I had the opportunity to make many flights in these as an observer (and sometimes pilot) on the search missions and worked on the recovery teams that went in to crash sites to bring out whatever we could. First, the man or bodies, then salvage the plane itself, if possible. There was a lot of swampy wooded area there making salvage of the plane impossible sometimes. I learned about all I wanted to know about alligators there, too. They're very easily mistaken for a fallen tree limb. That tree limb comes to life very suddenly when stepped upon.

In late 1942, after doing everything there was to do on the field, I was promoted to staff sergeant and was squadron line inspector for a little while. The inspector put his "ok" on mechanical work done on aircraft by other mechanics. Our maintenance staff was small—about 15 men as I remember—but we took care of three BT-13s, two L-4s, and 2 AT-8s, plus all transient aircraft that landed on our base. The alert crew was on duty twenty-four hours a day and was made up of three men from our maintenance staff. This crew serviced and did minor repairs on the transient aircraft from other bases. I was even in charge of basic training for raw recruits who came to our base directly from civilian life. We didn't get many at one time, so they took this goof-off duty away from me. I think they quit it altogether.

I was given what I considered a much better deal. I was made a flight engineer on a C-87 transport plane that delivered air freight all over the Southeast Training Command area. We delivered various aircraft components such as rebuilt engines and new engines, too, new and rebuilt accessories, generators, magnetos, propellers, hydraulic pumps, etc. We'd pick up new and rebuilt parts at Middletown Air Depot in Pennsylvania, deliver them here and there, and bring back a load of worn engines and parts to be overhauled at Middletown. The Depot was run by the Army Air Corps, but all work was done by civilians. I didn't understand why, but I didn't care enough about it to find out. The depot was a huge place and thousands of people worked there. It was there that I first saw WACs [Women Army Corps] or women soldiers. They were working in different places doing mostly secretarial work. I didn't see anything but civilians in the shops themselves, but the head man in the offices was a full colonel of the Army Air Corps.

The C-87 was the cargo version of the B-24 and would really carry a load, but we really had to keep an accurate weight record to keep our load balanced and within limits. It didn't take many engines or 24-volt generators to weigh a lot. We had good range, too, and we hopped up and down the Southeast region from Pennsylvania to Florida and on down to our bases in the Caribbean and even down into South America, too, into Brazil. Once we went even as far as Ascension Island, a tiny dot in the south Atlantic about midway between South America and Africa. This island was used as a refueling and maintenance base for shorter range planes being ferried across to Africa. It was very hush-hush at the time.

This was a real good deal, too good to last, and early in 1943 I was called in and interviewed as a prospective pilot for troop-carrying assault gliders. I guess my record indicated that I was desperate enough to fly anything. I had cooled off a bit, though, and I really did like what I was doing then. So, I took the physical examination which I think I passed but an interviewing officer—a head shrink, I guess—asked me how I felt about the deal, and I told him I guessed that the results of the physical examination would make the decision for me. He became terribly hostile and said my attitude was not good at all, and that I was just unsuited to be in the program. I got quite a lecture about it.

I don't know if this incident had any bearing on it or not, but soon after this I was relieved of my good deal which, with flight pay, made me the fabulous sum of $144 per month. I'd never had it so good. It was like being a millionaire.

About this time, I went home on a fifteen-day furlough and returned with the car my brother [Harold] had bought us just before he went into cadet flight training. It was a little jewel, a 1941 Chevrolet coupe, black, beautiful, and practically new. He couldn't take it to cadet training, so there it was just gathering dust when I went home.

Harold had deserted the farm, and he with my brother, just younger than I [Wiley Jr.], had gone into flying cadets together. Harold was older than most at 25, I guess, while my younger brother was of about typical age, at 19. I was really proud that they had both chosen to join the Army Air Corps!

We had talked our oldest brother [Gerald] who was 28, an old, stable married man with children, into coming to run the farm and to join our partnership as the third Allison brother. Had it not been for him, I guess we'd have lost the blooming farm.

As Oscar comments, he and Harold formed a partnership with Gerald, who agreed to manage and work their farm while they served in the army. They were delighted in the arrangement in that they had a knowledgeable and trusted man to do this. Thus, the Allison Brothers farming partnership began and persisted as they moved after the war to Muleshoe, Texas, and farmed there. We are not sure what type of financial arrangement was made here. One family member believed that they agreed to give Gerald one third of the 180-acre farm. Gerald, upon hearing of the Pearl Harbor attack, had anted up for military service. He was then 28 years old, married, and had three children. The draft board, in light of these circumstances, advised Gerald that his service in home front agriculture was the best place for him to serve.[25] This was fully as important for victory as joining the military to fight. The nation and its allies needed food, as did the military. It was essential for fighting the war. Gerald and millions of home front Americans worked and sacrificed to undergird Allied victory.

Gerald and family—wife, Ethel; sons Jimmy and Winston; and daughter, Sherry—settled in a small house near the farm.[26] This move put him close to Wiley. All the farms were worked more or less as a family operation. So, Gerald, while farming his own land, also farmed Harold's and Oscar's and assisted Wiley with his farm. This was probably required as equipment, farm supplies, machinery, and farm laborers were in short supply during the war. It was necessary to pool resources. This indicates that reconciliation was effected or had been effected between Wiley and Gerald, at least to the degree necessary to work the farms together. So the home front situation caused normal relationships to be resumed on behalf of the war effort. Gerald, Wiley Sr., Ollie Mae, Mary, and Jim worked and farmed diligently to support the drive for victory.

This is not to say that the females of the family did farmwork. Although it was very common for women to do farmwork in those days, I have found no evidence that the Grizzle women—Ollie, Ollie Mae, and Mary—did except for minor chores like feeding the animals or gardening. Their work was generally confined to housework, shopping, cooking, cleaning, and canning or preserving food. These latter tasks were all the more important during the war. Although families had habitually canned and preserved food in the Depression, it was continued or resumed during the war. These and other measures minimized the consumption of store-bought food. More food, therefore, could be sent to the military and the Allied nations.

Now that their farm was in good hands, Harold was free to join the military. He and Wiley Jr., like millions of other young men and women, were anxious to defend the nation. While the family at home worked and sacrificed, Harold and Wiley Jr. put farming behind them and set off on an adventure. For them there was only one way to serve in the military and that was as a pilot.

Chapter 3

Harold and Wiley Jr. into the Army Air Forces: 1943

While the family at home worked hard at farming and doing what they could to help win the war, Harold and Wiley Jr. were anxious to get into the military and join the fight for freedom. They had waited through all of 1942, the year that is considered the dark days of World War II. In early 1942 the Axis nations were at their peak of success and influence. The Germans occupied most of Europe and in 1941 had invaded Russia. By late 1941 the German army was at Moscow's doorstep. The Japanese had successfully conquered a large part of the Pacific and the islands therein. They were within 2,500 miles of Hawaii. Japan had conquered the Philippines—an important American territorial possession—a good bit of Southeast Asia, and islands in the South Pacific. Their conquests in Southeast Asia had severely curtailed the availability of rubber to the United States. Their conquest of South Pacific islands directly threatened New Zealand and Australia, important American allies. But during the year 1942, the tide had begun to turn. Germany failed to take Moscow and, indeed, was beaten back by the Soviets, who recovered a lot of territory that had been lost. Critical battles were fought in the Pacific: Midway in June 1942 and Guadalcanal beginning in August 1942. These two battles, or campaigns, put the Japanese on the defensive; momentum shifted and the Allies began to advance toward Tokyo. Perhaps Harold and Junior thought the war was moving toward an end. They did not want to miss their chance to fight.

They both wanted to fly, a strong family instinct. So in December 1942 they traveled to Santa Fe where they joined the AAF as aviation cadets. A few weeks later, they entered training. Their first stop was Sheppard Air Base in Wichita Falls, Texas. Here they met the military. They got their first uniforms, an armful of shots, and indoctrination into military life. Sheppard Field was one of four basic training centers that the AAF used for boot camp–type military training. In the four-week course, recruits received training and instruction in military courtesy, personal hygiene, the Articles of War, wearing the uniform, mathematics, interior guard, government, and School of the Soldier. The last category, School of the Soldier, by far consumed the bulk of the recruit's time. This was basic infantry training, and although there was no weapons training, it included physical training, squad drill, platoon drill, company drill, marching and ceremonies, and field marches.[1]

The next month, Harold went directly to the San Antonio Aviation Cadet Center (SAACC), where he underwent the AAF's classification process to determine what aircrew position he would be assigned: pilot, navigator, or bombardier. Of course, almost everyone wanted to be a pilot. The classification did not mean that one was a pilot but that he entered the pilot training pipeline. The chances of becoming an actual AAF pilot after about a year of intensive training that included preflight, primary, basic, and advanced flight training were not that good. The AAF graduated 193,440 pilots during the war. Another 40 percent above this number of those selected for pilot training washed out somewhere along the way. But in the AAF, the pilot was at the top of the social ladder, "highest in prestige and responsibility and prized by the organization."[2]

Just to be selected for pilot training was the first of many hurdles. An applicant must pass a qualifying examination, perform satisfactorily in "a psychomotor test that evaluated eye-hand coordination, reflexes, and ability to perform under pressure," meet exacting physical standards, and pass a mysterious psychological examination.[3] One's subconscious was investigated by interviews and tests to determine if they were psychologically pilot material. The psych exams seemed ridiculous to some of the young men. One pilot specified the type of questions that were asked by one psychiatrist: "What was your childhood like?"; "Exactly what did you study in college?"; "Do you attend church regularly?"; "Do you have a girlfriend?"; then the subject turned to sex: "Did you ever have sex with your mother or sister?"[4]

In actuality, the battery of tests proved effective at predicting success or failure.[5] Those selected for pilot training tested well "on factors correlated with perception and rapid physical reaction, and they exhibited an ability to discriminate between visual objects and to visualize mechanical movements. They were well coordinated and were judged to be interested in and informed about aviation."[6] Pilots had to be of appropriate size to fit cockpits. Fighter pilots had to be at least sixty-four inches tall, but no more than sixty-nine inches (Junior barely slipped by here, as he was sixty-nine inches tall). The max weight for a fighter pilot was 160 pounds. Of course, vision had to be at least twenty-twenty.[7] Harold, to his great joy, was classified as a pilot and became a part of Class 44-C. For whatever reason Wiley Jr. had to wait to get that classification. They both, however, went into the College Training Program (CTP).

The CTP consisted of 153 colleges contracted to provide additional instruction in aviation-centric subjects—physics and math, for example— while also providing basic military instruction and indoctrination. Actually, CTP was a means to sequester a large number of promising young men out of the clutches of the other services until they could start flight training.[8] The AAF hoped to train fifty thousand pilots a year, a virtual tidal wave of men to meet the war demand for aviators. In contrast, consider that the largest class of new pilots the air corps graduated before 1939 was 246. To support their training, the AAF had to build facilities, bases, airfields, training centers, and maintenance facilities in rapid fashion to produce trained combat aviators.[9] The AAF just could not train that many new pilots in such a short time, so some were pooled in the CTP and went to college classes appropriate for aviators. Harold and Junior had both attended college after high school, although neither graduated. For CTP Harold went to Ouachita Baptist College in Arkadelphia, Arkansas, and Wiley Jr. to Southwest Texas State Teachers College (now Texas State University) in San Marcos, Texas.

Junior wrote home about life in CTP. In these letters we can gain an understanding of what this initial stage of training was like for AAF inductees headed for commissioning and a pair of wings:

March 1943
Dearest Mom,

Well, Harold and I busted up Monday. He went somewhere [SAACC] and I am now at San Marcos. I didn't think we could stay together for long, the Army doesn't do things like that. I suppose you're wondering why I'm here, no? Well, I'm here to go to school. We're to be here at least six weeks, or the most 5 months.

Boy, I got off K.P. [kitchen patrol] at Sheppard [air base]. I was to go on K.P. at 2:50 AM, but I got shipping orders so that left me out. We left Sheppard at 7:00 [a.m.] and got here at 1:00 [a.m.]. We ate dinner in Ft. Worth and supper on the train.

Listen to this. We have 3 hours off a week and that's on Sat. I mean, we can't leave the campus to go to town. I guess that is all right.

Love to all, Wiley Jr.[10]

April 1943
Dearest Mom,

Got a letter from Harold today. He sure has it easy. O.P. [open post] every weekend. We get only 3 hours. And study, we have about 2 hours each night. We're lucky to get that tho. Sometimes we don't. Have to shine shoes for 30 minutes each night. Have to have our rooms ready for inspection at all times. Boy it's pretty hard. I'm making pretty fair grades considering time we have for study. Boy, I'm telling you, a guy that finishes as a lt. [lieutenant] is really going to be a good officer. An educated one at that.

Love to all, Wiley Jr[11]

The same month Wiley wrote:

Dearest Mom,

Well I guess I'm here for a few months. Maybe. You never know what will happen next. We may start school Monday, and we may not. We've been here almost two weeks now. Haven't done a thing yet. A little drill is about all. I moved up to Harris Hall last Wednesday. Really a nice place here. We had personnel inspection today. We have this every Saturday.

Say, have you heard what Oscar is doing? He won't say eh? Wonder what it is? He must be doing something really important since he won't tell us. [Oscar was at this time at Wendover, Utah, for gunnery training, which is described in ch. 4.]

Well sweetheart I got another letter from you just now. You did get the money order didn't you? I'm going to try to save about $25 a month if I can. I kind of doubt it though. Ought to have quite a little, time the war is over. Just in case you didn't know it, this is Sat night. Couldn't get any passes cause there were too many in front of me. I guess I'll go to the show tomorrow instead. I've been making pretty fair grades. Made 22 on a Physics test. The class average was around 13. Not so bad, eh? I'm now taking Physics, English, Geometry and History.

Well Mom dearest I guess this is all I can write now.

Love to all, Wiley Jr.[12]

Before he left the CTP, he wrote his 13-year-old little brother Jim:

[June 1943]
Hi ya bud,

How's it going around home? Hope your keeping everything in good shape. Sure was glad to hear from you. Really never expected to hear from you. Guess I was fooled, eh? How's farming going? I guess you have to work pretty hard right? Well hard work never hurt anyone.

Well I'm through flying. Finished up a week ago Monday. Got 10 hours to my credit. Boy, I can't wait till I get in another plane again. But first I've got to pass tests & stuff at SACC.

Boy I'd sure like to be flying again. You don't realize at the time how much you like it. We had a little dog fight the last day we went up. Lots of fun. We could have shot one guy down several times. Then we dived at an ole boy on a tractor. Missed him about 10 ft. We did stalls, spins, snap rolls, etc. Course you can't do much with a T.A.C. That's what we were flying. They are just plain Aeroncas—Tandem Aeronca Continental is what T.A.C. means. Well it's almost time for me to go to radio, so I guess I'd better sign off. All I gotta say is keep 'em flying. I'd like to hear of a good crop this fall which is not too far off you know. Well kid keep your nose clean and write.

Love to all, Wiley Jr.[13]

This letter to his little brother indicates they had a warm relationship (although Jim attested that Junior was always picking on him—normal for brothers), as Jim had written him and Junior responded with a longer-than-usual and informative letter. Junior asks about farming and hard work. This indicates that Jim—now that Junior, Harold, and Oscar were gone—probably had more farmwork to do. He was out of school for the summer, and June was an especially busy time. Cotton was up and growing, but so were the weeds. There was plowing to be done. If the weather was dry, which it usually is in eastern New Mexico, irrigating was necessary, a very labor-intensive chore. Cotton and alfalfa both needed watering, especially alfalfa. So indeed, Jim, Gerald, and Wiley would have been busy.

Junior mentions flying while at CTP. The AAF was endeavoring to find out which cadets might not be comfortable flying or have no "air sense." This was done in light civilian aircraft such as the tandem Aeronca Continental, as Junior mentions. This airplane was introduced in the late 1930s as a competitor to the Piper Cub. It looked like a Cub and gave most cadets their first taste of flying. It had tandem seating (front to back), with the instructor's seat behind the student. The instructor sat about nine inches higher so he could see the same instruments as the student. So in this letter Junior, in saying "we," means that the instructor was with him. Continental built the engine for this particular Aeronca. It had about forty to fifty horsepower. The US military used derivatives of the Aeronca trainer for frontline liaison work. They were designated originally as O-58s but later were L-3s. But having cadets flying, even very early on in their training, had a purpose.

He wrote again to his mother from CTP:

[June 1943]
Saturday afternoon
Dearest Mom,

Well I'm almost through with my flying. We're leaving in about a week going to San Antonio for classification. Doing alright in my flying and really liked it. I'm going to have to stand guard tonight and on Sat. night at that. I'm not doing anything this afternoon. Had to stand inspection though. Heck mom I don't know anything to write, but I guess I could tell you about guard duty though. Well first you learn your general orders,

11 of them. You carry a rifle and allow no one to enter your territory without proper authority. That's all there is to it. Like heck. There's much more but it's too technical.

Say I'll bet the cotton really looks pretty by this time. How much do we have now and what else do you have planted? I'd really like to know.

I got your card today. Oh yes, I got the money, and I really did appreciate it too, and I appreciate everything else you have done for me. I'll send it back as soon as we get paid. We're getting flying pay this month. $75 instead of $50. Have you heard from Harold lately? [Harold was at preflight training at San Antonio.] Guess I'll write him one of these days.

Well Mom dearest I guess I'll quit now, cause I can't think of anything to write.

Love to all, Wiley Jr.[14]

After spending a lot more time at CPTP than he had expected, by July 1943 Junior was out of CPTP at San Marcos and assigned to the SAACC. Here he underwent the aforementioned tests to determine his aircrew classification.

July 1943

Well here we are at classification. Got here Saturday. Pretty good place. Think I'm going to like it here. We're quarantined for 15 days, so we can't get out. I'd sure like to see Harold, but I can't get around yet. . . .

Well we start taking tests tomorrow. We take a seven hour mental exam, then the next day we take our 64 physical. Sure hope I don't wash out. If I get through here I probably won't wash out anywhere along the line, I hope.

How is everything around Roswell now? Still the same I guess. And how is farming coming along these days? Sure is hot here. I guess it is there too. Got a letter from Oscar about a week ago. Seems he likes gunnery pretty good. I think I would too, but I like flying better.

This field is just like Sheppard, except that the dirt doesn't blow. We don't have many trees here, but we do have some grass. There are a bunch here from Miami, and they don't know which way is up. They don't even know what G.I. means. Such a dumb bunch.

Well Mom write and tell me all that's happened there lately.

Love to all, Wiley[15]

He waited with great anticipation to determine if he would get classified as a pilot.

July 1943
Dearest Mom,

Got your letter yesterday . . . I am not yet classified as a pilot but hope
to be soon. I had a tour of K.P. yesterday. I was cook's helper. Didn't
have much to do though. We don't do much here after we are classified
except detail work. I like this place pretty good. We have lots of grass,
but few trees. Pretty nice barracks too. Kind of hot here at night though.
Well, almost chow time so I'd better quit.

Love to all, Wiley[16]

July 1943
Dearest Folks,

Well at last I'm classified. Just what I wanted too—Pilot. Boy I'm really
glad too. Harold came over yesterday. He sure looks good with his
brass on.[17] Guess I'll get mine in about two weeks, or more. Then, after
that, two more months of school at pre-flight. Then I start flying.
I sure hope to make that commission, cause that's what I got in for.
That and flying. I'll be flying [training] for seven months before I get it.
I haven't gotten to the place where they wash-out so many. Ten % are
washed out here. In fact, 12% were washed out here.[18] That is in our
bunch of 50 from San Marcos. Some were washed out on the physical,
and some by the psychiatrist. They ask you the most foolish questions
too. They determine whether you can stand up under the combat strain.
Guess I better quit, almost 9:30 [p.m.], time for lights out.
       So good night to all.

Wiley Jr.[19]

Wiley at this point began preflight, as had Harold a couple of months earlier.
Preflight was a nine-week course and was also at the SAACC, one of
three such training centers established by the AAF. Preflight included more
military indoctrination and training, including drill, physical conditioning,
calisthenics, shooting, and leadership. Classes pertinent to aviation and the
military continued also.

Despite Wiley Jr.'s relaxed tone, preflight was rigorous and demanding. A cadet's day began at 5:45 a.m. with a morning formation. The cadets were dismissed and rushed back to their rooms to clean up and make their beds before marching to breakfast. Chow was overseen by an upper-class cadet table commander who insisted on good decorum and minimal talk. The business of eating was the priority. Any hazing that was done was by the upperclassmen. After breakfast it was back to the barracks to prepare their rooms for inspection, which could occur at any time. The day was then filled with classwork in physics, math, map reading, aircraft recognition, code, physical training, drill, and athletics. The evening could include more classes, chapel attendance, or sports. Lights-out occurred at 9:30 p.m. Little off-duty time was allowed. The best personal time away from the military was when (and if) open post was granted on weekends. Cadets left base and went into town, had a good meal, or socialized at the Cadet Club in downtown San Antonio.[20] While preflight was stressful, it was also frustrating to the aviation trainees as they looked forward with great anticipation to flying, getting those cherished pilot's wings, and then going into combat.

Here is Wiley's first letter home from preflight:

[Aug. 3, 1943]
Dear Folks,

Well here I am in pre-flight. Moved over yesterday. Guess I was pretty lucky to leave classification so soon. Some of the guys had to stay there 8 or 9 weeks. We haven't done anything much as yet, but we will soon. I imagine that it's going to be pretty rough here. We are going to be here 9 weeks as far as I know. Then primary, where we start flying. I can hardly wait.

By the way, Harold came over yesterday. I don't know how he ever finds out where I am, but he manages someway. Guess he goes from one barracks to another. Speaking of barracks, we've really got a nice one. All painted inside and everything. . . .

Love to all,
Wiley Jr.[21]

But there was waiting to be done. The AAF had so many cadets to train that a backlog had developed by late 1943, and Wiley Jr. and thousands of other cadets were caught in it. Harold was barely ahead of this logjam and was moving forward in his training. Harold had finished primary flight and the next month, December 1943, began basic flight training. Wiley Jr. was anxious to begin flight training but instead had to wait.

Dearest Mom,

We have finished our classes and have nothing to do these rainy days. I hate to say this, but I guess I won't go to Primary this month. I flunked my "Blinker Code."[22] However, Harold did too and he wasn't held over. You know that code is something you can't study for. I passed [Morse] code O.K. taking 12 words/minute. That's easy, but blinker is pretty rough. Well enough of my troubles. I'll know tomorrow whether I ship or not.

Oh, these damned Yankees. They are crazy as heck. Can hardly understand them. Especially the ones from Brooklyn. And they talk so funny. I can't help but laugh in their faces.

Say, did Oscar tell you that I've got a fraternity brother here? Yeah, he's in group H, I think.

Well, the shipping destinations have come in, but not the names. I'll know tomorrow. I was sure counting on going this mo. But guess I won't. Too many men here. The biggest class here than ever before.

Love to all,
Wiley Jr.[23]

Wiley writes home the next month still hoping to get out of preflight soon:

September 1943
Dearest Mom,

Got your letter yesterday Mom. I happened to be on Mess Management or K.P. However, it's pretty easy. I was in charge of one wing, and it was more work than if I was just one of the boys.

Well Mom, I finished my tests Tuesday. I passed everything O.K. I guess I'll leave soon. We've got an open post next Wednesday.

We had it pretty easy this morning. Had one class which was [Morse] code.[24] I think I passed the 12-word test, but they didn't call me off. In fact, I know I passed it. We only had to pass an 8-word test to qualify.

By the way, we go to the firing range this afternoon. Pistol firing for record. I think that I can qualify. I hope so anyway.

Say, have you heard from Oscar? [Oscar continued in B-24 combat crew training, which will be described in the next chapter.] He hasn't written in a long time. Guess he's pretty busy.

Love to all,
Wiley Jr.[25]

As he feared, he was held over.

October 1943
Dearest Mom,

I know you haven't heard from me in a long time, but everything has been in such a mess. I've had to move around so much. I now live in tarpaper barracks, they're not much, but we get along O.K. Yeah, I'm going to be here another month. They had such a big class that they had to hold over 2,000 men. That's a lot. Well, that puts Harold two months ahead of me. Well, I guess I can't have good luck all the time. Too bad, eh?

I'm barracks guard today so I have nothing to do, but sit around in the room here.

Love to all,
Wiley Jr.[26]

As Wiley Jr. observed, a large class of cadets had preceded his and clogged up the flight training pipeline. Indeed, late 1943 was the peak number of cadets in flight training, seventy-four thousand cadets total, in varying stages of flight training. The need for cadets to meet the war effort was diminishing after this point, and the number of cadets trained was reduced until at the end of the war, August 1945, only five thousand cadets were in the training pipeline. Harold had gotten ahead of this wave of cadets and was a training stage ahead.

Days later, he wrote about the discouraging situation at preflight:

October 1943
Dearest Mom,

Got your letter day before yesterday. Needless to say that I was glad. And I really did like those pictures too. Jerry [Gerald] also wrote me a letter, and I got one from Harold. All the same day too. I'd really like them to be scattered out tho.

Well Mom looks like I might leave this month. That is if nothing happens. Things get harder and harder every day. They've added several things to Physics to make it harder and the same with the other classes. We've got two more days to go on classes now. They didn't hold any men back on blinker until I came along with class 44-E. Blinker is really extra anyway. Well I'm going to make it this time, or know the reason why. I don't know what I would do if they washed me out here. However I'm not worried so much anymore.

Well I guess Oscar is doing ok. He's in charge of all the crew and really second in command. Not so bad, eh? Yeah he's doing ok.

Oh yes, we're doin ok in basketball too. We have one more game to play for group champs. Then we get a SAACC letter. Sure hope we get it.

Well I guess I'll stop now. Only a line or two but it helps a little anyway, I guess.

Love to all, Wiley Jr.[27]

[October 1943]
Dearest Mom,

Congratulate your little boy. He passed everything this time. Yeah I passed 12 words per minute code and 4 in blinker. Boy am I happy, now I'll get to leave this place. That is if nothing happens. There's no reason why I can't go to primary. I've got an 88 average in my classes. Not bad, eh? Guess I had a stroke of bad luck. Well that's water over the dam now. Enough of my troubles. How's everything on the home front? I really hope everybody is fine, and that the crops turn out well.

Say, did I ever tell you about my buddies from Oklahoma and Texas? Good guys too. I have to make them study though. They're sure lazy. I am too for that matter.

By the way I got your card today but no packages. I really appreciate your trying to help out Mom, but you know how soft tomatoes are. Of course you could send some cookies, etc. you know. But that's ok, letters are plenty ok for me. I know this is a short letter but there really is nothing to write. I'm sending a "Tale Spinner" for you to read. Hope you like it.

Love to all, Wiley Jr.[28]

Wiley did in fact finish up the preflight course and was ready to begin primary flight training. This began the next month (November 1943) at a primary training base in Oklahoma. During 1943 Oscar had progressed significantly in his AAF career. He would also enter a training regime that would prepare him for combat.

Chapter 4

Oscar, Liberator Training: 1943

While Harold and Wiley Jr. were in the early stages of their AAF careers, Oscar continued his flying career. We left Harold and Junior in late 1943. We will back up to the spring of 1943 to catch up with Oscar, who was at Shaw Airfield in South Carolina. His army career was about to change. He was to train as a gunner for bomber aircraft and also to become a flight engineer, which was a prestigious position.

"Exceptional mechanical aptitude was an engineer's most important characteristic."[1] Oscar had this in spades. On a bomber the flight engineer was the top ranked enlisted man. The crew was in his charge. Besides being a gunner manning the top turret, the flight engineer's main responsibility was to be an "in-house" mechanic, ensuring the mechanical functioning of the aircraft. The flight engineer had to be thoroughly knowledgeable of all aspects of the mechanical workings of the aircraft. When something went wrong with the aircraft mechanically, the engineer is who the pilots turned to, to fix it. The importance of the flight engineer is emphasized by the AAF policy instituted in 1945 that the flight engineer became an officer's position and was rated equivalent to pilot, navigator, and bombardier.[2]

Oscar was to be a gunner also, in the top turret of the B-24. Gunnery training was at Wendover, Utah, and was one of the most difficult assignments the AAF tackled during World War II. There were no specialized schools for gunners, called flexible gunnery, when the war began. So these schools had to be established under the harsh glare of wartime demand. Remember, the aerial warfare in World War II was all new, fought with modern aircraft that were increasingly faster and more complex. There was also the manifestly larger role that aircraft assumed when the United States committed to strategic bombing as a priority for winning the war. It meant that bombers carrying a crew of ten each had to fly hundreds of miles deep into enemy territory. Here, the enemy would naturally throw up a stout defense of fighters and antiaircraft fire, or flak, to protect their homeland. Gunners were the protection for the bombers from enemy fighters and therefore had an essential mission. If the gunners could not hit enemy fighter aircraft, the mission would not succeed. Training gunners, however, was difficult in that it was a new science. New geometry had to be learned to hit a fast-moving, small target that had the advantage of surprise, speed, and maneuverability in three dimensions. Fighters flew at speeds nearing 400 miles per hour while the gunner's own aircraft went 250 miles per hour in a different direction.

It is difficult to understand the swiftness, fury, and sudden destruction and death incurred when German fighters attacked. Pilot Walter Cubbins of the 450th Bomb Group provided an admiring perspective of the German fighters:

> I'd never seen anything like it. It was beautiful airmanship, a veritable flying circus. So daring were their maneuvers, so great our surprise, that I doubt that a single gunner got an effective shot at them. I tracked one fighter. He came racing through . . . a shiny yellow-nose [Messerschmitt] 109 dancing on air as the pilot skillfully avoided colliding with the bombers. The sunlight reflected his face, a face that seemed to look directly at us as his oxygen mask dangled to one side. I saw him for only the briefest moment, but I was certain that he'd smiled as he sped by.[3]

A 483rd Bomb Group radio operator, Merle Perkins, recalled another fighter attack:

"Systematically, in close arrowhead formation, with cannon and rockets firing, swarms of six fighters at a time would curve into the lowest box [a formation of bombers]. After six of these attacks, that squadron's planes and crews, seventy men, were gone: one plane exploded, another was totally shot to pieces, a third . . . went into a spin."[4]

The AAF worked and experimented with various means to make the gunners' training as realistic as possible. Prospective gunners came from a variety of backgrounds. Some were gunners by specialization. Others had other duties and being a gunner was a secondary role, as in Oscar's case. Every crewman on the bomber, except the pilot and copilot, had to get at least some gunnery training. The schools were not a cakewalk, and some classes had as much as 20 percent attrition. The training regime at Wendover at the time Oscar went through was six weeks long and besides gunnery training included some basic military and physical training. Training focused on operating the Browning .50-caliber machine gun, maintaining it, and firing it. Various attempts were made to develop skills for firing at enemy attacking fighters. Targets were pulled by jeeps, or trainees rode in trucks while firing at pop-up targets. Trainees got in-flight practice by shooting at towed banners. Aiming and sighting were the most difficult skills to learn. The guns at this time had iron sights or optical rings, not the sophisticated computing sights that came later on B-29s. Synthetic trainers were used to teach turret operation and sighting. In one sophisticated method, film obtained from actual combat flashed images of real fighter attacks on bombers. The student gunner fired at the image, and his gun simulated the sound of firing when the image was in range (six hundred yards). Outside of range, a bell rang. But despite the AAF's best efforts, gunners' training was never realistic enough to meet the actual demands of combat. Bombers suffered under the attacks of German (and Japanese) fighters throughout the war.[5] But it was not entirely one-sided. American gunners stayed at their guns and shot down hundreds of German fighters. Enemy pilots developed tactics that minimized the effectiveness of the bombers' guns, the most effective being the head-on attack at just the right angle such that the only guns that could be brought to bear were the two in the nose, and with a closing speed of nearly six hundred miles per hour, there was precious little time, indeed only seconds, for the nose gunner to hit the fighter.[6]

Oscar's story continues:

I'd been back to home base in South Carolina for about two weeks when I was ordered to Wendover, Utah [April 1943] to go through aerial gunnery school there and to become qualified to be a flight engineer on some type of bomber.

They wouldn't let me take my car with me or even take it home. It was, "Onto the troop train, old chap, and off you go!" We had a terrible time getting the car back. My mother and sister-in-law [Ethel Allison, Gerald's wife] finally rode the bus to South Carolina and drove it back to Roswell. It made me pretty unhappy. I had lost $48 a month in pay already, and now they were really messing me up. I went on to Wendover on the troop train, though.

There I learned many things. All about the .50 caliber Browning machine gun. We learned to completely dismantle it into its many separate pieces and reassemble it blindfolded. I learned aircraft identification. We could identify many different planes in the flash of 1/50th of a second. We learned ballistics, the effects of aircraft speed and direction as it relates to the trajectory of a projectile, and many more lessons on aerial gunnery.

Wendover was on the Utah-Nevada line at the great salt flats. The town wasn't much. There was a building right on the line. On the Utah side was a restaurant, and over in Nevada was a bar and gambling casino. A couple of gas stations and a half dozen houses seemed to be the whole thing. There was an air base there separate from the gunnery school. The base was close by the city, but the gunnery school was about ten miles away in the mountains.

We were there only a short time, two months maybe, and I only went to town once to call home and to my friends in South Carolina about the car. Oh yes, there was a telephone exchange there and maybe a lot that I didn't see. It was no resort area, though, and I was glad when we finished there.

The boys' mom, Ollie, maintained a close relationship with her first husband's (Oscar) sister, Annie Allison, and her brother Ed who lived in Eastland, Texas, throughout the war. They corresponded and even visited on occasion, even though it was a drive of more than 350 miles. This was quite a journey at the time, especially in the war when tires and gasoline were rationed.

Oscar's mother wrote Annie about Oscar's progress in training:

Dear Annie,
25 July 1943 -

Had a letter from Oscar when I got home dated 17th [July]. He said he had one more week of school and he would graduate and get his wings. Oh, how I wish I could be there but guess he got his wings Sat or today and I didn't have time to go if I could have. Had a letter from Harold too and he had gotten to see Jr. He was sure happy about it.

Ollie[7]

Oscar continues:

About a dozen of us were put on a regular passenger train at Salt Lake City with orders transferring us to Clovis Air Force Base in New Mexico. We had a few days to get there and when we got to Denver, we decided to spend a day or two there. I was in charge of the group and had their train tickets and meal tickets for the dining car on the train. I should have known that we'd never all get together again. We separated at the railroad station in Denver with instructions to meet at train time the next night. When that time came, four men were missing, so we decided to wait another day, and I told those that were there we were leaving for damn sure and if they saw the missing ones to let them know. Twenty-four hours later, we met in the station and with only two missing. We got on board. I don't remember if the two we left were of the original four or not. I never got to know any of them very well. I remember one of the two thought it was cruel of me to have left without him. One man came the next day, but one was missing for more than a week. He got busted back to private. So, we proceeded on to Clovis Air Base, all that had showed up.

In about July 1943 we went into first phase combat training on B-24Ds at Clovis Air Force Base.[8] I was to be a flight engineer and top turret gunner of a later model with a nose turret where the D model had only one .50 caliber gun operated by hand. The B-24 was identical to the C-87 except for the bomb bays and bottom door [bomb bay door] on the B-24. The C-87 had big side doors in the cargo space where the bombs in the B-24 were hung. At the time it was our biggest aircraft: sixty-eight feet long, high wing monoplane with a 110-foot wingspan. It was powered by four Pratt and Whitney R-1830 14-cylinder, double row air-cooled radial engines of about 1,200 horsepower each. The B-24 sat very close to the ground on its tricycle landing gear, and I guess it really wasn't pretty.

Oscar's assessment of the B-24's looks were not peculiar to him. Many noted that it was not aesthetically pleasing to look upon, but those who flew the Liberator, nicknamed the Flying Boxcar, loved it. It had many redeeming qualities. It carried more bombs farther and faster than the AAF's more famous and eye-pleasing B-17 Flying Fortress. It was reliable, mainly because its engines, Pratt & Whitney R1830 Double Wasps, were excellent. It could take battle damage and get the crew safely back home. It was flexible and could fly a range of missions in various conditions. That is why so many were built and flown in virtually all theaters of war by all the services.[9]

One distinguishing feature was its twin vertical stabilizers and rudders—twin tails. Behind the bomb bays was the waist section where the waist gunners manned single .50 caliber guns firing through the open waist windows, one on each side. A tail turret, hydraulically powered, was located between the twin tails and fired two .50 caliber guns backward with about 150 degrees travel sideways and up and down. In the floor of this section was the ball turret, powered hydraulically, and had to be lowered into firing position after takeoff, and it was the most confining position of all since the operator had to get into it before it was lowered and couldn't get out until he raised it into the waist section in landing position. He could do this manually or hydraulically from inside or outside the turret, and it could also be raised electrically by anyone in the waist section. The ball turret had nearly 360 degrees of travel laterally and almost 180 degrees vertically, more than any other guns on the ship. Forward of the bomb bays was the flight deck where the radio equipment was located and where the radio operator worked. Many modules for different radio frequencies were stowed behind and above the flight deck just under the wing. Each of these weighed thirty or forty pounds and it wasn't easy to change frequencies. Each module had quite a range of frequencies, so he didn't have to change many times in the air anyway. In this same area just under the wing was the manually operated gearbox and winch that lowered the landing gear if we lost hydraulic power.

On the flight deck were the instruments and controls of the flight engineer—the ammeters and voltage controls of the four generators, one on each engine, the fuel gauges and fuel flow meters. Directly above the flight deck in the ceiling or roof of the plane was the top turret. Electrically powered and operated by the flight engineer, it had 360 degrees of lateral travel, but the guns only had about 120 degrees vertically. Automatic stops kept the gunner from shooting his own plane.

In combat the radio operator moved straight forward into the nose turret which had twin .50 caliber guns, was powered by electricity, and moved laterally about 180 degrees and vertically about 120. All turrets had automatic stops to keep them from being fired when our own plane was in the line of fire and both waist guns had physical stops for the same purpose. You couldn't shoot yourself.

The pilot and copilot compartment was just ahead of the flight deck and of course just above and behind the nose. In the nose also was the bomb sight. Ours was a Norden and top secret, which was said to be capable of dropping a bomb in a barrel from 40,000 feet altitude.[10] So, the bombardier position was in the nose compartment and also the navigator's worktable was there and the little astrodome that the navigator used for shooting the sun and stars in his celestial navigation problems. It was a clear plastic bubble in the top of this compartment. The copilot had most of the engine instruments on his side (right) of the cockpit, all in fours, for each engine: oil pressure, cylinder head temperature, oil temperature, tachometer, manifold pressure, and others. They all together made quite a display on his instrument panel. On the pilot's side were other instruments: air speed indicator, turn and bank indicator, gyro compass, artificial horizon, and others. In the center were, for both pilot and copilot, the landing gear indicator lights, flap position indicator, and other warning lights. I never did count the number of instruments and gauges but there were a bunch. Between the pilot and copilot were the landing gear position controls and flap controls.

While taxiing on the ground, I usually sat on top of the fuselage just behind the pilot and copilot with my feet hanging down through the open top hatch where I had a better view and could warn the pilot if we were getting a wing tip too close to anything. I came inside and had the hatch closed and locked before we started our takeoff roll. On landing, I'd stand behind the pilot and call out airspeed about once every second so he could keep both eyes on the runway. We usually made our descent at about 120 mph, and I'd like to have a dollar for every time I've called out, 115, 120, or 125. We'd touch down at about ninety-five or 100 mph.

The copilot manned the engine and propeller controls and on landing he was constantly moving all four engine throttles to keep our air speed at the proper rate. The propellers were Hamilton-Standard Hydromatic constant speed revolutions per minute (RPM) and controlled by a hydraulic governor for each one. Control settings were made by a small electric motor reversible, of course, and set by the copilot with four two-way, spring-loaded (to the off position) toggle switches on his control panel. A little bar moved them all at once then after getting them close to the proper RPM, he'd synchronize the props one by one, by sight and by sound. The turbo-supercharger controls were on his side, too. Actually, the copilot had more to do than the pilot it seemed. It was also his duty to take over the top turret if I were incapacitated in combat.

With its ten .50 caliber machine guns, we thought the B-24 was unsinkable, except for maybe a direct hit from an 88-mm anti-aircraft gun.[11] We already had great respect for this gun and later we learned the hard way to respect the fighters of the Luftwaffe (German air force).

On the C-87, a crew of five manned the aircraft: the pilot and copilot, navigator (these three were commissioned officers), radio operator, and flight engineer. These were always enlisted men with the rank of staff sergeant or higher. Our radio operator on the C-87 was a technical sergeant, five stripes on each arm. I was a staff sergeant with four stripes.

On the B-24 with a nose turret, it took a crew of ten. The four officers were the pilot who was aircraft commander, copilot (second officer), bombardier, and navigator. The six enlisted men were usually staff sergeants or higher. I imagine I was the lowest ranking engineer in General [James H. "Jimmy"] Doolittle's Fifteenth Air Force, but that part comes later.

Regardless of rank, the flight engineer was number one enlisted man. Next the radio operator, third the chief armorer in charge of guns, ammo, and bombs. Number four was my assistant engineer, usually a waist gunner. The tail turret operator came next, then the other waist gunner. It really didn't make much difference though; everyone knew what to do and usually did it without orders from anyone. It was very informal and friendly. I don't remember, or maybe I never knew, just how a combat crew was put together or by whom.

One day, shortly after arriving at Clovis Air Base, a tall, thin second lieutenant came into our tent (all engineers there lived in tent city, four men per tent) and announced that he was looking for me. I admitted who I was, then he told me he was Bob Bird and that he was my pilot, and I was his engineer. I'd called "Attention!" and saluted when he came in, he said, "As you were." We shook hands all around. I remember the name of only one of my tentmates. Everything had suddenly become so temporary, but I think it always was and always will be. Nothing is permanent.

We talked a bit sitting on my bunk. Then he suggested we go down the flight line to see what the operations office had in mind for us. He told me his home was Stow, Massachusetts and I told him I was from Roswell, New Mexico, about 100 miles southeast of Clovis.

We exchanged other bits of information. He had just been transferred from flying B-26s from a base in Florida. I told him I was a green aerial gunner just in from Wendover, Utah but that I'd had some experience as an aircraft mechanic and that I was familiar with the C-87.

I knew if he was still alive after associating with the man-killing B-26 that he could probably fly anything.[12] I liked him immediately. He found our check pilot and we three went lightly through the flight manual of the B-24. Two or three hours later, we boarded an ancient-looking B-24D and took off. Bob was in the copilot's seat, and I was standing in the middle right behind him and the pilot.

I had started the auxiliary generator, "putt-putt," before we started the four main engines to save our batteries. The auxiliary generator was under the flight deck just like the C-87. It ran all the time we were on the ground and sometimes in flight. The pilot had told me to let it run awhile, and I had just come back up from shutting it off and taking up my position behind them. Bob asked me where my home was in Roswell. It was located on Highway 285 about seven or eight miles south, and a few minutes later I was looking down from about 5,000 feet at my home. Unknown to me, Bob had suggested that we fly to Roswell and the check pilot, a first lieutenant, was very agreeable. I liked Bob even better than before.

In no time at all, Bob was ready to solo in the B-24, so he found our copilot, Second Lieutenant A.F. Hughes from Sac City, Iowa, fresh from advanced training at some AT-11 base. The AT-11 was the twin Beech with twin tails and two R-985 engines. It looked a lot like the B-24 but much smaller. He was just a kid, 20 years old but like-able and very easy-going. Bob was only 21, and both he and Hughes had married after graduation from cadets. Bob had been married about a year but Hughes was newly married. They both had left their wives at home.

We three flew around together a few days, then the bombardier Deane Manning, from Stillwater, Oklahoma, joined us. He was only 19 and not married. Professor Vic Harris from New York was our navigator and an old man of 26, married and with a son, but his family had been left at home in New York. He was pretty quiet and absentminded because he was a professor, I guess. He didn't quite seem to fit in the Air Corps somehow, and I never decided I liked him until 1973 when we all met again in Kansas City. But that is another story. It took a smart guy, I knew, to be a navigator, and he was a good navigator, and if we were ever lost, he didn't tell me about it.

Next, we picked up our radio operator Jack Dixon from Birmingham, Alabama. We immediately started calling him Jackson and "static chaser" which applied to all radio operators. He was 21, I think, and not married. I really got to know him later and he was a great friend. We went through a lot together. Then, along came E. T. Szymanski from Brooklyn, our chief armorer and ball turret operator. He was immediately named "Skeets" and still is to me. Richard Leaf, my assistant engineer, showed up one day and claimed the left waist gun. Skeets was only 18 and Leaf was 19. Those three [Dixon or "Jackson," Szymanski or "Skeets," and Leaf or "Leafski"] and I helped "unroll the whole ball of yarn."[13] We were together to the end. Leaf we changed to "Leafski." Why, I don't know. He was young but a big, tall 6-foot Swede who was just too much man to fit into the turret. So was [Frank W.] Watkins, our other waist gunner from Seneca, South Carolina. We called him "Whistler" because of his constant imitating a train whistle. That's about all we got out of him. He was as quiet and withdrawn as the navigator. [James W.] "Pretty Boy" Blake filled the tail turret. He was from Chattanooga, Tennessee, and got his nickname from the combing of his dark, wavy hair anytime his head was uncovered. This completed our crew.

We spent a very short time at Clovis Air Base but long enough to get to feeling close to each other like a family. A truly great crew.

Everyone called me "Pete," a handle that was put on me in South Carolina by some Yankee who thought New Mexico was a foreign country of Mexicans only and surely my real name must be Pedro Something.[14] New Mexicans were rare, I guess. In the whole time I spent in the Army, I never met another one.

I'm a naturalized Texan now and proud of it, and I was proud then to be a New Mexican. Well, I am still proud of it.

Incidentally, the first time I went home was about the first weekend I was at Clovis. My tentmate Joe hitchhiked with me and we stayed overnight, and I brought the car back to Clovis with me. So, I got around quite a lot. I discovered Muleshoe [Texas] right away although I didn't have much business there.[15] In fact, one night Joe and I, with a pair of sweet young girls, were parked on Main Street about where Lud's barbershop is now, and the night watchman or city constable told us, "You soldier boys ain't got no business here, and you better take the girls home and get back to Clovis." It wasn't very late, but that's what we did.

Muleshoe, Texas, across the state line and about twenty-five miles deep into the Texas panhandle, was a boomtown of sorts at the time. Founded in 1912, it was named after the Muleshoe Ranch. During the war it had about 1,500 residents, with many more farm families nearby.[16] Evidently young ladies, farmers' daughters, abounded. Once the Comanche Indians had been ultimately defeated (1875), this area had attracted ranchers such as those that had established the giant XIT ranch. A shallow and huge underground source of water, the Ogallala Aquifer, had been discovered. Well technology developed by the 1940s allowed this crystal-clear, ice-cold, and nice tasting water to be pumped in massive quantities to the surface. The flat and fertile land was perfect for large-scale farming operations. With irrigation and modern and efficient tractors and farm equipment, Muleshoe and the Texas panhandle were turned into one of the world's most productive farming regions.

Oscar continues:

We came back several times to Muleshoe. My oldest brother Gerald came to see me with his wife Ethel and children one Sunday, and we drove around the country some. We were both impressed with the potential of irrigation here [Muleshoe] where the water was so shallow and so plentiful. In 1944, my dad [Wiley Grizzle, Oscar's stepfather] bought two quarters [of sections of land; two quarters would be 320 acres] of land here and Allison Brothers [Gerald, Harold, and Oscar] bought a quarter and an eighty-acre block, all this in the Pleasant Valley community [east of Muleshoe]. My home place was still in grass and part of the Warren U-Bar Ranch. The Allison Brothers got a two-mile long section [1280 acres] in 1948. I came to Muleshoe in 1945 as soon as I was discharged from the Army. Now, Muleshoe has been my home for more than half my life, and I hope to live here many more years. But that's another story, too.

In about October 1943, we finished our first phase training, and while the rest of the crew was given a fifteen-day delay enroute to Bruning Air Force Base in Nebraska, I was given the same amount of time to report to a new B-29 group being put together in Kansas. I was to train to become flight engineer on this latest heavy bomber of the USAAF.

It was called the Super Fortress, much bigger and faster than the B-17 or B-24. It was built by Boeing.[17] I'd never seen one. I would be promoted to flight officer, a new rank equal to warrant officer. Not a commission but quite a step up for me.

I would have to give up my staff sergeant rating and go through training as a flight officer candidate. If I flunked out, I'd be a private again, and no telling what they would put me to work on. I was sure I could make the grade, though, so, off I went.

When I arrived at Wichita, Kansas, after being away from my old
crew, I wanted to change my mind and go back to Nebraska with the
others [of my crew] to pick-up a new B-24H for the final phase of
combat training.[18] I felt like I was divorcing my family, and I just didn't
want to do that.

The brass in personnel was upset, to say the least, and told
me it was too late to change my mind. But I remembered what the
doctor had said about my attitude when I was going to gliders, and
I hung on to my bad attitude. We finally compromised and I went
back to Bruning as a private and was charged with seven days of
lost time. I was happy to be with my crew, and I've never regretted
making the decision that I did. Those kids just couldn't get along
without me and vice versa.

Oscar's sense of responsibility for "those kids" was partially due to his
being older. At age 25, he was the old man of the crew. Oscar's decision that
resulted in a drastic demotion is also a powerful testimony to the "band of
brothers" concept—that force that binds fellow warriors together in the face
of shared danger. Although Oscar's crew had not been to war, there was a
bonding process brought on by shared danger that stirred a reliance and trust
in other crewmembers to do their jobs because everyone had a role in the
preservation of all. This was true especially in combat, but when it came to
World War II flying, it was also very true in peacetime training. Flying was a
dangerous business without the sophisticated and precise instruments extant
in today's warbirds. The accident rate was extremely high.

For Oscar to be willing to take a three-rank demotion speaks volumes
about the powerful sense of belonging and family he, and probably the
others, felt. Oscar also had to consider that his reduction in rank to private
would make him the lowest ranking enlisted man among the crew. As flight
engineer, he remained in charge of and responsible for the other enlisted men.
He did not have trouble resuming his leadership duties, as he had won the
crew's respect. These were citizen soldiers. Rank was not that important;
competence and good leadership were.

Oscar continues:

The winter of 1943 was bad in Nebraska. Maybe they all are. Cold, snow,
and wind were much more disagreeable than here in Muleshoe. But life

and training went on. Several times we had to sweep an inch or two of snow off the wing before taking off. There was a lot of area there.

We flew simulated bombing missions with real bombs and fired at two targets with real bullets. At Clovis, we used flour-filled bombs and never fired a gun. We flew all over Nebraska, Kansas, and Oklahoma, a long mission to White Sands, New Mexico, landing at Alamogordo Air Force Base. I don't know where all we went. The Professor had a job keeping us from getting lost, but we never were lost but once, and that about twenty miles from Bruning we landed at another base, but Bob saw his mistake just as we touched down and we roared away undetected, I guess. I think most of the crew didn't know what really happened.

We had mock battles with USAAF fighters—mostly P-47s and once with P-51s. We used gun cameras on these missions, and it was much like the real thing.

Before we resume with Oscar's training and deployment into a combat theater, let us look at how Harold and Wiley Jr. are progressing in flight training and preparing for war. This will bring us to the end of 1943, a year in which the Allies had made significant progress in defeating the Nazis and Japanese. The Germans had been stopped and rolled back in North Africa. The Allies then invaded Sicily and Italy, which resulted in an armistice signed with the Italians, formerly a German ally, on September 3, 1943. In the Pacific the Allies were following up their victories at Midway and Guadalcanal by advancing against Japanese strongholds on New Guinea and initiating a drive through the Central Pacific with the battle of Tarawa in the Gilbert Islands. The Allies also sought to drive the Japanese out of the Aleutian Islands.

Pivotal battles at Stalingrad and Kursk on the eastern European front were won by the surging Soviet Red Army. These represented turning points in this theater of the war. The Soviets in 1944 and 1945 would push farther west in German-occupied lands and indeed into Germany itself. Of pointed significance for Oscar and Wiley Jr., the strategic bombing campaign in Europe commenced with bomber raids on key German industrial and trans-portation sites. These raids in 1943, comprised of a few hundred bombers and escort fighters, were small compared to what would follow.

Chapter 5

Wiley Jr. and Harold, Flight Training: 1943–1944

While Oscar rejoined his crew at Bruning, Nebraska, for tactical training in their weapon of war, a B-24H, by November 1943 younger brother Wiley Jr. was finally flying. He went to Chickasha, Oklahoma, for the primary level of flight training. As noted earlier, Harold had preceded Wiley Jr. into the primary stage of flight instruction, taking his training at Hicks Field at Saginaw, Texas (near Fort Worth). He had already completed primary and moved in early November to Perrin Field near Sherman, Texas. He had begun the basic level of flight training. Flight instruction for cadets at the primary stage was done by private, contracted flight schools. There were fifty-six of them. Most were in the south, southwest, and west, where the weather was better for flying. At Hicks Field it was the W. F. Long Flying School. At Chickasha it was W&B Flying School.

The W&B school was the initiative of Ray Wilson. He later founded Monarch Airlines, which grew into Frontier Airlines. An associate was Maj. F. W. Bonfils, the *Denver Post*'s business manager. In addition to their own money (mostly Bonfils'), they got a substantial loan from the federal government's Reconstruction Finance Corporation. They recruited flight instructors from a cadre of pilots who had been Wilson's former students at a flying school he had operated before the war. An airport and facilities were built from the ground up. Farm or open-range land was scraped clean, making it windblown and dusty. The flying school built the requisite number of office buildings, barracks, maintenance facilities, and paved surfaces to support flight operations, all in rapid fashion. Flying schools were paid about $1,100 for each cadet who graduated and about $18 per hour of flight instruction that was given for each cadet that washed out. Primary schools had detachments of AAF officers and enlisted men as well as check pilots at each school. Otherwise, civilians were the instructors, both for flights and in the classroom.

The first group of fifty students arrived at W&B in October 1941. This illustrates how the United States was gearing up for war even before entering the war, which was still two months away. The school disbanded in July 1945, again anticipating the future when the war ended two months later. Thousands of cadets received their primary training at the W&B school.[1]

The relationship between the government and civilian-operated primary flight schools was a good one. Gen. Henry H. Arnold, who commanded the AAF in World War II, commended the civilian-military partnership: "Training of personnel in time of war can be done on a large scale only by utilizing all the nation's facilities and experience. . . . The armed forces will never have all the facilities required to meet war programs. Civilian agencies must, in some way, be kept aware of their responsibilities, especially during peace when planning and preparation for war are so distasteful to Americans."[2]

Primary lasted nine to ten weeks. Cadets obtained about sixty hours of flight time, half solo and half dual (with an instructor). Primary was impor-tant. The fundamentals were either solidly learned or glossed over. Either way, it was significant and bore on the skill and competency of a pilot throughout his career. Military training continued, turning the cadets into military officers, as did physical training and classroom work. At Chickasha and Saginaw, cadets flew the Fairchild PT-19. There were more washouts during the primary stage than any other—27.5 percent. If a cadet made it through primary, he had a very good chance of earning his wings and commission. Only 13 percent of cadets washed out in the next two levels, basic and advanced, combined.

Primary was tough for cadets because the AAF was in a rush to turn out pilots. One AAF officer commented, "There was an extremely high washout rate . . . I think, not so much that the people they washed out couldn't learn to fly, but they couldn't learn to fly fast enough. You were expected to solo within eight to ten hours, and if you hadn't done it by 12 or so, they would wash you out. They just simply didn't have the time. They had more people than they did time."[3]

Cadets believed that the system of evaluation was arbitrary. Evaluation and elimination seemed to occur just because an instructor did not feel the cadet was pilot material. One Navy pilot who underwent similar training remarked,

> There were tests, but not like any test that I had taken at school or university. You couldn't cram for it, and you couldn't fake it. You weren't even being tested on something that you had studied, really, but on what you were. If you were a flier, you passed; if you weren't, you washed out—fell out of the air, and became a lower order of being. It became clear that some people were natural fliers, and some weren't. The athletes usually were; they used their bodies easily and naturally, and they seemed to make the plane a part of themselves.[4]

In November 1943 Junior wrote his first letter home from his primary training field, Chickasha, Oklahoma.

> [November 1943]
> Dearest Mom & Dad,
>
> Well here I am at Primary. Boy is this a swell place. Food is really nice, the quarters are the best, and the beds are wonderful. We got here yesterday at noon. We had to sleep in a chair car Wed. night. In fact I didn't sleep any. We're treated like kings here. And we have been issued flying clothes. Helmet and goggles, heavy flying jacket lined [at this point in the letter a censor has cut out most of the paragraph, and it ends with] . . . blue blankets for our beds and a porter to clean up the place. Well that's what I've been working for, for 8½ months. I guess we'll start flying Monday. Boy, sure don't want to wash out here. Fingers crossed.

Say, do you know where Harold is? [Harold was at Perrin Field near Sherman, Texas, in the basic phase of flight training.] I'd sure like to know. And how is Oscar getting along? [Oscar was in combat training with his B-24 crew in Bruning, Nebraska.] He never stays in one place long. Well, just a line to let you know where I am. Write soon.

Love to all,
Wiley Jr.[5]

In the above letter, as well as others before, Junior consistently asks about his brothers. Other letters between the boys and with other family members reflect a strong family bond.

December 1943
Dearest Mom and Dad,

Got your much welcomed letter yesterday Mom. Glad to hear everyone is ok. Well I guess winter is really here now.

Boy, am I tired. We have been flying 2 hours every day now, and it's really hard work, but I like it. I have about 22 hrs. now. About 8 solo. I shot my stages, or spot landings yesterday. Solo of course. Passed it o.k. Nothing to it. I have a 20 hr. check Monday or Tuesday. It's really nice to be up there by yourself and do whatever you want to. Spins, stalls etc. My spins are pretty good now. These PTs are really nice ships. I was up yesterday about 5,000 [feet] solo and started to do some spins. Well here come 2 AT-6s. One on each side of me. I didn't know what to do, so I kicked it down. I had a pretty fast ship and they went by like I was standing still. Some fun this flying.

I got a letter from Harold yesterday too. He didn't have much to say. Said he had 20 hrs., and didn't know how he was going to get 70. [The basic course of flight instruction required seventy hours of flight time.]

He also said his landings were not so good as yet. I can land these PTs anywhere now. However I had a little trouble for awhile.

Your loving son,
Wiley Jr.[6]

In another letter home, Wiley wrote:

Friday
12/9/43
Dearest Mom,

I got your card today. Say sweetheart, I'm sending some presents home, and I'd rather you wouldn't open them till Christmas. I'll be sending some more later. Look Mom will you please send me Aunt Hannah, Aunt Pearl, and Aunt Gladys, and Aunt Angie's address. I've just got to send them some cards or something. And I'd like to have Oscar's too. I have no idea where he is or what he is doing. He hasn't written for a long time now. Guess he's pretty busy. [Oscar and his B-24 crew were winging across the Gulf of Mexico and into Brazil, headed for Italy and the combat arena. Oscar's story continues in the next chapter.]

Well I have about 55 hours now. We haven't flown but one day this week. Rains too much. They let us go into town yesterday to do some shopping. Oh yes, I had an hour of Link today. It's really instrument flying—worth $25 an hour. We have 9 here worth $9000 each. Expensive, no?

Well Mom guess I'd better close now, have some studying to do. You can send me some money too. A little short now.

Your loving son,
Wiley Jr.[7]

Junior mentions the Link trainer in the above letter. This was an early and primitive flight simulator by today's standards and was widely used in World War II. Ed Link invented it and obtained a patent in 1931. Its technology was based on air bellows on which the body of the trainer sat. The bellows inflated or deflated according to the controls the operator applied and very much gave the impression of flying. The government contracted with Link in the mid-1930s for his device to aid air mail pilots in developing instrument flying skills. In World War II, Links became a regular part of pilot training. Link trainers gave student pilots basic flying and instrument flying skills in a safe and economical manner. More sophisticated flight simulators do the same today.[8]

Christmas was close but Wiley Jr. would not be going home. He wrote his teenage sisters Ollie Mae and Mary.

Hi gals,

How's everything going with you all now? Say, there's a man shortage isn't there? Bad, bad! Sure hope I could be home for Christmas, but can't make it. We are behind a little in our flying.

Say, look, here's ten bucks [equivalent to $165 in 2022] you all can split. I haven't had time to get anything so get what you want. Well gals, guess I'd better study some now. So be good and have a good time over the holidays.

Your lovin' bud,
Wiley Jr.[9]

Wiley also had received a rare letter from his father, to which he replied:

Hi Pop,

Well by golly you did write, didn't you? Well it's about time, don't you think? Well how's farmin comin along now? Hope the crops are all gathered and stuff now. How much cotton and maize per acre did it make?

Well, I guess I won't be here too much longer. We leave the first of the year. And I can't make it home for Christmas. I have only 36 hrs. now and 65 is the customary amount given here. I have a recheck on 180-degree stages tomorrow. Had some bad luck Wed. I'm not worried cause I know I can make them. They're easy. That is if the wind doesn't blow too hard.[10]

Well Dad thanks for the money, however I didn't need so much. Send some home maybe. Write soon.

Your loving son,
Wiley Jr.[11]

By February 1944 Wiley Jr. had survived primary training and had started basic flight training at a freshly built base at Garden City, Kansas.[12] Here he, as did Harold at Perrin Field and most cadets in basic, flew the Vultee

BT-13 Valiant aircraft. It was a significant step up from the PT-19 in complexity, speed, and power. Cadets called it the Vibrator or Old Snarly. One cadet attested that it had a reputation as a "killer ship." Learning to fly the BT-13 was a challenge for the students, most of whom only had about sixty hours of flight time upon arriving at basic, and that was in the docile PT-19. One cadet attested that he had never met anyone who enjoyed flying BT-13s.[13]

The BT-13 was of all-metal construction, whereas the PT-19 was part plywood and fabric. Its landing gear, like the PT-19, did not retract, but the BT-13's 450 horsepower almost doubled that of the PT-19. The heavy BT-13 had a significantly greater sink rate than the PT-19, which made landing it with a dead engine quite tricky. This was something not to be taken lightly, as the engines were notoriously unreliable due to a faulty fuel system.[14] Takeoffs in the BT-13 were also tricky. Unlike primary trainers, the BT-13 had a variable-pitch propeller, which was another control that cadets had to master. It was important, though, as most tactical aircraft had propeller prop controls. Cadets could get in trouble by improperly adjusting the propeller's pitch from a high rpm flat pitch for takeoff to a more angled pitch soon after becoming airborne. Particular care was required in doing "touch and goes," repetitious practice landings followed by an immediate takeoff. As flaps were lowered for landing, the heavy nose of the BT-13 would tend to drop. Therefore nose-up trim was applied. After landing, full power was applied for the takeoff. With flaps still down and nose-up trim, the plane tended to climb abruptly and, if not countered immediately, could cause a stall. A stall at such a low altitude could easily result in a crash.[15]

Whereas the elimination or washout numbers decreased substantially from primary to the basic phase, the accident and mortality rate increased substantially. The mortality rate in primary was about two cadets for every one hundred thousand hours of flight. In basic the mortality rate was significantly higher. Every cadet knew a classmate who had been killed in flying. It pressed home the statistical truth that training to fly was almost as deadly as combat. A historian of aviation in West Texas noted that June 1943 began the bloodiest period ever when weekly crashes killed twenty-five cadets.[16]

In basic the military's insistence on precision flying was impressed upon cadets. Landings, takeoffs, and all phases of flight must be on altitude and on airspeed. Formation flying was taught, as was instrument flying, which was especially important yet had not been well developed. By 1944, however, the AAF had adopted the "full instrument" system of instrument flying, which the navy had used for some time. The full instrument panel system taught that when pilots are flying on instruments (i.e., in the dark or in obscured conditions), they should use magnetic compass, the rate of climb indicator, and the clock in addition to the needle (turn indicator), ball (bank indicator), and airspeed indicator. The army had taught cadets to use the latter three instruments only for instrument flying. The full panel system brought a "revolution in instrument flying and saved many lives."[17] Long-distance flights, or cross-countries, were flown to sharpen air navigation skills. Cadets practiced aerobatics to give them confidence in their skills and trust in the aircraft as they pushed it to its limits. Cadets had to work hard, and they were also pushed to their limits. Wiley wrote home soon after arrival at Garden City, Kansas, where he began basic flight training.

Dearest Mom

Got your letter yesterday and really glad to get it. I'm not feeling so good today so I'm waiting for sick call now. I have a cold that's pretty bad. Oh yes Mom, I'm to the point now that I wish I'd never seen an airplane. I flew 3:20 hrs. yesterday and I'm so tired I could sleep forever. When I get home I'm gonna sleep for a month. Well Mom guess this is all for now. Write soon.

Your loving son,
Wiley Jr.[18]

Despite the added dangers and challenges, Wiley Jr. was perfectly comfortable flying the BT-13, and enthusiastic.

February 1944
Dear Mom,

By golly you sure do write a lot don't you? Boy, I really like that. Yeah, I got the cake and also the cookies. They were really nice too Mom.

And who said I didn't like the Air Forces? That's the only thing I'm here for. If I didn't like it I could get out. In fact I could leave this place tomorrow. It only takes a few minutes. Of course it's not all glamor, but when you're up there by yourself you wonder why you haven't flown anymore. Boy, it's really nice. It's work, about the hardest there is. It's tiresome at times except on solo. We are still on instrument flying now, but almost thru. I have 4:20 of night flying. A little hard to land at night tho, but I like it. No, when I get tired of flying, I'll let you know. Of course, I wish at times that I had never heard of a plane, but when morning comes I'm ready to go. Boy when you learn to fly, and can take a plane up and do a loop, Immelmann, snap & ½ split "S," a slow roll in a chandelle and a lazy eight, wing over, Chinese "8," precision spins and make inverted turns, that's something. And you have to know how to fly. Lot's of fun too. If you're good you can do an inverted snap roll and barrel rolls. Of course, this is impossible in a box car. Loops have been done in [B-]24s and [B-]17s, but $11,000 of instruments were destroyed.[19]

Well, got a letter from Oscar. He is ok he says but you never know. Well, it won't be long before you write Harold as Lt. Harold L. Allison. How's that sound? Well Mom, I'm ok now. I still have a cold but not bad. Sorry I haven't written sooner; busy you know.

Your loving son,
Wiley[20]

In this letter Junior gives a great accounting of some of the aircraft maneuvers he was learning and how it generated confidence and enthusiasm for flying. It is interesting that he mentions a letter from Oscar and that Oscar said he was "ok," but Junior presciently cautioned that "you never know." It was exactly four days earlier that Oscar's B-24 had been shot down. He also mentions Harold and that he would soon successfully complete his flight training and be commissioned a second lieutenant, which, in fact, Harold did.

Training moved rapidly now for Wiley Jr. He was proving his mettle as an aviator and had been selected to be a fighter pilot, a cherished designation. It was one that the majority of cadets desired despite that the main focus was on strategic bombing, using big bombers like the B-17 and B-24. During the war 60 percent of cadets ended up in bombers and 40 percent in fighters.[21] As can be detected from the above letter, Wiley Jr. wanted fighters. He relished executing aerobatic maneuvers. It was during the basic stage that

cadets learned of the aircraft type they would be flying in the AAF upon graduation. Harold was selected for bombers.

Harold, in Class 44-C, was ahead of Wiley Jr. in Class 44-D. After
basic Harold went to Ellington Field outside of Houston to learn to fly
multiengine aircraft, preparing him to fly bombers. As cadets moved
forward into the advanced stage, they sensed that they were on the
verge of really earning their wings and going to war. And they were. If a
cadet made it to advanced, he had a very good chance of completing the
program, getting his wings, and being commissioned as a USAAF officer.
In advanced training instructors took a more mentor-type style instead
of a harsh instructor/student style. Discussions and question-and-answer
sessions replaced mandates and commands.[22]

At Ellington Harold trained in the Beechcraft AT-10 Wichita aircraft.
It was powered by two 980-horsepower engines, which could generate a max
speed of almost two hundred miles per hour. For the future bomber pilots,
the emphasis was on navigation, formation flying, and especially instrument flying in anticipation of flying at night and in the detestable European
weather. Cadets did not have to wait for bad weather to practice instrument flying in the sunny south and southwest. They flew "under the hood."
A canvas hood was fitted to go under the canopy to block the outside view
and force their reliance on instruments. Safety pilots flew alongside. Formation flying was essential for bomber pilots. One bomber pilot observed that
"he and his cohorts became very close during advanced training, mostly by
flying formation together: 'We had to fly on each other's wings from time
to time and that requires complete reliance upon each other. . . . When I hit
combat it didn't take me long to learn that in those days a pilot's life absolutely depended upon his ability to fly good formation, because its purpose
was mutual protection.'"[23] Formation flying was practiced in day and night
conditions. Five feet of clearance between wingtips was the desired standard.
Understandably, night formation flying was a dreaded high-pressure training
mission until cadets became adept at it; then, like everything else, they came
to be at least proficient in it and comfortable, if not enjoy it.

The curriculum of flight training for bomber-bound cadets is revealed
in Harold's breakdown of hours flown. He flew a total of seventy hours,

thirty-seven minutes (70:37) during the advanced stage, all in the AT-10. About twenty hours were at night and fifteen hours were under instrument conditions. Forty-two of the seventy hours were in the copilot position and twenty-three were as first pilot. He executed 111 landings. Harold also got more than ten hours of simulated instrument flight time in the Link trainer. His total time after all his training, all three stages, was 205.37 hours. It is significant that Harold got seventy hours of copilot time.[24] He evidently had already been targeted to be a copilot. This in no way reflected on his capability as a pilot. The needs of the service came first, and his entire group of cadets were designated as copilots.[25] He was extremely disappointed.

A new and important aspect of training for future bomber pilots was learning to work with a crew and being in a leadership position. Before, in flying single-engine trainers, it was man and machine only. A bomber pilot had to be a leader of a team, a crew commander. Flying competency was vitally important. This established confidence and trust in the pilot by crewmembers. Pilots and copilots learned the duties and responsibilities of an officer, their roles in relation to crewmembers, and the duties and responsibilities of each crewmember.[26] Bomber pilots were expected to be effective military leaders in addition to being superb aviators. Yet leadership of a bomber crew was not the standard military rank-conscious relationship. Effective bomber pilots trusted their crewmen, each in his own way a specialist. It was democratic, up to a point. The crew respected and relied on each other's knowledge and skill. In combat each crewman was essential to mission success.

Harold completed his flight training and received his wings and his commission as an army officer on March 12, 1944. He left Ellington Field immediately and headed home. He had big plans, and they did not involve the AAF. He planned to marry his sweetheart, Jean McKinstry.

Harold and Jean began dating before Harold entered the army. Although they grew up together, Harold had hardly noticed Jean, as he and Oscar hung around with Sammy and their clique of friends. As noted above, Jean and Wiley Jr. were considered boyfriend and girlfriend in junior high and high school but were not going steady. Jean and Junior graduated from high school in 1941 from different high schools. As noted, the Grizzles had moved to East

Plains, outside of Roswell. Junior started college at New Mexico State A&M after graduation. Any romance they might have had was ended.

Soon after graduation, Jean attended a dance that changed her life. She went with one of her boyfriends, M. C. As it turned out, she hardly danced with M. C. at all. Instead, Harold and Oscar (the two seemed inseparable) discovered Sammy's little sister Jean. At this dance at Lake Van near Dexter, New Mexico (close to Hagerman), their eyes were opened. They kept cutting in on dances. Oscar: "Wow. When did you get so pretty?" Then Harold cut in: "Where have you been hiding? What have I been missing?"[27] Harold eventually, by playing it cool but nice, won out, and they began dating.

Jean, as noted above, worked as a secretary in the Roswell Army Airfield (in 1948 it was renamed Walker Air Force Base) transportation office from 1942 until she was married in March 1944. The big Roswell base was a vibrant enterprise, a major training base for bomber crews. It was an exciting time for Jean. When Harold left to go into the army in January 1943, even though they had been dating for over a year, he was cool about it and encouraged her to date other men. And she did.

She was popular among the soldiers on the base. She jitterbugged at the enlisted men's USO dances as well as at the Officers' Club. Jean recalled that the music was wonderful! "It was the big band era and I loved hearing Glenn Miller and many others."[28] Busloads of girls were driven to the dances from the surrounding towns. The USO dances were closely chaperoned and had strict rules. Once at the dance, girls were not allowed to leave with one of the soldiers. This, of course, did not mean they could not date a young man they met at the dance. None of Jean's would-be suitors, however, compared to Harold. When he returned to Hagerman in March 1944, a freshly commissioned second lieutenant sporting pilot's wings, he did ask Jean to marry him, and she enthusiastically consented.

Jean introduced him to the men she worked with in the transportation office. Jean recalled, "They were ground soldiers, and they always let it be known that they did not like the 'fly boys.' I introduced my 'fly boy' all around and they were nice to him but were surprised I would no longer be working there and would marry soon. Yes, they assured me, they would attend our wedding."[29]

With orders to report to his replacement training unit in only a couple of weeks, Harold and Jean had to hurry. They got married exactly two weeks after Harold had completed his training. Immediately after the reception they set out driving to Harold's next duty station, Columbia Army Air Base, South Carolina. Here he would transition into the North American B-25 Mitchell bomber. Harold was a happy second lieutenant. Things were looking up for him. He had the good fortune to fly one of the best bombers of the war, the B-25, and now was married to his sweetheart.

Due to the demands of war, Harold and Jean only had a brief window of time to get married. For the same reason, Oscar and Wiley Jr. were not able to attend this joyful event, as much as they might have wished to. The three boys were all engaged in the deadly serious business of training for air combat. Indeed, Oscar and the crew of the Sophisticated Lady were on the cusp of deploying to a combat theater. For this account we will resume his story in the following chapter.

Chapter 6

Oscar and the Sophisticated Lady to Italy: 1943–1944

acking up chronologically, we will pick up Oscar's progress in training for combat flying in the B-24 Liberator bomber. His crew completed training in Bruning, Nebraska, in December 1943. With a combat crew in place and a brand-new B-24H Liberator assigned to them as their aircraft, Oscar and crew flew to Italy to join the recently commissioned Fifteenth Air Force. The Fifteenth Air Force would be another major force that, along with the Eighth Air Force flying from England, brought American airpower to bear against the Nazis. The Fifteenth could easily range German military and industrial targets in occupied south and east Europe, southern Germany, and France, whereas the Eighth, flying from England, would be range limited to hit these targets. The targets—transportation, industrial, and especially petroleum production and refining sites—were vitally important for the Nazi war machine.[1] Oscar's crew did not participate in these air raids. The war had different consequences for them.[2]

Oscar resumes his story:

Not long after, I guess about December 1, [1943] or so, we flew our plane to a modification center at Topeka, Kansas to make it ready for ferrying overseas. Baggage racks were installed in the bomb bays, and for some reason we named her Sophisticated Lady and had a life-sized pin-up girl painted on the forward side near the nose. A huge number 214 was on the opposite side. Here, engine cowlings and vertical stabilizers were painted red to identify her as belonging to the 716th Bomb Squadron, 449th Bomb Group (H), Fifteenth Air Force under the command of the famous General James H. Doolittle. Of course, we didn't know what this meant at the time. We had no idea where we'd be going from there.

Oscar was impressed with General Doolittle, and he should have been. General Doolittle was, or is, one of the most famous aviators of American history, one of the "finest airmen to ever live," opined the aviation historian Barrett Tillman.[3] He was a popular and successful air racer before the war. He was also smart; he had earned a doctorate in aeronautical engineering from MIT. He became world famous as a lieutenant colonel in the AAF and led the astonishing 1942 raid on Tokyo by sixteen Army B-25s bombers flying from an aircraft carrier. He received the Medal of Honor for this remarkable mission and rose in rank. In March 1943 he was given command as a major general of the North African Strategic Air Force. A powerful and inspirational leader, he continued to fly combat missions in bombers and fighters despite his high rank. In November 1943 he became the first commander of the newly established Fifteenth Air Force, headquartered at Foggia, Italy, which lay about 150 miles east-southeast of Rome. Doolittle turned over command of the Fifteenth Air Force to Lt. Gen. Nathan F. Twining on January 1, 1944, and then took command of the Eighth Air Force.[4]

Oscar continues:

The modifications to our B-24 took several days and we commuted almost daily to Kansas City, Missouri on the fast streamliner train *Rock Island Rocket.* It left about noon from Topeka, which gave us plenty of time for roll call and to get the orders for the day. Kansas City wasn't very far away and in less than an hour we'd be at maybe our last party stateside. Three men from our crew made this run every day: Jackson, Skeets and me. A fourth would join us sometimes, a crazy Hungarian waist gunner in our squadron [but a different aircraft crew] named Daniel Buda. We four became inseparable. Sometimes Leafski or Blake would go with us, and Whistler, too, but they'd wander away from the group, leaving the four of us together. About the first night we found a small, cheap nightclub The Indiana Tavern, which we made our headquarters in the city. After a couple of trips, the live five-piece band would stand and play the official Air Corps March when we came in the door. This caused some jealousy in the naval clientele, so they would obligingly play "Anchors Aweigh," and we got along with the sailors pretty well. We never had a brawl like so many movies showed. We were all very peaceable and innocent. We decided the Marines must be the troublemakers, and no Marines ever came in. We were having a great time and still got plenty of sleep if we'd catch the *Rocket* back to Topeka about midnight, which we didn't always do, but we had to stand roll call and get the orders for the day every morning at eight o'clock. This went on several days, and our financial condition was getting in bad shape.

Pretty Boy Blake met his wife there in those few days, a beautiful Italian girl who could really put on a show dancing jitterbug style with Blake. He went back to Kansas City in 1945 and they live there now [1973]. His being in the veterans' hospital there determined our meeting place for our 30th anniversary. I wonder if we'll ever have another.[5]

Topeka was indeed a break for the airmen from the hard training endured the months before. The 449th Bomb Group's historian, 1st Lt. Damon A. Turner, wrote in his diary/log on the twenty-third and twenty-sixth of November, "A wonderful place, this Topeka. Except for appointments, the men are free to go as they please. Parties, juicy steaks, plenty of liquor—Topeka is a paradise; Kansas City a happy playground."[6]

Oscar continues:

Just a couple of days later Bob [Bird] announced at roll call that there would be no trip to Kansas City that day—we were moving out for parts unknown. It was a bitterly cold December day—cloudy, windy, and snowing a little. Very unpleasant. We didn't want to leave really. But we did, and a few hours later, we were sweating and slapping mosquitos at Morrison Field in West Palm Beach, Florida. We spent the night there.

Our number of men had grown to thirteen. We were taking a pilot from another crew with his radio operator, and we had Master Sergeant [Clarence B.] "Red" Davis, line chief and head of maintenance of our squadron. Red Davis we already knew from working with him in Bruning. He admitted thirty-five years of his age and seventeen years in the Army, not all in the Air Corps. He was a real character and had adopted our crew about the middle of our stay in Bruning. I was glad to have him aboard. He could be a big help to me, knowing just about everything on the B-24. He was a crazy likable old man whose only advice to everybody was, "Make sense, men, make sense." This he repeated several times a day.

Next day, we filled up all fuel tanks, gave everything a thorough daily and preflight inspection, got everyone on board and took off into the "wild blue yonder" with only a heading of 135 degrees [southeast] as a clue. Our orders were sealed and not to be opened until thirty minutes after takeoff—very dramatic but not really very hard to figure one's final destination.

The first aircraft of the 716th Squadron departed Topeka on December 3, 1943. Some of the 449th Bomb Group's aircraft had left earlier. Col. Darr H. Alkire, flying with the 719th, led a formation out of Topeka on November 28. Others left later. The 717th and 718th Squadrons left Topeka on December 8.[7]

The heading 135 degrees, or southeast, from Florida started the journey to Italy by way of South America, then across to North Africa and into the Mediterranean and Italy. Here the Fifteenth Air Force gathered for attacks on German forces in southern Europe. But the initial heading given to aircrews did not necessarily mean the destination was what one might think. Another B-24 crew of a different group, flying from a California base, got an initial heading sending them west. They assumed that they were going to fight in the Pacific theater. They discovered upon opening their orders, thirty minutes after takeoff, that they were to reverse course and head east, with their ultimate destination the Fifteenth Air Force in Italy.[8]

Oscar continues:

So, after 30 minutes of flying, we found ourselves on the way to Trinidad, a British-controlled island in the Caribbean Sea. We were to land, refuel, and remain overnight and then to proceed to Belem, a base in Brazil, South America. The first leg was short but different by being all over water, and a B-24 won't float, so we'd had several dry runs of "ditching," or crash landing on water, in Nebraska which, believe it or not, has a larger percentage of water area than any other state. I learned that only recently. It sounds fishy, doesn't it?

We arrived early in the afternoon in Trinidad. Prof had no trouble putting us right on target. We just got parked and in came a flash flood. I think it does every day in Trinidad. It was warm and steamy after the rain, and pleasing smells came from the jungle that grew right up to the runways and buildings. Trinidad is about ten degrees north of the equator, quite a change from Topeka, Kansas.

Next day, the flight to Belem was in perfect weather and uneventful, maybe even a bit boring. I'd made this run before in the C-87 hauling "junk."[9]

The jump from Belem to Natal was about 900 miles and this was all over lush green jungle country practically on the equator. We flew high enough to be comfortably cool. We talked and played poker in the waist section or napped in the luggage racks. Hughes [the copilot], now called "Air Force" from his initials, A. F., let me act as copilot for a while but mostly we were on auto-pilot. Everything was okay.

We made an apparently normal landing at Natal, but in our inspection the next day, I discovered a tiny crack in a casting of the left main landing gear. I was sure it hadn't been there before, so after consulting with Bob and Red, we grounded ourselves and made it very official by having Master Sergeant Davis initial the red X in the plane's book.

It was a major operation and for two days we sweated and worked with maintenance men on the base there removing the faulty part to be ready when the new one came. We had to wait almost two weeks for it, but finally it arrived by air freight on a C-87 from Middletown Air Depot.

We didn't mind the waiting at all. For us it was a Christmas vacation in summer. We lay on the beach of the Atlantic and swam. I guess surfboards hadn't been introduced to Brazil. The city was off limits, but it was easy enough to cross the fence guarded by Brazilian soldiers and patrolled by the U.S. Army military police (MPs); the Brazilians would even hold the wires while you went through the fence. It was just an ordinary four-decked wire fence. Then you could walk across the adjoining Brazilian airfield and take a taxi into town about two miles away. If you got picked up by the MPs in town, they just hauled you back to the base, free of charge. A taxi was fifteen cents.

We didn't go into the city much. I only went once and thought it better to stay on the base that went right down to the beach. It was hot Christmas Day on the beach, and we bought fresh pineapples for a nickel each from a cheerful native peddler who carried them in two baskets, one on each side of an ancient looking, dirty white horse. He obligingly peeled them for us by holding them by the top and with a few quick strokes of his sharp machete, he expertly removed the rough peeling. Then, he cleaned his machete by wiping it on his horse's tail. We ate them anyway and they were good.

Finally, on December 27 or 28, we took off on our longest jump, about 2,000 miles across the Atlantic to Dakar in French West Africa (now Senegal). We left early but traveling against the sun, we lost about two hours of daylight, and it was late afternoon when we arrived. The Professor again put us right on the spot, just like we knew he would. Everyone had complete confidence in everyone else.

The next day, a "short" hop of about 1,300 miles over the desert took us to Marrakesh northeast of Dakar in Morocco. We were really "jelly-rolling" now—on to Casablanca the same day and landed there just so we could say we had been there, I guess. We did take on a little fuel and went on to Oran to remain overnight.

I think it was New Year's Day 1944 that we hopped on to Constantine in Algeria. As I remember, all those places were still under the control of the Free French. We stayed at the Constantine base about ten days. Most of our squadron and group was already there. The base there was the biggest in North Africa, I think.

Not all of the B-24s of the 449th Bomb Group made the trip from Topeka to Grottaglie as uneventfully as Oscar and crew, even though they suffered a major breakdown that cost them ten days of transit time. Indeed, the group suffered considerable loss during this transit. On December 8 the B-24 flown by the commanding officer of the 719th, Capt. David L. Councill, with thirteen airmen aboard, crashed into a mountain near Marrakech, killing all aboard—the first of many casualties the 449th Bomb Group would suffer. On December 14 the B-24 flown by Capt. Hiero Hays, the operations officer of the 719th squadron, crashed. All the crew bailed out and survived except for Hays (who was probably last out). His parachute failed to open, resulting in his death. On December 16 Lieutenant Zimmerman's B-24 crashed in Puerto Rico. Maintenance problems, weather, and other issues resulted in the 449th Bomb Group's sixty-two B-24s being scattered, as Turner wrote on Christmas Day, "all over South America, North Africa and Italy." Colonel Alkire's formation of the 719th was first in Grottaglie, arriving on December 17. It was a month later before all the 449th's Liberators were marshalled at Grottaglie, the former Italian air base from which the group would operate.[10]

Grottaglie became the home base for the 449th Bomb Group, the Flying Horsemen, consisting of four B-24 squadrons. Grottaglie was one of twenty bases built in southeastern Italy, an area known as the Foggia plain, from which the Fifteenth Air Force, with headquarters at Bari, was to operate.[11]

The movement into Italy by the Fifteenth had been rushed. The rapidity of Italy's collapse and surrender spurred AAF commander Henry H. Arnold on October 9, 1943, to ask for the Fifteenth Air Force. The Joint Chiefs immediately authorized it. Besides being closer to targets that were practically out of range for the Eighth Air Force, "Sunny Italy" was supposed to have good weather for flying, so the Fifteenth could fly when the Eighth Air Force was shut down by England's persistent bad weather. Furthermore, positioning another air force in Italy would force the Luftwaffe to fight on two fronts.[12]

They were wrong about the weather, though. It proved almost as bad as England's winter weather: cold, wet, foggy, and cloudy. This added another layer of danger and suffering for crewmen. Bomber crews had to deal with flak, enemy fighters, and now the weather with accompanying extreme cold at altitude. Although the men had special clothing, including electrically heated garments, wool-lined boots, and gloves, the tremendous cold could and did inflict frostbite on exposed flesh.

There were no facilities for living and working upon arrival. Grottaglie had been an Italian airbase and had been bombed regularly during July 1943 by, ironically, AAF B-24s prior to its liberation by British troops in early September 1943.[13] Virtually everything was destroyed that was conducive to supporting living, working, and flying. First Lieutenant Turner noted in his diary the poor conditions at Grottaglie. December 28: "Conditions at Grottaglie are bad. There were no lights, no latrines, poor food, no beds, bombed out buildings, no heat, no nothing! The closest showers are in Taranto. So, this is war!" January 1, 1944: "Will Grottaglie ever be a satisfactory base? To the newly arrived Group it looks doubtful. Long lines before latrines. Officers and EM [enlisted men] alike, take their turns."[14]

The rapid move into Italy meant that the bombers arrived at Grottaglie before engineering units. Thus the field was not really ready for flight operations before the arrival of the planes. The official air force history attests (in regard to all the bomber bases in Italy) that during the "winter of 1943–44 in the Heel was a nightmare of buckling runways, frenzied repairs, mud, water—and neglect of other construction."[15]

The ground crewmen and other support personnel of the 449th Bomb Group came into Italy via merchant ships in convoys. There were delays en route, and therefore the ground crews arrived, in many cases, after the bombers. The 716th's ground echelon arrived the same day as the Sophisticated Lady flew its first mission, January 15, 1944. Before they were ready to go to work, Oscar's crew did their own aircraft maintenance and even loaded their own bombs.[16]

With the interest in D-Day and the Battle of the Bulge, the popular knowledge of World War II in Europe is focused on France, Belgium, and Germany. Before D-Day (June 6, 1944) Allied armies saw a lot of tough fighting in Northern Africa and Italy. Italy had agreed to an armistice with the Allies in September 1943 due to the success of American and British armies in liberating southern Italy. The German army, however, continued to fight viciously for possession of north and central Italy. This was another reason the Joint Chiefs commissioned the Fifteenth Air Force. Once deployed on the Foggia plain, it could both strike Hitler's forces that fought the Allies there and participate in the strategic air campaign against Germany.

Oscar continues:

> [Grottaglie] had been an Italian air base but the battle that took place nearly destroyed everything. Not a building was untouched and only one was in condition to be used. It was a big building, well-built of stone with marble floors. It was taken by Colonel Alkire, our group commander, for his headquarters, officer briefing room, and most of the officers' quarters there. The six enlisted men of our crew made camp in a corner of a bombed-out building where two walls were still standing. We were issued six blankets each, but we nearly froze at night. Master Sergeant "Red" Davis decided to live with us. He was one of a small number of our ground crew who had come across from Africa, so we did our own maintenance and bomb loading for quite a while. Red had become one of the family.
>
> All crew members were issued a Colt .45 [semi]automatic pistol for shooting saboteurs but Red had a Thompson submachine gun that fired the same ammunition. He never did load it but was always pretending to shoot the enemy by pointing it high and saying, "Bang,

bang, bang! That was sure a tall Italian, but I got him!" After we got new living quarters built of wood, he didn't live with us anymore, but we heard that one day somebody loaded his gun. He came in, grabbed it, and shot about a dozen holes in one wall and the ceiling. The story was he never picked the gun up again, just put it under his bunk and left it.

We had left summer somewhere in Africa and Italy was much like Topeka, Kansas, being on about the same latitude, and it was really cold and damp. Some of those poor Italian kids went around bare footed. I could agree with General Sherman who said, "War is hell."

Things finally became better organized as the ground crews moved in. Our crew chief and assistant weren't the same that we'd had in Nebraska. I never knew what happened. Maybe they missed the boat. But we soon got acquainted with Martincech, our new crew chief that we called "Marty." His assistant was Joe. They took a load of work off Leafski, Red, and me. Red still spent a lot of time with us. Skeets, Pretty Boy, and Whistler were happy to have ground crewmen to load the bombs and to carry ammunition to the guns.

The group's first combat mission was January 8, 1944. The delay in Natal had put the Sophisticated Lady's crew ten days behind. They flew their first combat mission on January 15.

Oscar continues:

We flew several combat missions into Italy and had our first contact with the enemy: explosive shells from anti-aircraft guns on the ground [otherwise known as flak]. We saw our first enemy fighters. But they were Italian Fiat G-50s and not aggressive at all. We saw enemy flak for the first time, and it really scared me. There was absolutely nothing to fight back with—just sit there and take it. It gave me the sensation of being under a big metal tub while someone whacked it with a big hammer and another threw handfuls of rock against it. An odd sort of sound. A direct hit would be fatal, and if a shell exploded very close to a plane, a thousand or more pieces of shrapnel of various sizes could penetrate nearly anything except armor plate steel. Everyone but the turret operators could wear a flak vest that covered chest and back. They could also wear steel helmets, but many shell fragments penetrated even the vest or helmet. I guess more aircraft were lost to enemy fighters, and if I had a choice between flak and fighters, I'd choose neither one.

The rare appearance of enemy fighters is not surprising in that the German air force, in the Mediterranean theater, was greatly outnumbered. It had only 550 aircraft to cover an area from southern France to Crete. Opposing this was the Allied air armada of more than 3,000 operational aircraft in this theater.[17]

It is interesting that Oscar saw the Italian fighter, the Fiat G.50. It was a mainline Italian fighter aircraft, but Italy had surrendered to the Allies in September 1943. The Fiats he saw must have been from the National Republican Air Force (Aeronautica Nazionale Repubblicana) based in Northern Italy. Their pilots were Italian airmen who remained loyal to Germany. Only forty to forty-eight Fiats were still flying at the time. The Fiats were seriously outclassed by American and British fighters, P-51s, P-38s, and Spitfires that operated in Italy in late 1943 and 1944.[18]

Mail from home was the greatest morale builder for soldiers. Oscar got a letter from his mom soon after arriving at Grottaglie:

Sun. Jan 23
Oscar darling:

Got your letter Fri. Jan 21, just 2 weeks from the time you mailed it & that's the first I've had since Dec. 12th. I was so happy honey to hear from you, I nearly cried. Oh, you are so far away dear, I am always countin' up to see what time it is where you are & wonder what you are doin'. I do hope you & the other boys and the "Lady" are just fine.

Daddy has begun plowing for another crop. Gerald has been gettin' ready to go to work on another hay crop. He said we wanted to get ready to go to plowin' tomorrow but I don't think he did. He has been sick with the flu nearly ever since we came from seein' Harold & Jr.

Honey, your pilot has a sweet wife I bet (I guess she is his wife) anyway, Mrs. R. P. Bird sent me a picture like the one you sent me of the crew & the "Lady." I think it was so nice of her . . . tell all the boys I am thinkin' of them & praying you will all be successful & that everything will be ok.

Honey, I lost my wings you gave me, on my trip to see the boys. I cried for 50 miles after I found it out. Sweetheart I love you & think of you every hour. Good nite Oscar dear.

Mom[19]

In this letter Ollie reports on the home front farming. Although it was the dead of winter in New Mexico, there was always some work to be done on a farm. Gerald, and certainly Wiley and youngest son, Jim, were continuing to work, getting ready for next year's crop. Winter was when repairs were made on farm equipment. Due to a shortage of new agricultural equipment, any equipment or vehicles that might have been replaced with new purchases now had to be repaired.

She also reports that Gerald is ill with the flu. Gerald's respiratory problems stemming from his bout with tuberculosis years earlier left him vulnerable to respiratory illnesses.

Interestingly, Ollie also remarks on an informal and unofficial network of mothers and wives of Oscar's crew. In today's military there is an official network that provides support and information to the families of deployed service personnel. In World War II, such networks did not exist. Families nevertheless maintained contact with one another. We do not know who reached out to whom, but it very well could have been Mrs. Bird, who was the wife of the pilot and saw herself as the leader of the families at home just as Bob Bird was the leader of the crew.

Brother Harold, who was in advanced flight training at Ellington Field near Houston, also wrote to Oscar at this time:

4 February 1944
Dear Bud,

Haven't got anything much to do tonite now that Gypsy Rose Lee and her company didn't stay long. She came out about 7:30 tonite and at 7:40 she came out for her last bow. It wasn't worth what it cost to get in and it was free. Course she was fresh out of the hospital and I guess she didn't want to take anything off—afraid of catching flu or something. O well, I still have my pin-up girls.

Yeah, I see by the papers you boys are really givin' 'em hell and I reckon you're having quite a little fun. What do you think of me askin' for a B-24, I mean do you reckon it'll stand up under my landings? That's a tough one; I know you think the 24 is the best in the West & East but you're just a little reluctant to recommend it for the beating I'll give it. OK. I'll ask for a B-26 and let it kill me. All jokes aside tho, I think I will try to get one. I'm going up to instrument section tomorrow so I'll be P.O'd for about a week. Wish you luck & adios, son.

Harold[20]

Harold was nearing the completion of his training and would soon be assigned to an aircraft type. Here he mulls over his choices and then settles on B-26s. As he jokes, the B-26 had a nasty reputation. Harold evidently wanted a challenge and excitement. He could make his desires known but ultimately his aircraft type was decided by the AAF. The needs of the service prevailed.

He mentions Gypsy Rose Lee. She was a well-known performer in vaudeville and burlesque. Evidently here she is performing (or not) for the troops, who were disappointed that she did not show a little more skin. Harold mentions pinups, which were regular features in *Yank* magazine. His favorite was Betty Grable. Although not at all pornographic (by twenty-first-century standards), they pushed the envelope for propriety at the time. They also served as templates for aircraft nose art that proliferated among army aviation units in the war. Of note, the aircraft in other services, the navy and marine corps, generally did not feature nose art. This could have been because pilots in those services, in most cases, were not assigned a personal aircraft as were army pilots.

Oscar continues:

Most of the Italians were glad that we had liberated them from the Germans but there was still danger of sabotage. So, we took turns staying in the Lady at night to guard her.

Our new housing was about a mile from the flight line, a long walk. Officers rode on 6 x 6 trucks or weapons carriers like a pickup, but enlisted men furnished their own transportation. Jackson and I bought an old motorcycle to ride; it sure beat walking. I wonder who took it when I left. We thought nothing at all about the segregation of officers and enlisted men. It wasn't fair, but after all, what is? That was the Army way, and I doubt that it has changed much.

Our officers all lived together in one room of the HQ [headquarters] building and had rigged a stove fueled with 100-octane gasoline. Nearly every room had one, I guess, but one night their stove exploded burning "Air Force" [Lieutenant Hughes] and the Professor pretty bad.

I don't remember why Bob [Bird] and Deane [Manning] didn't get burned as badly. The fire swept several rooms and burned about twelve in all that had to be taken to the hospital at Bari about fifty miles up the east coast of Italy.[21] It was the Fifteenth Air Force headquarters.

None of them was badly burned. Bob and Deane were gone about a week.[22] The Professor [Victor Harris] and Air Force were gone a month or more.

Lt. Deane C. Manning, the crew's bombardier, wrote of this fire:

When we got there [Grottaglie], the four officers [of the Sophisticated Lady crew] were assigned to one room in the "L"-shaped, burned-out administration building, on the third floor near the corner and the circular stair. Our only furniture was six or eight G.I. blankets each, some of which we used to cover the open door and window which had long since departed. Since it was cold in mid-January even in southern Italy, we scrounged some items around, probably from the plane to make a stove for heat, with 100-octane gas dripping on rocks in a drum.

I remember the de-icer tank from the plane was our fuel storage tank was located about 10 feet away from the stove. One night, copilot Anson Hughes and navigator Victor Harris had stayed up playing cards while pilot Bob Bird and myself, bombardier Deane Manning were in bed on pallets of blankets on the floor. They decided to fill the tank for the night before going so we wouldn't have to make the "run" every day. It is not known if they turned out the stove before filling began or not, but quickly the funnel filled and overflowed and ignited the gas. Hughes and Harris were saturated and very severely burned, but due to the quick and effective action taken by the flight surgeon, both recovered in good shape.

Bob and I tried to get some of our clothes out of the fire—which we had just hung up on racks built that day, just inside the door opening. I assume that the fumes from the spilled gas had saturated both ways down the "L"-shaped corridor, for when someone yelled that "it's going to blow!", it really did, and sent sheets of flame roaring down the "L"-shaped corridors from about 5 feet above the floor, both ways. Many who were in the corridor, or even in rooms without doors, were burned from the neck up! Everyone tried to get out at once, many falling over each other going down the circular stairs in the dark, and several . . . were hurt bailing out of the third-floor windows! . . . It was over very quickly, and fortunately not many were seriously hurt, but . . . they did change the rules on stoves rather abruptly.[23]

Oscar continues:

We six enlisted men were left to fly with various strangers who came from the general pool of pilots without planes of their own. Some were pretty chicken and gave us a pretty bad time. One eager beaver pilot went to the squadron commander with the story that we were neglecting the Lady in various ways and that she should be taken away from us and given to him with a different crew of his own choosing. He accused us of not keeping our guns clean, they were just rusting away, that we didn't guard her at night, etc. Our squadron commander, [Maj.] "Smilin' Jack" Silverstein, came to see for himself. I was worried that we'd lose the Lady, but Master Sergeant Davis testified for us along with some officers of the squadron. We not only got to keep the Lady, I was promoted to sergeant that [very] day. We surely were happy when Bob and Deane came back. I just wasn't made to take a responsibility like that.

Oscar comments on the pressure that fell on him as senior enlisted man of the Sophisticated Lady's crew, even though he was only a private, in an attempt to "steal" the Sophisticated Lady away from the crew. As a flight engineer, he was responsible for the overall condition of the Lady. These charges were a direct attack on him and his performance as a flight engineer. This attempted "theft" was warded off and Bird's crew kept their B-24. There was more good news in that Oscar's rank was restored to sergeant. That Silverstein, the squadron commander, and other officers weighed in in support of Oscar and the Lady's crew says a lot about Sophisticated Lady's good mechanical condition and about Oscar's reputation as a competent and conscientious engineer. Evidently this reputation was known throughout the squadron.

Oscar continues:

Most of our missions were fairly close to home since Italy is only 700 miles or so from top to bottom and very narrow, but we were up early nearly every morning for breakfast and briefing of the day's mission. We made our pre-flight check and daily inspection as soon as it was light. Marty and Joe were always there to see us off. Sometimes they had worked all night.

British Beaufighters were based at this same field, and these twin-engine radar-equipped night fighters started flying nearly every night.[24] This made good use of the field night and day. The Luftwaffe had bombed us a few times at night, but they were not very effective, and we operated with very little opposition.

On a mission one day, the impossible happened. In the Browning .50 caliber machine gun, the bolt shuttled back and forth 800 times a minute to eject empty shells and to reload the chamber with a live round of ammo. To absorb the shock, limit its backward travel, send it forward again into firing position, a cylinder four or five inches long and about one inch in diameter was filled with a stack of thin fiber discs. Thirty or forty were held in compression in the cylinder by a threaded plug screwed into the cylinder, which was on the back plate. Actually, it was a part of the back plate. This plug had a detent device which was guaranteed not to let the plug back out. It just could not happen, it never had. But the one in my right gun of the top turret did! There is a first time for everything. This happened while I was wasting ammunition blasting away at an out-of-range Italian fighter plane. I shouldn't have been doing it, but I hate to sit and do nothing, and I did need the practice. This steel plug bounced around the turret a few times, then it hit me right in the mouth. My beautiful two front teeth were broken off practically right at the gum line. The discs flew everywhere, and several hit me in the face. I carried the mark of one on my right cheek bone for months after. It didn't hurt much, but my pride and ego were sorely wounded.

Even Skeets couldn't figure out how it could happen. We did put on a new backplate, however, and it didn't happen again.

By now, we had all been awarded the Air Medal for five combat missions with an oak leaf cluster for each additional five. I still have my Air Medal with one cluster. I'm proud of it. I think not many air medals were awarded to a private, but mine was with engraving on the back to prove it. Most combat crewmen had at least a staff sergeant rating. As I said, my rating was restored to sergeant at about this time.

Ollie wrote to her Texas relatives, Annie and Ed, to give them an update on her "darling boys."

Sunday, January 23, 1944:
Dear Ed & Annie,

Annie you don't know how mean I feel for not writing to you any sooner after being down there & couldn't come to see you and Ed [it had rained too much to get to their farm]. I have been so busy, seems like I'll never get caught up with my work and & I've been going twice a week to fold surgical dressings all afternoon. Harold and Jr were just fine but we didn't get to see much of them. They couldn't get out and we couldn't get in. Harold got out only about 2 ½ hours. The two nites we were with him and Jr. didn't get out at all. The first nite we all just sat in the car and talked till 8:30. Then the next nite we did finally get a visitor's pin and went in and had supper with Jr. at the canteen.

Harold has moved now to Ellington Field at Houston. He's taking twin engine training now & in Advanced. Jr. is in Garden City Kan. now, in basic. And Oscar, bless his little heart, is in Italy. I just got a letter from him Fri. He was okay he said. He spent Christmas in Brazil. He didn't say how long he had been in Italy, didn't say much of anything in fact. Said they could call it Sunny Italy if they wanted to but personally it didn't appeal to him, it was too cloudy and cold. Oscar's birthday is the 19th & I wish you & Ed would send him a card. It took his letter two weeks to come. . . .

Ollie[25]

Here Ollie relays that they (either all or part of the family) took a trip to Texas, probably the previous late summer, when both Harold and Junior were in San Antonio (about 500 miles from Roswell), when Harold was in preflight and Junior was in classification. They had attempted also to visit the Allison kin near Eastland, Texas (about 240 miles from San Antonio). This long trip would have been risky at the time due to rationing for gas and tires. To undertake a trip of this length would have required saving up ration stamps over a considerable period of time.

Ollie also mentions folding surgical dressings. This was one of many volunteer activities women undertook during the war and highlights women's important role on the home front. Indeed, the war had a profound effect on women. With men at war, and encouraged by the government, they went to work either on the farm, in industry, or in the military (335,000 women served in the military).[26] Women replaced men gone to war, both on the home front and in the military stateside. In the military a popular motto was "Free a man to fight." This meant a female soldier could serve in administrative or maintenance positions instead of a man. (Women did not serve in combat roles.) Ollie folded surgical dressings as a volunteer. Other common volunteering activities included working with the Red Cross, growing home gardens (victory gardens), hosting scrap drives, and supporting USO activities. With a large air base at Roswell hosting thousands of service personnel from all parts of the nation, there would have been many opportunities for Ollie, Ollie Mae, and Mary to help out with the USO.[27] The war changed society's perception of women to a large extent, from being child raisers and homemakers to having marketable and valuable skills outside the home. These skills were in addition to the traditional outside-the-home work activities such as teaching, clerking, and sewing.[28]

Oscar wrote the following letter to the folks two days before an eventful mission over the Anzio beachhead:

18 February 1944 - Still in Italy
Dear Mom and Everybody

Well here I am again, all there is to do is write letters. I got a V-mail from Harold today, not so very old, it was mailed Feb. 4th [see above, this chapter]. I haven't heard from Jr. in quite a spell now I guess maybe I should write to him. [Junior at this time was in advanced flight training at Eagle Pass, Texas. This will be discussed in ch. 11.] I guess I don't make much sense anymore, I'm becomin' slightly flak happy I think. Flak ain't so bad till it bursts too close, then it can do one helluva lot of damage. It's kinda pretty when it bursts quite a ways out. The bursts fascinate Dixon, our nose gunner, he stands up in his turret and watches for the stuff. Personally, I try to keep my mind off it by swingin' around lookin' for enemy aircraft. It doesn't exactly scare me but it gives me a funny feelin' every once in awhile, 'specially when it's so close you can hear it burst. Some of these nazi gunners come as close as they can without hittin' you I think. They must be tryin' to scare us off and break our morale. I don't think it'll work, do you? They're getting desperate enough to try anything though I reckon'.

Have y'all sold all your cotton yet? I guess you must have a pot full of money by now. I ain't doin' so bad myself. You should know I'm a Sgt. again now and that makes more money and my expenses are not anymore. There's nothin' to do with money here, in fact I started $175 home today. So you take the $40 per month allotment and make bonds out of it, but you keep what I send home till I tell you different. I may want some of it when I get back to the States.

How's your old Hudson doin' Wiley? I never thought you'd buy an off-brand thing like that. Why don't you buy a good Chevrolet and forget your car troubles. Have you got the Buick fixed up yet? How's the old pickup doin' now?

Harold thinks he wants to get into B-24s. I guess it's okay, but like I told him, I'd hate to have a crew like the one my pilot has. They're good boys but they're full of life you know and kinda hard to keep under control at times. He's [Bob Bird] the kind of man that could handle 'em though. Some of these guys are getting' worse by the minute. It's a wonder these Guinea barracks stand the vibration of some of these friendly arguments. I hope they're friendly. I'd hate to wake up some mornin' and see 5 or 6 corpses layin' around.

Oscar[29]

This is an interesting letter as it denotes his and his crew's response to the antiaircraft fire the Germans were throwing up. This was their first combat experience. The enemy fire as Oscar relates, although humorously, was no doubt eye-opening. Two 449th Bomb Group B-24s had been lost in combat by the time he wrote this letter.[30] Men from other crews whom he might have known, were gone, killed, or prisoners of war.

One of the planes went down due to a freakish and deadly accident. On January 14, on a mission to Mostar, Yugoslavia, the formation of bombers lost cohesion and the bombs of one B-24 were accidentally dropped on a B-24 below. The lower bomber exploded in a massive fireball, and nine crewmen were killed. Miraculously, two men survived and spent the war as POWs. The upper plane, its crew not realizing what had happened, thought they had been hit by flak when the lower B-24 exploded. The powerful blast seriously damaged their aircraft and five men bailed out. The pilot managed to keep the plane flying and flew it back to base with the other four crewmen aboard.[31]

Another plane had been lost, hit by antiaircraft fire on January 31 while bombing Aviano, Italy. It was the lead aircraft of the group flown by the group commander, Colonel Alkire. He was captured and remained a prisoner until the war's end. Col. Thomas J. Gent Jr. became the new group commander.

The farm was on Oscar's mind, and he was interested in the cotton crop. His comment about a "pot full of money" might reflect the good news on farm commodity prices. Farming was doing exceedingly well nationwide. In the period from 1940 to 1945, farm income rose from $4.4 billion to $12.3 billion. Individual farm income rose from $707 to over $2,000 per year. This was truly good news after the bleak years of the Depression. Finally, farm income exceeded farm expenses.[32] His pay also seemed fantastic for the times when one considers that in the desperate times of the Depression, men pounded the streets for jobs that might pay only forty cents an hour.

Finally, Oscar comments on life in the barracks tell us they were no longer living in a bombed-out building; better quarters were now available. The crew was quartered together and discussions could get lively. These men were dealing with a new environment, combat, rough living conditions, family separation, and any number of stressors. Whatever the cause, added to it was the natural propensity of young men to be adversarial. That they were hard to keep under control suggests that he, as the flight engineer and (supposedly) the ranking enlisted crewman, had some responsibility in this regard.

In the next chapter Oscar continues detailing his war experiences, including a mission in support of a massive Allied amphibious landing. In another mission his crew flies their first strategic mission—an attack into Germany in conjunction with the massive Allied air offensive called Big Week. The result of this mission had dramatic and serious consequences for Bob Bird's crew.

Chapter 7

Oscar into Combat and Anzio and Regensburg: 1944

At this point in his memoir, when combat turned deadly and dark, Oscar felt it necessary to include the following statement in his memoir. It represents a type of waiver. Hopefully, the reader will understand.

FOREWORD of WWII SEGMENT:
The following account has been written from my memory. Dates and places are therefore only approximate. I tried to pinpoint various things from a diary which was sketchily kept by Skeets, our ball turret gunner who was with me nearly the whole time, but it turned my thoughts into confusion, and I was unable to use it to any great advantage. He has written many things that I remember vaguely or not at all.

Unfortunately, I wasn't endowed with total recall, or even an exceptional memory. Some things that I remember clearly I can't write about, because I don't want to. Sometimes they say, "to protect the innocent," and some of the characters involved are just that.

Some stories, especially true stories, are better left untold. I will write about the things that I choose to remember and keep trying to forget those that I've been trying to forget since the beginning of 1944 AD.

Some of the untold stories might make better reading, but this account is true as I remember it from my place in the action and from my place in the audience. I've tried not to create any heroes or villains,

> so there will be quite a lot that won't be written. I don't think I have
> time anyway.
>   Locations of places and distances I have checked in Rand-McNally's
> *World Atlas* before I write them in this story. I'd never bothered to do so
> until I started writing this.

This is perhaps the most telling part of his memoir: what he did not write,
and his deliberate withholding of that information speaks volumes. I believe
he did it, as he said, to protect the innocent. A reader who never flew where
these men flew has no context to help them understand why things occurred
as they did. It highlights the ferocity of the memories that combat veterans
live with. Like most combat veterans, he does not want to perpetuate the dark
memories he has, to give them life, potency, and eternity in ink. Oscar here,
forty years later, is still dealing with them. He relates what he deems suitable to protect his fellow participants and himself. He also wants to protect
us, those who never experienced war in the air, who would be shocked and
disillusioned by the reality of war. It is an appropriate introduction to
the next three chapters. Oscar pulls back the curtain on some of the events
he experienced—a sanitized version. To enhance readers' awareness, I have
included comments from other veterans of the time and place that provide the
between-the-lines information and give readers greater understanding.

Oscar is to be commended for even writing these memoirs. It required
that he resurrect some long-buried memories. I believe he did this for his
family—his crew—whom he wants to honor by telling this story that depicts
their bravery and sacrifice. There was not a tighter band of brothers than that
of a bomber crew.

The ground fighting in Italy had devolved into a stalemate. German forces
had stopped the northward drive of Allied infantry divisions in the southern
part of Italy. To break that stalemate, leaders decided to land a large force
amphibiously behind German lines at Anzio (Operation Shingle), on Italy's
west coast. The thinking was that a large Allied force coming ashore there
would force the Germans to choose between two unsavory courses of action.
One was to pull forces out of their defensive positions in the south to resist
the landing. This action, however, would risk an Allied breakout in the south
due to weakened German defenses. The other choice was to not oppose the

Anzio landings and keep the Allied armies bottled up in the south. This action, however, would put the Anzio-landed Allies behind them, causing them to fight on two fronts and have their lines of supply interdicted. They chose to oppose the Anzio landings and, to a significant degree, were successful.

The Germans effectively bottled up the beachhead, creating a precarious situation for the Allies. The Germans could leisurely shell them from the high ground around the beach, wear them down, then drive them into the sea. Air support was critical for the American forces trapped on the Anzio beach. While the principal mission of the Fifteenth Air Force was to participate in the Combined Bomber Offensive against Germany, a strategic air campaign, the land battle in Italy forced a deviation from that main mission. It was imperative that the Fifteenth Air Force support the Allied troops on the Anzio beachhead as well as those fighting in the south.

The Fifteenth Air Force surged sorties in support of the Anzio land-ing. For the heavy bombers, B-24s and B-17s, this meant attacking enemy transportation lines that fed troops and supplies to the Germans at Anzio. German-held railroads were often targeted. Oscar's B-24 hit marshalling yards on seven of the twelve missions it flew during January and February 1944. Another key target for heavy bombers was German air bases in Italy.

Bob Bird's crew flew eleven missions on Italian targets before they ever flew a mission into Germany on a strategic target. These were: Prato (north-central Italy) on January 15 and February 8 and 14; Arezzo (north-central Italy) on January 17 and 29; Pisa (on the northwest coast) on January 18; Perugia (northeast of Rome) on January 19 and 23; Quidonia (ten miles east of Rome) on January 20; Genzano (an airdrome near the west coast, fifteen miles south of Rome and fifteen miles north of Anzio) in February; and Anzio beachhead on February 20.[1]

A mission flown by the Sophisticated Lady and twenty-six other bomb-ers of the 449th Bomb Group on January 19 gave the Nazis a sharp poke in the eye. These Liberators dropped sixty-five tons of bombs on the German long-range reconnaissance base at Perugia in north-central Italy. By hitting this base, the Allies severely reduced German knowledge of Allied activity. This was especially important because it occurred just three days before the Anzio landing. Anzio was a tactical surprise because the enemy had been effectively blinded by this strike.[2] Nevertheless, in the following fighting, the Germans stopped any breakout from either the beachhead or Allied positions in the south.

On February 16 the Germans launched a massive attack on the Anzio forces with the aim of throwing the Americans back into the sea. Ground commanders asked for the heavy bombers to add their punch in direct support of the troops. The Sophisticated Lady flew one of these close support missions.[3]

The very next day, Oscar's twenty-fifth birthday and the day before the mission to Anzio beach, he wrote home again. Perhaps it was the increased dangers associated with an Anzio mission or that the 449th would soon be flying missions over Germany for the first time. At any rate, he was in a reflective mood.

Feb. 19, 1944 – Somewhere in Italy
Dear Mom and everybody,

Well, here it is Sat. the 19th day of February, today I'm 25 years old, boy I'm getting' old ain't I? Here I've given three of the best years of my life to Uncle Sam. I hope he appreciates it. I'm not complainin' though, I guess he's treatin' me the best he can under the circumstances.

They got our movie set up again finally, in the mess hall and I went over tonite with Skeets and Daniel, the two Brooklyn bums. We saw "Claude" and they liked it. But I had the toothache [probably because of the incident with his machine gun malfunctioning described above] and I just couldn't get in the mood for pictures . . . but there is nothin' else to do. Not even any beer to drink. I haven't had any beer since I left N. Africa and that was quite some time ago. Nothing will take its place either, I tried this Italian wine and it's definitely no good!

I got your letter of Feb 4th yesterday and also two from Jerry [Gerald]. Mighty happy to hear from you folks. You asked what I was doin' mom. Well I'll tell you. I'm still engineer on the Sophisticated Lady and naturally I'm an aerial gunner and I man a Martin turret in the top of the Lady. As far as the country goes, no, it's not like N.M. It's the crowdedest place you ever saw. More dam little old towns around here and nothing in any of them. The farms look like so many little gardens, it's kind of pretty alright but you can have the best part of it,

I don't want it. The weather here is stinky, the least little bit of moisture makes the ground sloppy and it's always rainin' and the wind blows like hell and it's cold even on the ground. At 20,000 ft. it's colder than you can imagine. A lot of the boys got frozen ears and spots on their faces here one day. I didn't though 'cause I'm too tough I guess.

Everybody be good and I'll write more later. Adios amigos—I'll be seein' you.

Love from Oscar.[4]

Oscar gives us his perspective on Grottaglie and Italy in general. Not surprisingly, it is not a positive opinion. The base was not ready to support intensive air operations. Its austere and expeditionary condition is described in the above passages. Many men who went into the AAF because of the glamor associated with flying were discovering there was hardly anything glamorous about what they were doing in Italy.

He notes the cold at altitude and jocularly dismisses it. After undergoing a boyhood of farmwork and well drilling, Oscar indeed was tough. But in actuality the cold was hardly funny. B-24s were open to the brutally cold wind as it lashed through the fuselage. Temperatures of negative thirty degrees was not uncommon. The missions were long, at least five or six hours in length. The AAF was doing all it could to deal with the cold, providing insulated and electrically heated flying suits, fur-lined flying boots, and more. But still it was bone-chillingly cold. Oscar could be referring here to the mission flown on February 14 in which the official record notes that "several of the men returned with frostbitten faces."[5]

Oscar continues:

I celebrated my twenty-fifth birthday February 19, 1944 by flying to the aid of our troops at the Anzio beachhead who were hanging on by their fingernails and about to be pushed back into the Tyrrhenian Sea [actually, this mission occurred on February 20]. The beachhead was just south of Rome on the west coast of Italy. It was only about 200 miles away, and we made three trips carrying anti-personnel bombs against the defending German and Italian forces there.[6] We went in at a low level for better accuracy, not wanting to bomb our own troops. The lines were very close, and I think we took flak from both friend and enemy. It was the heaviest I'd ever seen. We had no opposition in the air so all that I could see from the top turret was burst after burst of flak everywhere and very close several times. I couldn't shoot back, and I just sat there petrified with fear.

The Lady staggered through it shuddering and bucking. I could hear our other guns strafing the enemy below. One burst of flak was just too close, and I knew something bad had happened. Skeets didn't respond to Bob's call on the intercom, but everyone else was ok. Leafski reported from the waist that the ball turret where Skeets was had been hit and losing a lot of hydraulic fluid. He and Blake and Whistler (as soon as we cleared the battle zone) started bringing up the ball turret manually. Hydraulic pressure had been lost there and in other places. It now came to me why Bob had insisted on several occasions that Leaf and I should lower and lock the landing gear manually for practice. This time it was a necessity, and we knew how to do it. Surely we could this time.

The worst damage was to the ball turret where Skeets was. It was being flooded with hydraulic fluid, and while Blake and Whistler continued bringing him up, Leaf and I crawled into the space above the flight deck under the center section of the wing and attached the hand crank to the cable winch shaft for emergency lowering the main landing gear. I think it was twenty-six revolutions of the crank that unlocked it from the up position, and a lot of power had to be applied to unlock it. The crank turned harder and with more resistance as the winch tightened to the cables that went to each side. It took a lot of force to unsnap the locks, and the cables were adjusted not to pull them simultaneously, which would require twice as much torque on the shaft. I started sweating as the cable tension increased but finally one lock unsnapped, and I turned it over to Leaf for the other one. As soon as the gear was unlocked, the wheels fell into the down position but did not lock until the cables were pulled hard enough to snap the down locks into position. The winch turned a few revolutions easily until the cables tightened to unsnap the lock on the other wheel. In just a half minute old strong-arm Leaf had unsnapped the other lock, and then it was freewheeling again until the cables got tight enough to snap the locks into position. Normally this was all done with hydraulic pressure by simply moving a short lever located on the floor between the pilot and copilot. Even when we had power, the down locks were always checked visually even if the green light on the cockpit instrument panel indicated all three wheels to be down and locked. When the down locks were engaged, you could see both sides through the waist windows, and the down locks showed about a five- or six-inch square of bright yellow about the middle of each side.

We finally got them locked and Leaf went back to make sure they were down and locked while I went forward to just behind the nose section to unlock and drop the nose wheel. This was not hard to do. So, now we had our wheels down and locked.

Skeets was out of his turret soaked in the red hydraulic fluid. He looked like he had been dipped in blood, but nobody had a scratch. By now we were getting close to home, and since nobody was injured, we were instructed to let the rest of the Group land before us. There was a possibility that we could in some way block the runway. Everything looked okay, but we couldn't be sure of our hydraulically powered brakes. We circled outside the landing pattern and kept our fingers crossed.

Our landing was normal. The gear didn't collapse as we touched down lightly, and the full weight settled on the wheels as our speed decreased. Bob applied the brakes gently, and they slowed us to maybe sixty miles per hour. Halfway down the runway when the right brake started fading and the Lady started to turn slowly to the left. Too much pressure applied to the brakes could put us into an uncontrollable ground loop, but if Bob let her roll straight down the runway, we'd surely run off the end. Bob somehow held just enough pressure for the Lady to make a graceful 360 degree turn across the runway (luckily it was dry) onto the field and back onto the runway again. After what seemed an eternity, we came to a stop with our right wingtip just a few feet from the control tower. The meat wagon (ambulance) rushed in to claim Skeet's bloody body and seemed to be disappointed to find all that flood of red stuff was hydraulic fluid.

Nobody but Bob could have done it so perfectly. I think he had some help from Him. The Lady was perforated thirty-two times by various sizes of flak fragments, mostly very small but some as big as my hand.

First Lieutenant Turner wrote about this strike to Anzio:

The men's spirits were high, a smile on their face and eager for the mission. Everyone was in a mood to strike a blow at the enemy forces on the beachhead. A few minutes after takeoff the sky was black with Liberators heading in the direction of the Axis-held territory. Thirty-seven B-24s were aloft within a limited time . . . YES . . . that is right! They ran into a complete overcast, snow and bad flying weather causing 19 to return early, but 18 of the pilots plunged on through the treacherous weather, to deal a terrific blow to the enemy. The results as stated in a few words by one of the pilots on the mission: "We really pasted the hell out of them." Unfortunately, bomb strike photographs failed to equal the enthusiasm of the returning pilots.[7]

As Turner relates, over half of the group's B-24s that took off were forced back by the miserable weather between Grottaglie and Anzio. Yet pilot Bird, flying the Sophisticated Lady, hung in and got through the weather and over the target so the Lady's bombs could be brought to bear. As was often the case, however, the crew's optimistic assessments of damage done were not reflected by the hard evidence. This was a condition evident in all war zones, by all antagonists.

Oscar continues:

The crew took two days to recuperate, then February 22, 1944, we took the Lady's twin sister, Pistol Packin' Mama, to Regensburg in Germany proper to blow-up the [ME-]109 factory that Willy Messerschmitt had there. It was our first and our last trip to Hitler's Fatherland.

As for Sophisticated Lady, we never knew how long it took Red and Joe and Marty to get her ready to go again, but she did fly again only to be shot down and crashed somewhere in Yugoslavia. [This story is recounted in the next chapter.] "Air Force" Hughes was flying as copilot. Tito's[8] underground system had them back to home base about two weeks after that running battle with some other 109s. I'd like to read a tale of that mission, written by Hughes [this story is recounted in chapter 8 below].[9]

Until February 20, 1944, the Fifteenth Air Force had directed its might toward supporting Allied land forces battling the Germans in Italy; direct support was provided at Anzio. On February 20 the mission changed to strategic bombing, hitting targets that would hopefully cripple Germany's war effort. Named Operation Argument, or Big Week, it was the beginning of one of the war's most important bombing campaigns.

The 449th Bomb Group's first strategic mission, a sortie into Germany, was highly significant. Regensburg was the hometown of Messerschmitt BF-109 production, a veritable Detroit of fighter manufacturing. The Messerschmitt fighters were a serious threat to the strategic bombing campaign. The ME-109 (its official designation was BF-109, or Bayerische Flugzeugwerke 109, but it was and is commonly called the ME-109 after its designer Willy Messerschmitt) was indeed a killing machine. Designed in 1934 and first flown in 1937, its first combat was in the Spanish Civil War. The idea in its design was to build "the smallest airframe that could be wrapped around the most powerful in-line aero engine available and still carry useful armament." It was the most prolifically produced fighter aircraft of the war. About thirty-five thousand were built. The model that flew against US bombers at the time was the BF-109G. It was powered by a 1,400-horsepower engine. It had two 13 mm (.51-caliber) machine guns in the cowling, and a 20 mm cannon firing from the propeller spinner hub. Another two 13 mm machine guns could be mounted beneath the wings, as well as rocket launching tubes.[10]

Destroying the two big factories at Regensburg would seriously hamper the Germans' ability to defend against bomber attacks.[11] The significance of the Regensburg attacks equaled that on the ball-bearing factory at Schweinfurt, Germany. The Germans were sure to guard the factories ferociously with antiaircraft guns, cannons, and fighters.

This Allied air assault on German aircraft manufacturing was deemed Big Week. Lasting six days, it was an all-out effort that included the US Eighth Air Force and the RAF flying from English bases and the US Fifteenth flying from Italian bases. During Big Week about 3,800 missions were flown, almost ten thousand tons of bombs were dropped, and about six hundred German fighters were claimed shot down. It was costly, however. More than two hundred bombers were shot down by the German defenders, incurring 2,600 casualties.[12] Historians and analysts who studied the effect of Big Week determined that the strikes started an irreversible decline in Germany's fighter production. It was the beginning of the end for the Luftwaffe.[13]

Fatefully, for Oscar and crew, the Luftwaffe positioned more of its fighters to confront the Fifteenth Air Force than the bombers coming from England. Making this doubly dangerous was that at this time in the war the Fifteenth, unlike the Eighth, lacked long-range fighter protection.[14] The Fifteenth Air Force bombers suffered under this situation with eighty-nine bombers lost during the Big Week, 82 percent of them under the guns of German fighters.

This mission to Regensburg, the first Oscar's crew had flown into Germany, dramatically altered his experience of the war. Oscar tells us why:

> The B-24H Pistol Packin' Mama was a twin sister of our Sophisticated Lady.[15] For some reason, which I don't remember, three days after the Lady had been so badly injured on her third trip to Anzio, my crew and I, except for copilot Hughes and navigator Vic [Harris], was chosen to take Pistol Packin' Mama on her first trip to Germany. It was our first trip, too, and February 22, 1944 just wasn't a very good day for it. In southern Italy where our base was located, it was cold, windy, and cloudy with a fine mist of rain, but we were supposed to be able to see the aircraft factory of Willy Messerschmitt in Regensburg well enough to really give it a good going over. We'd never met the ME-109s that were built there, and in many other factories in Germany, Austria, etc., by the thousands. More than 33,000 109s of different models were made in the ten years from 1935 to 1945. More fighter aircraft of a single design ever to be built by anyone.
>
> We were up early for a long briefing of the mission since it was our first into Germany and, in cooperation with the Eighth and Ninth Air Forces based in England, was to be one of the biggest. Later, figures showed that more aircraft (the total count) were lost by both the Allies and the Axis than on any other day of the war.
>
> The weather was bad, and we flew above an overcast most of the way to Regensburg. Very few clear patches showed anywhere, and the target itself was so heavily overcast that the decision was made to leave it and go to our secondary target, somewhere in Austria. I don't know what was there but I'm sure it needed bombing.
>
> The flight was long and tiresome. We flew above 20,000 feet and saw nothing but other B-24s and some B-17s in the distance headed in the same direction that we were. We had never flown with fighter escort on a mission. We'd never needed it, so we didn't miss it. The Axis air arm in Italy was very weak. We had never been really bothered by it except for a few "nuisance" bombing raids by the night boys of the Luftwaffe which actually did very little damage, but they did keep us nervous and sleepless sometimes.

It was about midday and I was tired, hungry, and badly needing a cigarette, but we were on oxygen and the "No Smoking" rule was in effect. I was sleepy, too, and I guess not very alert. It had become boring. We were not in really close formation and not ready for those deadly 109s that came out of nowhere, striking us head-on and almost level, five or six of them in very close formation with the leader just a few feet higher than his followers, not high enough for me to get them in my gunsight and not low enough for the ball turret in the belly of the ship. Jackson in the nose turret was the only one who could do anything effectively. He later described the sight as a "gunner's dream," but to me it was a frustrating nightmare in bright sunshine. I could see them clearly, but my tracers showed my fire to be too high and my guns were bumping on the safety down stop. Any lower would cause my fire to hit our own ship. I think those yellow-nosed boys (the propeller spinners were bright yellow, and fire flashed from the 20mm cannon firing through the center of the spinner) seemed to have more experience at this sort of thing than we did. We had heard of the "Boys from Abbeville," the yellow-nosed group of ME-109G fighters that were reported to be the favored, hand-picked hot shots, the pride and joy of Air Reich Marshall Hermann Goering himself. Their record from our point of view was very bad.

Their 350 miles per hour plus speed added to our own of about 250 miles per hour kept them in the range of our .50 caliber guns a very short time, and the five or six that came almost in single file were in range and gone in probably less than ten seconds. The nose turret guns were already chattering when added to the noise and vibration of mine. The Mama was shaking from the recoil of our guns, and vibration continued to increase as the 20mm shells from the 109s slammed into her.

Our number three engine [inboard engine on right wing] exploded into a ball of smoke and several feet of the right-wing tip just disappeared. The Mama started to roll to the right but somehow Bob hauled her back into an almost level attitude. The number three engine had been ripped out and where it had been was a gaping crater, filled with twisted, smoking metal that had a few seconds ago been a powerful smooth-running Pratt & Whitney R1830, 14-cylinder radial engine of about 1500 horsepower. On the other side, number two engine [inboard left wing] was smoking badly and I knew we'd lost two engines, we couldn't stay up.

It all happened so quickly but it seemed that time stopped, and I can still see it as a "stop action" picture. The fighters coming in nearly head-on in close echelon formation offset a bit to my right and each just a few feet lower than the one ahead of it. Jackson's four or five hundred rounds of fire in the few seconds had their effect on the second 109. It shuddered and staggered, then dropped out of sight below. Jackson got him for sure. The leader dived under us just inches short of a head-on collision, and the others took their turn in quick succession.

I was a hypnotical spectator. My guns kept chattering until the last 109 broke under us. We were kaput. I don't know how Bob kept her level. She was shaking all over, and we were going down at an alarming angle. I heard Bob on the intercom tell Deane to salvo the bombs. This would take a lot of weight off the Mama and buy a little time. I swung my turret to the left as quickly as I could and saw other planes of our squadron and group, some smoking and tumbling out of control. One disappeared in a red ball of fire. For all practical purposes we were alone and at the mercy of these little gray devils that came from nowhere, and by the time I could turn, they were gone.

I caught sight of some, the same ones I guessed, behind us and off to our right already above us and turning in our direction but out of range and still climbing. They knew though, as we did, that it was all over for us, and they went on to strike someone else. I continued turning and searching the sky for more. None appeared and Bob called, "Prepare to bail out." We were going down fast. I unplugged oxygen and heated suit and intercom, climbed down to the flight deck, found my chest pack chute, and snapped the two snaps to my harness. I was ready to go. I wondered if my chute would still work after being thrown and kicked around for months. It was unreal. I'd never thought I would need it.

I went down onto the catwalk of the forward bomb bay. The bombs still hung there. No wonder we were going down so fast. We were still carrying our full load of bombs. I managed to open the bomb bay doors about halfway with the manual control located by the catwalk in the forward bomb bay. I saw Jackson coming back from the nose section. Blood was pouring from his forehead and face, streaming down his chest. Behind him came Deane, being helped along by the substitute navigator who seemed to be all right, but Deane's right ankle had been shattered by a 20mm shell. Jackson's face and forehead was full of glass fragments from the "bulletproof" glass in the nose turret. A cannon shell had barely penetrated it, and he said later that it landed (the shell) smoking in his lap. None of the glass had penetrated deeply and his eyes were not hurt, but pieces of glass came out for months.

Deane's leg had a tourniquet to stop the bleeding and he'd been given a shot of morphine from the first aid kit. He gave me a grin as I fell backward through the open bomb bay door and out of their way.

I didn't see Deane again until 1973. He lost his foot (he had surgery in Austria just a few days after going down) and was repatriated and sent home in June or July 1944. He walked without limping. He didn't talk about his foot, and neither did I.

Leaving Oscar and the other crewmen bailing out or preparing to, let us hear from others who experienced this attack by German fighters. First, the pilot, Bob Bird:

Since Sophisticated Lady was still grounded from the Anzio mission, we were assigned to fly #498 Pistol Packin' Mama, Gil Bradley's plane. Since Hughes and Harris were still off flying duty, we borrowed Gil's copilot ([2nd Lt. Philip J.] Sheridan) and navigator ([2nd Lt. Charles F.] Popken).

It was screwed up from the start in which our section never made rendezvous with other elements.[16] Aborts reduced our section to 13–14 ships. We lost several guns to freezing and jamming and the tail turret burned out the traverse motor by the time we were half way to the target which was never sighted due to clouds (solid). On our return to the secondary we were jumped by ME-109s who shot down at least four of our planes. We were badly crippled and could only fly in circles so we bailed out while under attack.[17]

And from bombardier Manning:

I was bombardier on Bob Bird's crew in the 716th squadron. We were scheduled for a mission to Regensburg, our first really long-range mission into Germany. As I recall, it had been scheduled the previous day, maybe two days, and had been scrubbed, and we were "standing by" this day, not really expecting to go on this one. I remember wearing plain G.I. coveralls rather than a flying suit and for the first time, didn't even wear a .45. We had been shot up a little by anti-aircraft fire some three days earlier and our plane was still being repaired. Our copilot and navigator were still in the hospital from the fire we had, so we borrowed a plane and copilot and navigator and went on this mission to Regensburg. Actually, we had gone to the hospital the night before and brought Anson Hughes, copilot back to the base with us, but talked him out of flying because he had no equipment.

It was one of those days—this was in the days before radar—we hadn't seen the ground for five hours because of solid clouds below, we could not see the target, our fighter escort couldn't find us—again because of the clouds—and we were on the way home and looking for a secondary target. We were flying at 26,000 feet, which was considerably higher than our normal 20,000. We were met head-on by German 109s and [Focke-Wulf] 190s, and although we took several attacks, the first one did all the damage. This one made a slicing head-on pass, hitting the main spar about 15 or 20 feet from the right wingtip, knocked out our #3 and #4 engines (they were only about half there), knocked out the nose turret just above me and hit me just above the ankle, plus the intercom—all in the first pass! A couple of our guns were frozen and the nose was out, so while we may have made some hits, it was too late—we were going down and like a rock—with drag and no power on one side. I don't know why we weren't spinning, but we weren't.

The nose turret operator, Dixon [nicknamed Jackson], got out of the shattered turret and crawled back to the flight deck. I knew that I had lost a leg [foot] because it was barely hanging on. I took off my oxygen mask to talk to the navigator, Popken, about giving me a shot of morphine from the nose first aid kit and putting a tourniquet on my leg. I then opened the nose wheel hatch in case we had to get out in a hurry. Popken did get the tourniquet partially on, but he was a little nervous by this time—understandable—and dropped the morphine out the nose wheel hatch. From the nose compartment one can see the feet and legs of the pilot and copilot. About this time, I saw the copilot get up and leave, so I guessed we were bailing out, and told Popken to bail out, and he did. Although I wasn't in any pain, I thought that I still ought to have some morphine, so I removed the small first aid kit from the parachute harness. Then I saw through the controls, the pilot get up and leave. Since I had to get out, I put the small first aid kit back in a chest pocket of my G.I. coveralls, got down on the floor of the nose compartment to bail out. I checked the altimeter and it still read about 17,000 feet.

We had flown to Italy via South America and Africa, and had thick emergency escape packs on the back of our parachute harnesses. When we got to Italy, we removed the packs, but neglected to tighten the parachute harness straps. It was more comfortable with a loose harness. Also, there were "dot" fasteners around the nose wheel well, which protruded about 5/8" above the deck, to receive a canvas screen when wanted.

Unfortunately, the loose harness caught a dot fastener as I bailed out, rip cord, ready to go—and I found my head, hands, and feet still attached—and no one left in the plane! I managed to squirm around and get my arms back inside and unhooked the strap. For some reason I looked at the altimeter again and it was about

14,000 feet. I got ready to jump again, but I do not remember opening the chute. I assume that I had been without oxygen long enough for me to pass out and the opening of the chute probably jerked me back to consciousness.[18]

Don Lapham, copilot of a 719th Bomb Squadron B-24, "Patches," in another part of the formation, witnessed what appears to be the attack on Pistol Packin' Mama at the instant that the German fighters sprayed it with shells. He wrote in his diary, "I glanced out of the side blister. Out about 2,000 yards was a tight formation of planes. B-24s I said to myself. One of the planes banked up sharply as seven of them peeled off. My eyes bulged; they had two engines."[19]

Of the Fifteenth Air Force's total bomber force that was sent to Regensburg (118), only ten were from the 716th Bomb Squadron. There were four aborts. These returned to base after takeoff due to various mechanical problems. This left only six B-24s from the 716th.[20] Of these six, three were shot down in this ambush attack. Another, the Wise Virgin, flown by Lt. Cecil E. Kinerd, was badly shot up but managed to make it back to friendly territory and the crew bailed out over Bari, Italy. The other two bombers that were shot down were Stinky the BTO (Big Time Operator), flown by 2nd Lt. Carl R. Browning, and Ramp Tramp, flown by 2nd Lt. Harry W. Moore. Bird's crew, fared the best casualty wise, with no crewmen killed. Three crewmen were killed among Browning's crew, and Moore's crew suffered seven killed. The six 716th bombers shot down nine or ten enemy fighters during this mission.[21]

Now back to Oscar at the bomb bay door:

As I fell out the door backward, I thought my helmet was going to blow away. I grabbed it with my left hand to hold it on. As I lay there on nothing, it was the softest thing ever, and I had no sensation of falling. A 109 passed slowly above me just a few feet away traveling in the direction we'd been going. I clearly saw the pilot's face as he leaned over to his left slightly and seemed to look me right in the eye. He was gone in a split second, but I'll never forget it.

I was still above the overcast and my right hand pulled the D-ring. I was still lying on my back, on that soft bed of nothing, not tumbling. The ring, with about a foot-long piece of small steel cable, came out of the pack, and it separated completely from the pack. I didn't remember if this was normal or not but since nothing happened, I dropped the ring and hung onto my helmet thinking I'd have to dig the chute out by hand. This was my first experience with a parachute, and I thought when you pulled the old ripcord you got jerked out of your shoes. I started to go into the pack with my right hand (it seemed everything was in slow motion, and the sound of silence was deafening) when out popped the little "pilot" chute, then the main canopy blossomed slowly. I was gently pulled upright and started floating down. Just as Mama disappeared into the overcast, I saw a chute open. I guessed it was Deane or Jackson, but it could have been someone from the rear section. I hoped everyone could get out in time. I don't know what our altitude was, but I had no trouble breathing.

All the things I'd heard about bailing out didn't happen to me. I never thought I'd have to jump but after the peaceful feeling of the softness and the quietness of free fall and the gentleness of floating down under that beautiful white nylon canopy that was like a huge, inverted magnolia blossom, I can see how one could easily become addicted to skydiving.

Everything disappeared for a minute as I went through the overcast. Then I could see Mother Earth coming up to meet me. Beautiful rolling hills and mountains covered with some kind of evergreen forest with small clearings here and there, and soon I could distinguish houses widely separated and some of the clearings. The slow-motion effect stopped, and one house started to come up just directly under me.

I landed in the middle of a steep rooftop covered with about six inches of snow, slid down the side, and landed softly in a deep drift of snow beside the house. I couldn't think and still, to this day, I don't know what I was thinking. I guess I wasn't. It's more puzzling to me as I write this than it has ever been. This is the first time I've seriously tried to bring the thing back to mind, and I find it a bit disturbing. I have an odd feeling that I'd rather just go on trying to forget it.

I remember wondering if anyone was in the house. I heard nothing. I hadn't heard a thing since the 109 roared above me just after I bailed out.

My ears were still covered by the earphones built into my helmet, but sounds were very loud in the plane before I jumped. I thought I might be deaf.

There was no wind at all, and my chute had just settled over and around me on the matching snow. I would be invisible to anyone not really close to me. I unsnapped the complete harness of the chute and crawled out into the open. It was a beautiful scene. I didn't wait to see if anyone was in the house. I plowed my way through six or eight inches of snow to the top of a small tree-covered hill. I didn't look back. I would be out of sight in the trees, and maybe I could think of what to do next.

I was wearing my heated suit which was like one piece, long-handle underwear made of material like an electric blanket. It plugged into the electrical system of the plane and usually kept one comfortable even when high altitude temperatures went to forty degrees below zero or worse. Heated gloves and shoes plugged into outlets on the suit, and I was wearing the whole works. Over my shoes were thick, heavy boots made of sheepskin with the wool inside and a zipper up the front, very loose fitting, and I was lucky not to be jerked out of them when I pulled the D-ring, but I've always been very lucky. I think my helmet was leather, lined with soft material. Earphones were built into the flaps that covered the sides of my head and face and were supposed to be snapped together under my chin, but it wasn't snapped and I nearly lost it. I've always been careless, too, I guess. I still had my throat mic around my neck, like a choker necklace, the latest thing at the time—very fashionable. This was mainly for conversation among crew members, but if the ship's radio was on group frequency, everyone in the group or anyone on that frequency could hear us and be heard by us. Most of the time we were on radio silence except for intercom. The Luftwaffe could home in on our group frequency if they knew what it was, and although it was changed every day and was given out to radio operators just before a mission at a secret briefing for "static chasers," only I think the enemy knew nearly every day what we'd use, so we just didn't use it much. I think everyone had been taking a nap. Not a word had been said for 15 minutes or more until Jackson yelled from the nose turret that they were coming in level and head on, a whole gaggle of 109s.

Waist gunners had enough room to wear flak vests and steel helmets, but power-driven turrets were small, especially the ball turret in the belly, and even though none of our turret gunners were more than five feet, eight inches tall or more than 150 pounds, there just wasn't enough space for this protection. Most turrets, though, had a little armor plate here and there, but only the Emerson Electric nose turret had the bulletproof glass, and I knew this saved Jackson's life. I didn't have a flak vest or steel helmet. Over my heated suit I wore an ordinary pair of OD GI coveralls with no markings of squadron or group and no designation of rank (I didn't have any rank until 1944 when I was promoted from private to sergeant. A lot of GI red-tape was involved when I changed my mind about going to B-29s, and I'm sure some of the clerks in Personnel loved me).

In one pocket of my coveralls I had my "Escape Kit," a little clear plastic box about six by eight inches and about two inches thick. In it were maps printed on light-weight, waterproof cloth, a compass, and thirty or forty pieces of bad-tasting hard candy squares. I guess the taste is what stretched them into a week's rations, although I had never eaten but one. I had a half of a pack of cigarettes and a book of paper matches. So, I sat down on a log, lit a cigarette, unwrapped a piece of candy, put it in my mouth, got out the compass and the map, and tried to guess where I was and what to do next. It didn't seem to be very cold. There was no wind, and I still couldn't hear a sound. I found Austria and Germany on the map (I'd like to have that map now. It was a beautiful thing, in color and great detail, about the size of an oil company road map, but much lighter. It must have been silk or nylon and would make a great thing to frame and hang on the wall of your den or trophy room).

I located Graz [Austria] and Regensburg and although I'd liked to have hiked to Switzerland to be interred there for the duration (we heard all kinds of fantastic reports about how American flyers were taken care of there. They couldn't be allowed to leave a neutral country, but they really lived it up at Army expense they said), I decided it was maybe not impossible but very impractical.[22]

I figured I was closer, but still not very close, to Yugoslavia which was partially occupied, as I recall, by Germany, but Marshal Tito and his communist guerillas dominated the country, and his underground had a very good record of evading the Nazis and cooperating with the Allies.[23] I guess I'd finally started thinking and remembering parts of the mornings' long briefing instructions. I didn't know exactly where I was and not even sure of my directions, so you might say I was lost. I seemed to be getting colder. I finished my cigarette and started walking through the woods on what appeared to be a narrow road for sleighs or wagons, but there were no tracks of any kind. I soon came to another clearing where another house stood. The ground floor was a semi-open shed with a closed room and door at one end. In the shed were two cows, a goat, and a small deer. I walked right into the shed and to the door of the room, and none of them did more than look at me and flap an ear or two. I thought to myself, "Well the animals aren't hostile," so I knocked on the door to see what would happen next.

Little boys. The three sons of Oscar and Ollie Allison (*left to right*): Gerald (5), Harold (3) and Oscar (1). They are all dressed up in their best, possibly for their father's funeral in 1920. Family photo provided by Larry Allison.

Little girls. The McKinstry girls (*back to front*): Sammy, Jean, and Mildred, 1931. Family photo provided by Austin Allison.

Well-drilling rig. Wiley Grizzle's rig for drilling water wells, which he probably built and engineered himself. It appear that it is the teenage son, Oscar, who is working aloft (ca. 1933–34). Family photo provided by Cindy Pennington.

Allison/Grizzle boys. A group photo of the Allison and Grizzle boys, taken around mid-1942. (*Left to right*): Oscar Allison (home on leave from the Army Air Forces), and in front of him is Jimmy Allison (Gerald's oldest son); Gerald Allison; Jim Grizzle (youngest of the Grizzle kids), and in front of him is Winston Allison (Gerald's second son); Harold Allison; and Wiley Grizzle Jr. Family photo provided by Larry Allison.

Gerald and Ethel. Gerald and Ethel Allison shortly before or after their marriage in 1936. Family photo provided by Larry Allison.

Nose art, B-24-H, Sophisticated Lady. This was the B-24H that Oscar and the Robert P. (Bob) Bird crew flew on most of their missions, except its last one. The Sophisticated Lady was shot down on February 25, 1944, on a mission to Regensburg, flown by 2nd Lt. Gil Bradley. Provided by 449th Bomb Group Association.

Bombs on an Italian target. Before the Regensburg mission, the 449th Bomb Group Liberators hit targets in Italy in support of Allied troops battling the Germans in Italy. USAF photo.

Bob Bird's crew poses in front of Sophisticated Lady. (*Kneeling, left to right*): 2nd Lt. Bob Bird, 2nd Lt. Anson F. Hughes, 2nd Lt. Deane C. Manning, 2nd Lt. Victor Harris; (*Standing, left to right*): S.Sgt. Richard W. Leaf, S.Sgt. Edward Szymanski, S.Sgt. Frank W. Watkins, S.Sgt. Jack K. Dixon, S.Sgt. James M. Blake, and Sgt. Oscar Allison. Photo courtesy of 449th Bomb Group Association.

Three boys from Roswell. Hometown publicity for the Wiley and Ollie Grizzle boys. Article was published on the front page of the *Roswell Daily Record* on April 25, 1944. Allison family documents.

716th Bomb Squadron Enlisted Man's Club. This is the sparse interior of the 716th Bomb Squadron's club for enlisted men at Grottaglie. USAF photo.

View of Grottaglie from the British side of the base as it was when the 449th Bomb Group began operations there in January 1944. The blasted-out hangars are clearly visible, as are a B-24 in the center and the ubiquitous mud. Photo courtesy of 449th Bomb Group Association.

PT-19s. This is the flight line at the Chickasha, Oklahoma, airfield where Wiley Jr. went through primary flight training. Photo provided by Katy Carter from the collection of her father, Gordon Compton, who went through primary there also and served in the 353rd Fighter Group. Gordon B. Compton Collection, 353rd Fighter Group Archives.

Crash site, Pistol Packin' Mama. The rough, snow-covered, mountainous terrain near Koglhof, Austria, as it appears today, where the B-24 flown by Bob Bird and flight engineer Oscar Allison crashed on February 22, 1944. Impact point is the ridge in the right foreground. There was only a single house there that day, a farmhouse on which fuel from the bomber splashed, resulting in the house catching fire and completely burning. There were no injuries because no one was inside. Photo by Christian Arzberger and used with his permission.

BF-109G. A BF-109G from the German squadron JG-27 in flight February–March 1944. This is the type of fighter that Helmut Beckmann flew that delivered the fatal blows to Pistol Packin' Mama, and the type of fighter that brought down Sophisticated Lady three days later. This type of fighter might very well have been the type that brought down Wiley Jr.'s P-51 in March 1945. From Wikipedia Commons. Photographer: Hebenstreit; German Federal Archive, Identification Code - Bild 101I-662-6659-37.

Koglhof. The small Austrian village of Koglhof as it appears today, which is not much different than how it appeared in February 1944. Here is where pilot Bob Bird was taken after he had bailed out of his B-24 and landed nearby. Photo taken by Christian Arzberger and used with his permission.

Oscar POW. Evidence of a rough couple of days, probably after a multiday train ride to Frankfurt from Austria, with little food or water. This is the paperwork that the Germans created as Oscar was processed into Nazi Germany's prisoner of war system. Done early on, probably at Dulag, this form followed him as he was moved from one Stalag to another. From Oscar Allison's personal files, provided by Sam Allison.

Moosburg. This shows living conditions for American airmen at Moosburg prisoner of war camp (Stalag VII-A) in April 1945 when Oscar was interred there. Used with permission from Moosburg online (www.moosburg.org).

Kriegsgefangenenpost

GEPRÜFT Postkarte

3 Zn

Mit Luftpost
Par Avion

-2.3.44 ∙ 15

Mrs. Ollie Grizzle

Gebührenfrei!

Absender:
Vor- und Zuname: *18035086*
Oscar I. Allison
Gefangenennummer: *Not Allotted*
Lager-Bezeichnung:
Dulag Luft

Deutschland (Allemagne)

Empfangsort: *R#1, Dexter*

Straße: *New Mexico*

Land: *U.S.A.*
Landesteil [Provinz usw.]

Kriegsgefangenenlager

Datum *2/27/44*

Dear Mom & Everybody

Down safe, and everything is fine.
The Red Cross is doing a good job here.
Had my first real cigarette in quite
a spell, sure was good. Don't worry too
much about me, I'm still sweatin'
the duration. Love to everybody
This is not my permanent station Oscar

Kriegsgefangenenpost. An example of the German POW mail allowed prisoners during World War II. This is Oscar's first letter after he had been captured, the one that gave his mother, Ollie, so much relief. Oscar Allison documents, provided by Sam Allison.

Wiley Sr., Wiley Jr., and Ollie Grizzle. This photo was taken during Wiley Jr.'s last visit home in July 1944, before he deployed to England for combat. Family photo.

OTU class. This is the 353rd Fighter Group Operational Training Unit that included Wiley Jr., December 1944–January 1945. Members were (*top row, left to right*): Lt. Howard H. Hakonen, 350th FS; F/O Robert C. Hassell, 352nd FS; Lt. William Harbin, 352nd FS; Lt. Lindsay Grove, 352nd FS; Lt. John L. Guthrie, 350th FS; Lt. Bernard Greenfield, 350th FS; (*kneeling, left to right*): Lt. Richard E. Hahn, 351st FS-POW; F/O Richard N. Gustke, 350th FS; Lt. Wiley Grizzle Jr., 350th FS-KIA; Lt. Roy C. Gordon, 350th FS. Note that Flight Officer Gustke has his arm around Wiley Grizzle Jr. Judging from Wiley's letters home, they were best of friends. Family photo provided by Austin Allison.

Wiley Grizzle Jr., 350th Fighter Squadron. Wiley Grizzle Jr. poses in front of a P-51 Mustang showing the checkerboard cowling emblematic of the 353rd Fighter Group, Eighth Air Force. Family photo provided by Cindy Pennington.

Honor Roll. This eye-catching artwork highlighted the aces of the 350th Fighter Squadron. Other members of the 350th are listed in the columns. Wiley Jr.'s name can be seen in the first column to the right of the photos of the aces. This display was on the front wall of the squadron ready room. Graham Cross Collection.

Officers' Club, Raydon. The nicely appointed interior of the 353rd Fighter Group Officers' Club at Raydon. Wiley Jr. would have spent time here socializing, resting, and reading. Graham Cross Collection.

Rimerman brief. Lt. Col. Ben Rimerman, the commanding officer of the 353rd Fighter Group, briefs pilots on an upcoming combat mission. Graham Cross Collection.

Harold's B-17 crew. Harold Allison and the B-17 crew he trained with pose in front of a B-17. Harold is kneeling, second from left. Family photo.

Ollie and Harold. Ollie Grizzle with son Harold Allison, probably taken when Harold was home in March 1944 to marry Jean McKinstry. Family photo provided by Austin Allison.

RHINE RIVER

350th planes in formation. Two Mustangs of the 350th Fighter Squadron fly over the Rhine River in Germany. The wingman aircraft might possibly be flown by Wiley Grizzle Jr. The P-51 designated LH-S was the aircraft he normally flew. Wiley flew two missions to the Rhine. Graham Cross Collection.

Blickenstaff after briefing. Lt. Col. Wayne Blickenstaff determinedly exits the briefing room headed for flight equipment to suit up for a mission over Germany on March 24, 1945. "Blick" was leader of a nineteen-plane formation to support the crossing of the Rhine River by Allied infantry. Two 350th pilots were killed on the mission; one was Wiley Grizzle Jr. Graham Cross Collection.

P-51s over Raydon. A large formation of P-51 Mustangs over Raydon, England, home base for the 353rd Fighter Group. Photo was taken from Raydon's control tower. Several copies were made and provided as souvenirs. This photo was with Wiley Grizzle Jr.'s effects and provided by Austin Allison; enhanced version is from the Graham Cross Collection.

Sattenhausen crash site. Over this peaceful and quaint German village, savage air combat occurred on March 24, 1945. Fighting at a low level, forty-nine roaring aircraft twisted and turned, climbing and diving, fighting with lethal intent. Wiley Grizzle Jr. was shot down and crashed in flames about ninety meters east of town. The site is marked with a white spot in the upper left of the photo. As can be seen, it is farm country, entirely appropriate for Wiley Jr. Photo is from the town's website, http://www.sattenhausen.de/, and permission was granted by the photo's owner, Mr. Willi Ollech, and the village mayor, Peter Schulze.

Harold and Jean, San Antonio. Harold and Jean Allison near the picturesque San Antonio River as Harold was in San Antonio for out-processing at the end of the war. Family photo.

Sammy and little kids. Sammy Allison (to be) with her children from her former husband, Aubrey Hewatt. Her children (*front to back*) are Mack, Susan, and Nan. Here she is living in Las Cruces, New Mexico, just prior to her marriage to Oscar Allison. Photo provided by Mack Allison.

M tractor. The much-heralded Farmall M tractor. It seems to be
Oscar in the driver's seat, so this photo was taken shortly after the war.
Photo provided by Cindy Pennington.

Bird-Beckmann meeting. Robert Bird (*center*), Deanne Manning (*left*),
and the German fighter pilot Helmut Beckmann (*right*) at a special
meeting of adversaries organized by citizens of Koglhof, Austria, in
1984. Koglhof was very near to where Pistol Packin' Mama crashed after
being shot down by Beckmann and was also where Beckmann's BF-109
Messerschmitt crashed after being shot down by gunner Jack Dixon of
Bird's crew. Photo given to Oscar Allison by Robert Bird; provided for
this publication by Mack Allison.

Oscar with his sons. Oscar Allison holds his son Sam while Mack stands in front, ca. 1950. Family photo provided by Sam Allison.

Sammy and Oscar later in life. Sammy and Oscar Allison, ca. 1970. Photo provided by Sam and Kathy Allison.

Chapter 8

Oscar Captured: February 1944

Oscar and his crew were fortunate to bail out over rural Austria, where civilians were not as hostile as in Germany indeed, in many cases, were near-friendly. The German population, on the other hand, was "strongly encouraged to kill airmen when they were captured."[1] Civilians who had suffered under Allied bombing were much more likely to be aggressive toward Allied airmen, those who manned bombers that brought havoc, death, and destruction to their neighborhoods. In these situations, ironically, the most-welcome individuals for Allied airmen were German soldiers whose job was to capture and protect the airmen. As prisoners of war, they were valuable and negotiable commodities, whereas German civilians were known to attack, harass, and even lynch downed airmen.[2] We can imagine Oscar's trepidation as he approached this house.

After a minute, the door opened slowly just a bit and I raised my hands and stepped back. The door opened wider, and I saw a woman looking out at me. In just a few seconds, she opened the door wide. I started talking to her in English. I knew very little German, but she motioned for me to lower my hands and come in. She was about 40 years old, I guessed, nice looking, with dark hair and eyes. I stepped inside and saw two young girls there, about 12 and 15 years old. I spoke to all of them in English and sign language, trying to tell them who and what I was. They didn't say anything or make a sound, but I heard my own voice, so I knew I wasn't deaf. The woman motioned me to a chair, so I sat down, took the map from my packet, and handed it to the woman, all the while trying to explain my situation. She took the map, said something to the older girl, and handed it to her. She unfolded it slowly and spread it carefully on a table, and the two girls started studying it intently. The woman looked me straight in the eyes for a long minute it seemed, then turned her back to me and joined the girls at the table.

I think they understood the situation, although they couldn't have seen any of the action above the clouds. Surely so many planes had gone down that they had seen or heard something. By the time I landed on the house, though, it was all over. I hadn't seen or heard anything since getting below the overcast.

The woman left the map and went to the door, opened it, and went out. The older girl kept studying the map, and the younger girl turned and stared at me. I wondered what I looked like. She didn't seem to be afraid or even surprised. Maybe this sort of thing happened often. The girls were really cute kids.

The woman came back in and said a few words to the older girl, who shook her head, folded the map, and handed it back to me. They kept talking for several minutes it seemed, then I heard dogs barking and soon I heard men's voices shouting not very far away. The woman cried out and motioned for me to follow her up the stairs, but the older girl said in words with the unmistakable meaning of, "No, no, Mother!"

The sounds outside grew louder, the door burst open, and four men (one with an old rifle that I expected was loaded) rushed in and surrounded me. The dogs stayed outside but the men took charge. The woman and the girls backed away, said nothing, and did nothing while the men chattered and grunted. The man with the gun made business-like signs with the gun, and I raised my hands above my head while one of the men searched me thoroughly, taking everything I had, including my watch but leaving all my clothes. They didn't seem angry or hostile, but they were excited much more than the woman and girls had been.

(Our intelligence section had determined that downed flyers who were unarmed had a much larger life expectancy than those who were armed. We had all been issued Colt .45 [semi]automatic pistols but we were urged not to carry them on bombing missions. They were to be used only for guarding against enemy infiltration of our airfield and sabotage to the aircraft. Crewmembers took turns guarding their own ships each night.)

The men seemed to be disappointed that I didn't have more equipment of some kind, and they consulted with each other for a long time before they opened the door and indicated that I should go with them. I looked back at the woman and the girls who still hadn't said anything. The men hadn't asked them anything, and it seemed to me that they all three looked a little sad about the situation. I still like to think that they were not wholeheartedly cooperating with even the local authorities. A lot of Austrians were not in love with Hitler and his iron-handed control of their country. I've thought about the people of that house and about what their thoughts were at that time. I'll never know but I hope they're OK now.

It is possible that this family did not support Hitler. Most Austrians were not Nazis, but support for Germany by Austrians remained strong early in the war. In later years it weakened as Austria began to distance itself from Germany. Civilian resistance was never on the level of those in other Nazi-occupied nations, like France or Yugoslavia. What resistance there was came from left-wing groups—mostly Communists, socialists, and conservative resisters: conservative Christians, Christian Socialists, and monarchists.[3]

The men headed me back to the road and on in the same direction that I'd been going. After an hour or so we came to a small town [it is not certain what small town this was; it was no doubt close to the village of Koglhof, about twenty-five miles northwest of Graz, the village where Bob Bird and other crewmembers were first taken][4], and they took me into one of the beer halls, I guess you'd call it that. They sat me down at a table and stood around talking with a few other men already there, not really paying much attention to me. The one gun was still all I could see. Some were drinking beer and finally one man brought me a mug of beer and a big piece of coarse, dark bread. I ate and drank, and I must say the beer was very good and the bread was better than anything I was to have for quite some time.

Finally, a man of authority arrived and took charge. Who or what he was, I don't know, but he spoke English probably better than I did. He seemed to be very interested in me and started asking many questions. He wanted to know who I was, so I told him I was an American Army sergeant, serial number 18035086. He wanted to know more. Where did I fly from? What kind of plane, what I did on the plane, where we had been going, etc., etc. I reminded him that according to the Geneva Convention, I had already given him all the required information and was forbidden by my superiors to tell him more. I showed him my dog tags which he read to a young man taking notes for him in some other language. He was very polite and had someone bring a mug of beer for him and another for me. By now there was quite a crowd in the hall, and it seemed to be getting dark. Day was turning into night, and although it wasn't very late by the clock, it had been a very long day. I didn't know the night would be even longer.

I sipped the beer, and he kept asking questions about everything in general. I almost felt that I was among friends, not happy about the situation, but he was succeeding in getting me to relax. I asked him if I could have one of my cigarettes, and he had the man bring the pack of Old Golds (short and unfiltered and a little musty). I took one, and he passed them around until they were all gone.

My interrogator kept trying to get more information from me, but he knew I didn't have to tell him anything more. He seemed to be enjoying it, so I just shook my head once in a while and sipped my beer. I was kind of enjoying it, too.

After some time, another group came in with Blake, the tail gunner. They were half carrying him. He was limping along and dragging his right leg. They sat him down beside me. He was dazed and in shock. He ignored them and started telling me about his chute having been caught in a tree, slamming him into it and hurting his leg, back, and head. I asked him if he was injured in the plane, but he just kept telling me how he'd hurt his leg and back, over and over. He said he was knocked out maybe for a while because the men had helped him get down from the tree where he still hung from his chute. Even in 1973, his story of that first night was just about blank. But he was unhurt when he bailed out, he said.

The man did get his name, rank, and serial number from his tags. I could tell that he knew that Blake and I knew each other, but he didn't ask me any questions about Blake. He knew that the professional interrogators at Dulag Luft in Frankfurt would get all the poop from all of us.[5] This was the Luftwaffe intelligence section, and praise the Lord they still ran the show without the SS [Schutzstaffel] or Gestapo.

They bought beer and bread for Blake, and he ate and drank. It didn't seem to help him much and I asked the man if Blake could see a doctor, but he said they didn't have one in the village, maybe tomorrow. We'd just have to wait. I felt sorry for Blake and that I could do nothing for him. Blake was dressed exactly like I was, but he had lost one heavy boot. After a while they took us to the village jail. I guess it was one, a small, one-room stone building about

10 feet square, two blank walls and one with a heavy door, and a small, barred window high up in the other. Inside was a pile of straw and one old quilt made mostly of holes.

It was still calm, but I could tell it was getting colder. Blake didn't seem to notice anything. He just fell onto the pile of straw when they shoved us in and locked the door. I hadn't any idea what time it was, but I guess it didn't matter. All we had to do for the moment was to make it through the night. It was really dark without the lanterns carried by the men. I rearranged the straw a little, making it as thick as possible and big enough for two. Blake sat up and looked around, asking where we were now. I told him all I knew about that, then I asked about Leaf and Skeets, and Whistler. He didn't know, he said. He just remembered bailing out and slamming into the tree. He didn't ask me any questions. I knew he was in too much pain to care. He lay down on the straw and I lay down beside him. Working slowly by feel—I was totally in the dark—I put a little straw over both of us and pulled the quilt over all. It kept getting colder. Blake moaned and shook with the cold. I huddled as close to him as I could and put my left arm over him to pull him even closer.

I think one man alone would have frozen to death, but now the thought just came to me that Blake and I owe our lives to each other. I'd never thought of that before.

Finally, daylight came and soon a group of four, now with two guns, came for us. We boarded a two-horse sleigh and off we went to a big town, maybe, Graz, Austria [actually Weis, Austria].[6] I didn't see any signs on the road anywhere. They turned us over to the Austrian home guard after about an hour's ride that wasn't too bad. The sleigh was a two-seater and they put Blake in the middle of the front, and I took the middle back seat with a rifleman on each side of me. They gave each of us a blanket, but we never did get warm until we arrived at the big town jail, in a building much like a county courthouse.

They took us inside and put us into a room about 20 feet square, the floor of which was wall-to-wall Americans. I didn't count them but there must have been thirty or forty in all. Bob [Bird] and Jackson were there, Skeets and Leafski, and now Blake and Bob said no one was missing except for Whistler and Deane who was surely in a hospital with his shattered ankle. It seems that Deane and Jackson were the only ones injured on board the ship. By pooling our information, we decided everyone had bailed out, but what might have happened to Deane and Whistler after landing we couldn't be sure. Bob assured us that everyone would be okay.

After seeing Blake and talking with him and with me, Bob went to the door and pounded it with his fist until a guard came. It wasn't long. The guards seemed to be very curious and concerned. Bob told the guards that Jackson and Blake needed a doctor—Jackson wasn't nearly as bad as he looked; he was still covered with blood, but the bleeding had all stopped. He said he was in no pain at all and was very alert and excited, going through the battle all over again with every one of the crew verifying that he shot down the 109 for him. Everyone including Jackson knew who got him. Skeets and Leaf were without a scratch. So was Bob and the copilot and navigator. We were all pretty lucky. Deane and Blake were the worst that we knew about.

It wasn't long before they took Jackson and Blake out. We hoped they would see a doctor. Blake doesn't remember any of this. His memory starts with seeing the doctor but doesn't know how much later it was or what the doctor did. He says he didn't do anything. Jackson said all they did for him was to wash his face and pick out three or four pieces of glass just under the skin.

After a short time, they brought us some of the dark bread and some of the imitation coffee for breakfast. It was pretty good. Most of them hadn't had anything since the morning before and refused to believe my story about drinking beer the night before. Blake was gone, and he didn't remember it anyway. Most of the men had spent the night right there in the city jail without anything to eat and only water to drink, but they were a lot warmer than Blake and me.

By now, the chief of police or officer of the guard or whatever, we never knew for sure what the uniform was, had all the poop about us. He started taking us out one at a time, about fifteen or twenty minutes apart. I don't know if everyone went through the same room or were dealt with by the same people that I was or not, but when my turn came, I was taken to a room about like the courtroom in a county courthouse. We had already noticed that no one came back after being taken out. We didn't know what to make of this, but I wasn't worried. The people all in uniform now seemed friendly enough, just more business-like than the small-town boys.

Well, they told me to take off all my clothes except for socks and underwear, and one of the men carried it all out. Three or four other men were in the room, but they ignored me. I asked the head man for a cigarette since he was smoking one, and I was surprised when he gave one to me. The tobacco was dark and strong, more like a cigar. It had a good taste but it made me a bit dizzy at first, but I enjoyed smoking the whole thing. I hadn't had a cigarette since the night before, and I really needed that. It seemed odd though to be sitting there in my underwear smoking a foreign cigarette. I remember the name well. It was an Elegante. We never knew where they were made but we did see quite a lot of them later in Germany.

It wasn't very long until they brought my clothes back to me minus the heated shoes and gloves, helmet, and coveralls. So, after getting dressed, there I was in my one piece, long-handled heated suit over my underwear. The suit was complete with a one button rear opening. It was light blue, two plies of blanket-like material, with dark blue knit cuffs and neck. They had cut off the electrical cord which I didn't care about, but I did want my coveralls back. The heavy boots were very loose without the heated shoes. I had to just shuffle along to keep from walking right out of them. He said that was all I could have, and they took me into another room where we were all getting together again. I noticed two other men had lost their coveralls, too, but they were strangers to me.

I must say, we three were the most distinguished looking of the whole lot. We finally decided they took only those coveralls with no stripes on the sleeves, but never knew why. The heated suit was sort of like a space suit, really heavy with zipper front, and I'd rather lose my coveralls than my blue heated suit. It was much better than coveralls alone would have been. It was pretty warm, even without electricity. My coveralls were identical to others except for stripes on the sleeves that designated one's rank. Mine had none, and we decided this was the reason they were taken. Some others without stripes had been confiscated also.

The heated suit was sort of like the modern space suit, only it was much closer fitting. Well, let's face it. It looked just like long underwear of the one-piece kind. It was warm even without electricity, and I'd much rather have it than coveralls alone. They took also my helmet. I wouldn't know how I looked until after VE Day, when my individual file with my pictures like a convict complete with numbers was found in the camp office and given to me. Many of the prisoners' files had been left there.

They put us all back into the first room except for the few who had been taken out for medical attention. We still didn't know anything about Deane or Whistler. We knew they were not far away, and that Deane was surely in a hospital and old Whistler was okay. He almost was okay. He was in a hospital, too, with a broken leg that he got when he hit the ground. [Whistler had two broken ankles, and shell fragments in his scalp]. Those big guys just landed harder than we little ones (of course we didn't learn about this until much later).

They kept us there in the crowded room all that day. They gave us all the water we wanted, but bread and coffee only once more. We were allowed to go to a men's room, not connected with the cell, one or two at a time under guard. We stayed in that room through the night, and nothing else was said or done. We didn't have too much conversation, for security purposes, and didn't feel much like it anyway. It was very uncomfortable in the crowded room, and we couldn't understand why we were all kept there. I guess it might have been the only cell in the building.

The next morning, we were given coffee and bread again, then herded through town to the railroad station. Many civilians lined the sides of the street to watch us as we were marched under guard to the train—to where? We didn't know. [This train took them from Weis, Austria, to the city of Graz, Austria, where they were processed by German officials—a distance of about thirty miles.][7]

By our standards, the train was antique—narrow-gauge with very small cars and the shrill whistle typical of European trains. It was a passenger train, and we rode like ordinary passengers with some of the natives mixed in with the prisoners, very informal except for the guards—a lot better than the cell but as the train went along, it stopped at every small town and got more crowded. At our first stop, a Luftwaffe pilot boarded the train carrying his loose parachute bundled in his arms. He wasn't exactly friendly, but he wasn't angry or hostile like some officers that we'd run into later. He was resigned to the war as a way of life. He was older, about 30, I guess, and had been at war so long that he was used to it and philosophized that "I shoot you down, you shoot me down." He spoke very good English and wasn't at all reluctant to talk to us about himself. We learned that he was from the yellow-nosed bunch, and he admitted that a B-24 had got him and that he was lucky to be alive. He seemed tired and soon closed his eyes and rested. He might have been the guy that Jackson shot down.

The German fighter pilot was Helmut Beckmann. He was a member of the Luftwaffe's fighter wing Jagddivision 27 (JG-27). On the day of the Regensburg fight, the Regensburg area was defended by JG-27, which had a solid reputation and had fought in the African campaign before deploying into the Mediterranean theater. JG-27's mission that day was to protect the Messerschmitt factories in the region.

Eight BF-109s from the fighter leader school near Wels-am-Wagram were scrambled. Flying one of the Messerschmitts was Helmut Beckmann.

They assembled over Vienna and flew to Linz. This would have put them in the path of the bombers coming out of Regensburg and headed into Austria. The eight BF-109s joined up in an attack formation over Vienna, then flew south and into the path of Bird's B-24 and the other bombers. Near Graz, the Messerschmitts ambushed the bombers. Lightning-fast, they struck and tore through the bombers, head-to-head and guns blazing. The Messerschmitt pilot that shot down Pistol Packin' Mama was Helmut Beckmann.

Beckmann, like the American flyers he attacked, was a young man, 23 years old. He was, however, much more experienced in air combat. He had joined the German military in January 1939, two months before he turned 18, and almost nine months before World War II began when Germany invaded Poland on September 1, 1939.[8]

By 1942 he had been assigned to the first group of JG-27. In June 1942 JG-27 was in combat fighting the British Army in North Africa when Beckmann got his first victory. He downed a British Supermarine Spitfire V during the battle of Marsa Matruh on June 26. This battle was the last German victory during the North African campaign. The British Army stopped their drive and began to push the Germans, led by Gen. Erwin Rommel, back west. The day after his first kill, Beckmann, flying over the British-held Sidi El Barrani, was seriously wounded in a dogfight against a British Hawker Hurricane fighter. He was shot through the shoulder and right foot and lost his big toe. He was evacuated to a hospital in Innsbruck, Germany, where he remained in recovery until August 1942.[9] Once back in combat, and within days of his release flying from Dortmund, Germany, he dropped a B-17 just inside the western border of Germany. Pistol Packin' Mama was his fourth kill.[10]

Oscar continues:

Nearly all the prisoners on the train were from B-24s, many from our group. [This train took them to Frankfurt, Germany, to the large processing center for POWs, Dulag Luft—a distance of about four hundred miles.][11] We were on the train all that day and all the night, too. Sometime during the night we must have crossed over into Germany. We were taken off the passenger train and herded into box cars of a freight train, bare floors and walls and very crowded, not enough room to lie down. It was miserable and was a long time between drinks of

water. It was cold, too. We hadn't eaten since morning, and I could feel
my stomach shrinking and my body melting away. To be without water
is worse than to be without food. Water is very necessary.

Morning came and the train had stopped several times. At each
stop we called for water but never got enough for everyone. We could
hear air raid sirens, but I don't remember being afraid of being bombed.
The RAF was busy, but they were our friends. Very clear thinking.

I think I had become intoxicated with fatigue, thirst and hunger.
I lost track of time, but I think we were three days and nights and
part of another night in reaching Frankfurt. Somehow, we knew we
were going to Frankfurt for interrogation and assignment to prison
camps.[12]

Back in Roswell, Ollie was worrying. She had been notified by the War
Department that Oscar had been shot down and was missing in action.
She wrote to Annie and Ed in Texas months later:

April 9, 1944
Dear Ed and Annie,

I should have written sooner but I have been so worried & upset &
I kept thinking I'd have better news to tell you but I won't wait any
longer.

My sweet little boy, Oscar, was reported missing in action over
Germany Feb. 22. I received the telegram Mar. 15, the day after Harold
came home on furlough.

The only other news I've had was from the pilot's father, last Thurs.,
in a letter from him he says he has a friend in headquarters in Italy &
the friend said our boys' plane went into the target in formation but it
was not in formation when it left the target. He says no explosion was
noticed. That's all we know. It has hurt all of us so much. I never sleep
very well & I am thinking of my darling all the day long.

Ollie[13]

Oscar continues:

We were unloaded in a blackout with guards and dogs, divided into
groups of ten or twelve, and held in a wide hallway between rows of
cells. The guards here were Luftwaffe personnel, many spoke English,

and we were given water and allowed to lie on the floor. I actually went to sleep. I don't know how long I slept, and it seems all the men in my group were strangers. Then we were taken outside. It was very cold and beginning to get light. I thought, "When the sun comes up, we'll be shot." It just seemed to be the logical next step, being herded along by the guards and their dogs. It didn't seem to bother me at all.

We just went to another building and had coffee and bread. Then we were taken one by one into the photo room where a numbered card was hung around my neck and my picture and fingerprints were taken.

From this room, I went into the office of a captain of the Luftwaffe. He was sitting behind a desk, and the guard indicated for me to take the chair opposite, then he left. The captain put on the friendly act, gave me a cigarette, and told me his name—Schroeder, I think. It was a good cigarette and I enjoyed it but thought that it was becoming ridiculous how much time and trouble they would spend to get the same information over and over. This man was more subtle, though, and confided in me that he had lived six years in the United States, in Chicago. I thought it was harmless enough to tell him I'd never been there. He continued to talk of irrelevant matters, but I didn't have anything else to say, and he soon dismissed me.

I was taken by the guard to a big bathroom where several men were taking showers. He told me to take off all my clothes and join them. When I was finished, I went out through another door into a supply room where I was given a Red Cross box of clothing. It contained a U.S. cotton khaki shirt, U.S. OD [olive drab] wool pants, long blue wool socks that came up over my knees (we later learned these were of Australian issue). A pair of black high-top, lace-up shoes (Britain), a little big. The underwear was U.S. GI, OD shirt, and shorts. There was a U.S. tan cotton belt, a suit of plain striped pajamas (the first I'd ever had), and a pack of Camel cigarettes, but no matches! Everyone in the room was getting dressed, so I did, too. The pajamas I put back in the box and took with me. I went out into a fenced area where already many men were standing in groups talking and smoking. I got a light from one and wandered around trying to find someone I knew.

I wasn't surprised to see so many prisoners that I knew slightly. From our group alone many ships and crews had failed to return from missions over the past two weeks or so.

I talked with several men, most of them were from the Eighth Air Force flying from England. They were all friendly and sympathetic, but none could help me. Finally, I spotted Skeets (he was so short he was hard to locate, but I was surely glad to see that kid again).

He had found several men from our group and talked with some who had been on the February 22nd mission and other recent missions in Italy. We exchanged information and talked with an engineer from our squadron who had been hit at Anzio. He thought he was the only survivor of his crew. He said his plane took a direct hit of flak and he remembered nothing until he'd been brought to Dulag a few days before. I heard some really weird stories of survival there at Dulag and was to hear many more during the next year that seemed impossible, but I'm sure most of them were true. Some of these unbelievable tales would take so long to tell in detail that I dare not start one here. You wouldn't believe it anyway.

The prisoners at Dulag seemed to separate into groups of six to ten men. Of my crew, Skeets, Leafski, Jackson, Blake, and I finally found each other after a day or two. The lone engineer from Anzio was Polish named Zeroweitz. He joined us and became "Zero."[14] A tech sergeant from our squadron who went down on the 22nd of February we had known a long time joined us. His name was [Technical Sergeant, or T.Sgt.] Daniel Buda [the same Daniel Buda mentioned in ch. 6] and his ball turret gunner they seemed to be the only ones left of that crew so we took them in. [Buda and crew had been shot down on February 25.] The ball turret gunner we didn't know so well but he was a good boy named [Sgt. Lloyd T.] Wright so we called him "Wrong." An Eighth Air Force B-17 engineer was a little five-foot loner named Moore, and usually B-17 men thought themselves to be superior to B-24 men, but he was an old timer who had been a B-18 engineer when that Jap submarine surfaced in San Francisco harbor and shelled the city. His story of taking off in the B-18 that night to bomb the sub was a very funny story that showed how disorganized the Air Corps was at the first of the war just after Pearl Harbor.[15]

His name being Moore had to be changed to "Les" because of his size. He was smaller than Skeets or me. In the summer of 1944, his weight went down to 80 pounds from a normal of 120. Nearly everyone lost 30 or 40 pounds, and I was a 97-pound weakling for a while.

We stayed at Dulag several days, and things there were not bad. Each man got the clothing suitcase plus a full food parcel on arrival. Rumor had it that Dulag had a full-time inspector of the International Red Cross, so this explained some of it.

Thus Oscar's prisoner of war experience began, an experience like none other. It lasted fifteen months—a waste of time (in his opinion) where the daily reality was hunger—and left him with dark memories regarding human nature and man's capacity for cruelty.

Chapter 9

Oscar into the Stalags: March 1944–April 1945

A fter processing at Dulag, Oscar and the fellow crewmen—except for Deane Manning and Frank "Whistler" Watkins, who were hospitalized for treatment of their injuries—entered the German prisoner of war system. German policy was to separate officers from enlisted men and keep them in separate camps. Captured airmen were kept in Stalag Lufts, which were run by the Luftwaffe. The Germans made an attempt at following the Geneva Convention's rules for maintaining prisoners in a humane manner.[1] The big problem for prisoners was the lack of food and other supplies. These shortages resulted from the war itself as Germany was ground down by Allied attacks in the air and on the ground. As Oscar describes, there were other hardships beyond the lack of food, but that was the worst.

In sum it was a miserable experience for the prisoners because of the lack of food, poor living conditions, boredom, an uncertain future, and, of course, the loss of freedom. Extreme hardship resulted as prisoners were moved from one camp to another as the Allied armies closed the noose on German occupied territory and, eventually, Germany itself. Prisoners suffered in these moves, overloaded into box cars and/or the holds of ships or forced to march from one location to another. Some marches were extremely long and performed under dire conditions; prisoners were hungry, poorly clothed, and subject to harsh weather.

Oscar describes his fifteen-month prisoner of war ordeal as he recalls it. There is a lot he has forgotten or deliberately chooses not to tell. As one can perceive as they read of his experiences, that key to survival for him was keeping his "family" together.

Oscar continues:

> One night about midnight, we were called out and a trainload (several boxcars anyway) was marched in the darkness with our usual guards with their dogs. We carried all our possessions in the little Red Cross case some distance to the waiting train. We had very little to carry. With the pajamas, some of us had a few items of food from the full, one-man Red Cross food parcel that had been given to us on arrival at Dulag. A can of Spam or corned beef, a can of jam or a chunk of the dark bread, that was to become our staff of life. Our Red Cross parcels came from different Allied countries and the contents varied some. The American parcel was our favorite of course but many things in the British, Canadian, Australian and New Zealand parcels were different and very good.

Red Cross parcels were a most welcome commodity for prisoners. They provided supplementary and good tasting nourishment. This was especially true for men who had spent weeks on end consuming bleak and tasteless, if not foul, rations provided by the Germans. The Red Cross parcels came in boxes ten inches square and about four inches deep and weighed eleven pounds. They contained "nonperishable items like biscuits, raisins, coffee, powdered milk, and canned beef and fish."[2] They also contained toiletries and that all-important medium of exchange and pleasure, cigarettes. Distribution of the parcels, which was determined by the German camp commandant, was uneven. Other factors such as the interdiction of transportation lines and the overall war situation might impede their arrival at the Stalags.[3] As Oscar says, the POWs never got what the Geneva Convention agreed upon: a box per week per man that provided 1700 calories per day.[4]

Oscar continues:

Trading of items was a brisk business on parcel day. The Convention agreement called for one parcel per man per week, and that would have been very good with just a little German bread, potatoes, vegetables, and a little beef or horse or pork or dog meat. But we were lucky after we left Dulag to get one parcel for two men per week, and at times there would be none for a month or more. Then we'd be on the starvation rations of the Germans. This was our worst complaint and hardship, along with the cold and the unsanitary conditions of most camps. As far as I know, very few Allied POWs were physically mistreated. Many were disciplined with solitary confinement ranging from twenty-four hours to sometimes two or three weeks, depending upon the mood of the commandant. A few were killed, most of them for trying to escape. I thought anyone who considered escape from Heydebrug [Heydekrug], (our first home in the far north, which I guess was in the territory of what was once Lithuania) was nuts. He would freeze to death in twenty-four hours. But some were nuts. I was in my own way. I helped in digging a tunnel, but under the building the sand continually caved in, and when we finally reached the outer wall, it was frozen solid and hard as granite. I don't think anyone there was absolutely sure of anything except that he was cold or hungry or both. Mostly it was a way to kill time. It wasn't too popular; it consumed too many calories. We had a critical energy crisis. But I'm getting way off course and too much ahead of my story.

We left Dulag in darkness, not knowing where we were going, but I had lost the idea of being shot and I just went along, trying not to think too far ahead. It was common knowledge that conditions in general were better at Dulag than in most other places in Germany, but no one stayed there for long. Maybe some high-ranking officers would be held there for two or three weeks of intensive interrogation which I'm sure was no picnic, and in some cases, we heard they used unfriendly persuasion to obtain information.

We did hear that after Dulag when officers and enlisted men were segregated that the camps for officers-only were much better than those for enlisted men. Our own officers confirmed this when we met in Kansas City in 1973 for our 30th anniversary celebration.

However, at the end on liberation day, April 29, 1945, at the final place of our confinement at Moosburg, near Munich, it was very much integrated. Officers and men of all the Allied countries lived together in an ideal atmosphere of democracy.

Our little group of nine managed to stay together and board the same car. Skeets, Leaf, Jackson, Blake, Zero, Les, Wrong, Daniel, and I huddled together while another dozen or so were crowded on with us. We finally started rolling and before we could figure out how to arrange ourselves in positions comfortable enough for sleep, night turned into day. Our progress was slow even though we didn't stop much. Once or twice we were held up outside some city during bombing raids. The trip was boring and uncomfortable. Every time we stopped, we cried out for water and sometimes got it, but never enough.

Back home, Ollie received a telegram from the War Department reporting that Oscar had been captured. This was good news. In a letter to the Allisons, she expresses the emotional turmoil she endured for almost a month awaiting news on Oscar's situation. This must have been the longest month of her life yet. We can only imagine the anguish she experienced and how hope and prayer were essential. In our imagination we can see her sitting, staring at the War Department envelope, fearing the bad news that it might contain.

April 12, 1944
Dear Ed and Annie,

I got good news today about my darling boy. A telegram saying he's a German prisoner. God, that was good news, & I knew you'd want to know, cause you love him too. I have prayed so hard, I just knew he wasn't dead. Now I'll get to see my sweet little boy again. I sat for 3 or 4 minutes before I could open the telegram wondering what was inside that envelope. I am still so nervous.

Gerald & Ethel are fine, but Gerald has been blue & worried these last 4 weeks & you can't imagine how terrible these last 4 weeks have been for me & how I've suffered, not knowing.

Ollie[5]

Gerald, who lived close by, shared her worry, causing him to be saddened as he worried about his little brother. The war had become very personal.

German authorities allowed prisoners to write and receive letters. Cards called Kriegsgefangenenpost were provided. This was a beneficial service for the prisoners, but it also served their purposes. The mail was highly censored and scrutinized for sensitive information to be used against the Allies. The bureaucracy and special channels between warring nations slowed the movement of mail and made it questionable whether the letters would even be delivered. Oscar complained often of not receiving mail when his family and other relatives wrote frequently.

This is his first letter after being captured. He wrote from Dulag Luft:

Kriegsgefangenenpost 2/27/44
Dear Mom & Everybody

Down safe, and everything is fine. The Red Cross is doing a good job here. Had my first real cigarette in quite a spell, sure was good. Don't worry too much about me, I'm still sweatin' the duration. Love to everybody—This is not my permanent station.

Oscar[6]

This was extremely good news for Ollie and the whole family. She in turn wrote to the Allisons:

May 2, 1944
Dear Ed & Annie

Oh, Annie, I got a card from Oscar last week & I am so happy. I am almost sick, or have been. I'm feeling better now. Oh, it was so good to see his printing (he printed all of it). It was dated Feb. 27, just 5 days after he was downed so I know he wasn't hurt much, if any. Thank God, tho' he is safe.

I got a letter from Harold last week. He broke his wrist playing football. Ain't that a heck of a thing for a married man to do?

I guess Jr. will graduate in about three weeks. I can hardly wait till he gets home.

Ollie[7]

June 4, 1944
Dear Ed & Annie:

I haven't heard from you in a long time but I tho't I'd write & tell you we are okay but just about "blowed" to pieces. I have never seen such a dry, windy, spring. We are plowing and [looking for] pickers anyway. They have shipped out all the German prisoners, you know they were only about 4 mi. from us & we had them last year to pick. Gerald got a pretty good stand of cotton & he has some fine oats. He is baling hay today.

I haven't heard any more from Oscar & I'm worried a little about my sweet boy. I have written all the crew's mothers except the copilot's and navigator's & have heard from 2 of them, real nice letters telling me what they know about their sons. All of the enlisted men are at the same camp, & they all write about like Oscar did, that they are okay & the Red Cross is doing a swell job. One boy said all they were doing (Mar. 7) was eat & sleep, so I guess they are getting along fairly well.

Ollie[8]

This letter addresses a home front issue that posed a problem for farm families. With sons, brothers, fathers, and hired hands in the military, farmworkers were in extremely short supply. Workers were lured by high-paying government and factory jobs producing war materials. The air base at Roswell no doubt hired many locals. In desperation, alternative sources of labor were sought. Women and urban young people were encouraged, and indeed promoted by the state and federal government, to work on farms. As a part of the federal Emergency Farm Labor Supply Program, a Women's Land Army—an agricultural version of Rosie the Riveter—saw about three million women go to work on farms. The highest numbers were in the South and Midwest. Few of these women worked on Great Plains farms.[9] This added to the already-changing roles of women in society: increasing work outside the home, more independence, and broader fields of work. Additionally, owners of businesses or factories were encouraged to close down during peak harvest times so that their employees could work the fields. The hard work and low wages, however, did not motivate many city folks to help the farmers. Farmers increasingly sought Mexican and Mexican American workers. The federal government addressed this by contracting with the Mexican government for workers who would work temporarily in the United States. This was the highly successful Bracero program, which persisted after the war.[10]

Another source of labor, and an unusual one, was using prisoners of war (POWs), which is what Ollie is referring to in the above letter. The German POWs probably came from the Orchard Park POW camp near Roswell. As Ollie notes, they picked cotton for her son Gerald in 1943. They were guarded by US Army soldiers as they worked. Farmers rarely had anything to do with the prisoners. Their daily quota for picking cotton was 150 pounds. At least one of the POWs that was at Orchard Park returned to live in Roswell after the war.[11]

There is no indication that the Grizzles employed women, braceros, or temporary workers from towns or cities. The farmwork was the business of the males of the family: Wiley, Gerald, and Jim, and occasionally local men, and when they were available, prisoners of war.

Although Oscar remained interested in the farm and frequently asked about it, his reality was much different than that of the family farm. While his thoughts of the farm and family no doubt gave him hope for the future, his immediate concerns had absolutely nothing to do with farming.

Oscar continues:

> We heard that the whole train was marked as a POW train with these huge letters and Red Crosses painted on the top of each boxcar. It was probably true. We heard many air raid sirens and exploding bombs but never close by. We worried more at night about this, but the worst thing was the lack of water and space and the terrible problem of sanitation. We were seldom let out of the car and used buckets for bathroom facilities. The air pollution was almost unbearable. I think we all lost track of time. I know I did, and even Skeets couldn't keep a record of anything while we were on the train. The majority decided that counting the first night we were eight nights and seven days enroute to Heydebrug [Heydekrug] which was to be our happy home until about mid-July 1944.[12]

Stalag Luft VI was indeed in the far north, the farthest north of any German POW camp. It was in what was known as East Prussia at that time. Today it is in Lithuania near the town of Šilutė. Prior to February 1944, it held British noncommissioned officers (NCOs) who had arrived at the new camp in September 1943. The first Americans arrived in February 1944, so Oscar's group were among the first US servicemen imprisoned there. By July 1944 an estimated nine thousand Americans were imprisoned there.[13] The first Americans initially depended on the British for food. The Brits generously shared their Red Cross parcels until additional parcels arrived for the Americans two months later.[14]

Oscar continues:

> No one died in our car, but we heard that eight men were lost on the trip of this train load of 450 men. Oh, the entire time I didn't seem to care where we were going or what happened. Skeets kept us informed with all the rumors he heard and I think some that he started.
>
> We were on our way to a newly built prison camp in the far north. We got the poop after a few days on the road, and Heydebrug [Heydekrug] seemed to verify the rumor when we finally arrived and were marched about two miles through more than a foot of snow to the practically new facility in a clearing of a Christmas card atmosphere. We knew it was way up there because the days were so short—only a few hours of sunshine even when it wasn't cloudy and those long, long, endless nights. There were four big brick buildings, low, long, and wide, about 200 feet long and 50 feet wide, one floor with about 12-foot-high walls and the roof not very steeply pitched.
>
> Each building would house about 500 men in single rows of double-decked bunks against each side wall, and a row of double-decked bunks on each side of a wide center aisle that had eight big brick coal-burning stoves with steel tops about 4 feet wide and 8 feet long. A good place to toast your bread if you had any. They burned very little fuel and were never very hot, but the inside temperature was fairly comfortable.
>
> A high row of small windows with double glass and iron bars were spaced 10 or 12 feet apart in the walls. The walls were about 2 feet thick, making very good insulation.

In early March Oscar wrote his first letter home from Stalag Luft VI. It was a surprisingly upbeat letter except that he desperately wanted mail from home or family, a lifeline for the prisoners.

Kriegsgefangenenpost
Germany, March 7, 1944
Dear Mom and Everybody,

Well here I am at a more or less permanent station. I feel fine & Everybody is okay. Not a scratch from my worst encounter with the Luftwaffe. Conditions are good and that goes for the food too. This is strictly an enlisted men's place and it's more or less run by NCOs. . . . Man, my money is on the red cross from now on. They're doing a swell job over here. It wouldn't hurt to give a little to them. Some of mine if it ever got there.

Love from Oscar.[15]

Kriegsgefangenenpost
Germany 4/17/44
Dear Mom and everybody,

Here we are again, everything still about the same. The life is a trifle boresome but I guess we can manage unless it's not for too long. How's everything there? How're H [Harold] & Jr. getting' along in their work? Wish I could hear from some of y'all.

Love from Oscar[16]

Kriegsgefangenenpost
Germany, 4/26/44
Dear Mom & Everybody

Time again for another card. Hope everybody is okay. Everything here is okay except the weather. I'd like to see a little of that good old sunshine there at home. I'd sure like to hear from somebody, that's one of the things I really miss. Guess the cotton is all planted now.

Love from Oscar.[17]

  Oscar continues:

The outside temperature was always cold until spring came about mid-May, and it snowed a lot but there wasn't much windy weather. We weren't outside very much during the winter. Once a week we were allowed to take a shower in a separate building. Many of us hated to do this because of the cold, but our barracks buddies saw to it that everyone did it who was well enough to do it.

We soon had a walkway pack in the snow just inside the warning wire where we took our daily walks for exercise. The warning wire was a single smooth wire about 2 feet high and 10 feet inside the inner fence which was about 12 feet high. The outer fence was about 20 feet further out, and loosely coiled barbed wire filled the space in between.

A prisoner was off limits if he crossed the warning wire and was fair game for the guards in the high towers at each corner of the compound and spaced about 300 feet apart around the perimeter. Each tower had two guards with their rifles, and a machinegun was mounted in the floor of each tower.

At this camp, only one man was killed by a guard from a tower. He was guilty of going outside his building before the proper time even though it was long after sunup on one of the long summer days. He was shot while running toward the big outbuilding that housed the showers and other sanitary facilities. Possibly he just had to go and the two barrels in his building for use during closed doors were already full.

Oscar is referring to the shooting of S.Sgt. Walter Nies that occurred on May 27, 1944. Nies had risen early and the door to his barracks had been mistakenly left unlocked during the night by the German guards. POWs were forbidden to leave their barracks during the night, until the door was unlocked at 6:00 a.m. Shortly after morning light appeared, near 4:00 a.m., another internee entered the barracks and announced that he had been to the latrine. Nies, thinking it was after 6:00 a.m. (since the door was unlocked) got a bar of soap and a towel and headed out to the outbuilding, evidently for a shower. A tower guard spotted him and shot him one time through his left side just above the waist. He died later that afternoon after being taken to a civilian hospital in Heydekrug.[18]

These two steel drums were the total of our inside plumbing. Each was about 2 feet in diameter and 2 feet high holding about 40 gallons each. One was a load for two men to carry each morning to the outhouse to empty, and the schedule for this duty was very carefully kept by each barracks leader and his council.

We had our own informal organization of government with an elected camp leader at the head and a barracks chief and council of ten who would meet to decide what to complain about to the camp commandant and to the Red Cross representative if he ever came. He didn't come very often. Once in six weeks or two months was about it.

Cigarettes served as money and every item of food or clothing had a value of a certain number of cigarettes. Cigarettes of different countries varied in value. All American brands were most valuable and about equal but were one and a half times the value of British or Canadian brands and twice that of the German Elegantes. Many cigarettes lost value from being handled too roughly in a poker or blackjack game.

Another POW at Luft VI, S.Sgt. Don Kremper, recalled the daily routine at Luft VI: "Dawn would bring the guards, and the doors and windows would be unlocked. Not long after, they'd blow whistles for us to fall out for a head count. This was performed twice a day, regardless of the weather. Often, we'd wait in the bitter cold while the ferrets searched our barracks for hidden radios, tunnels, and the like. After this annoying routine (the count was never correct the first time!), we went to the wash house–latrine and got ready for breakfast."[19]

Oscar continues:

We settled down to the boring life of living through the long dark winter, and how we managed to spend the two or three months is still a mystery to me. Finally, spring came, the days grew longer, there was less cloudy weather, the snow melted and made a sloppy mess for a few weeks. Summer came and the long, long days with eighteen hours of daylight, maybe more, were sometimes very pleasant. Some days seemed really hot—like 100 degrees—but nobody knew exactly.

Oscar wrote the following letter on D-Day, June 6, 1944. Oscar does not mention the significance of this date for obvious reasons but he was probably aware of what was happening at Normandy. There was a secret radio by which the prisoners received nightly radio messages from London in code. One prisoner ran from barracks to barracks proclaiming the great news until he was told to stop, as this would reveal to the guards the presence of the radio.

Kriegsgefangenenpost
Germany, 6/6/44
Dear Mom and Everybody –

How're y'all? The month of June now and everything is still about the
same here. Time goes pretty fast. It shouldn't be long now till I get
some mail from somebody. Boy that would sure help a lot. How's Ollie
Mae and Mary? I guess Mary is a senior. Ollie Mae are you goin' to
school this fall? Or are you gonna get all married up and stuff? [Ollie
Mae was going to college, at Texas Tech, and she did marry the dashing
George Didlake, but not until 1946. George had a passion for flying and
eventually became an airline pilot. He and Ollie Mae also raised four
children: Georga, Ted, Tom, and Tim]. Doggone I bet things are gonna
be different at home now. Even old Jim [a young teenager at this time]
will be a man if he grows to his feet. H. & Jr. will be big shot colonels
or sumpthin or and there I'll be, nothin' but an ex-kreige [slang for the
German word for prisoners of war: Kriegsgefangener]. I reckon I must
be the black sheep of our family.[20]

The next month Ollie wrote to Harold and Jean:

July 28th, 1944
Dear Harold and Jean,

Boy, oh boy, you sure got some fine cotton on your place this year and
its sure good cotton growing weather, so hot and no wind, just like in
SC. . . . I haven't heard from Oscar anymore and I'm sure worried.
I sent him his 2nd personal box the 19th and I've sent him cigarettes
three times. I doubt if he ever gets any of it though. I imagine they have
moved that camp since the Russians started their last drive and are
getting close to east Prussia. Gerald and Daddy think they will just go
off and leave them.
     The pilot's [Bob Bird] mother has never heard from Bob. I am
writing to all the moms and they are a sweet bunch of moms, too.
Mrs. Syzmanski sent me her picture and Mrs. Leaf sent me a clipping
of the wonderful job the "Lady" did on the 25th. They have the names
mixed up. Oscar was on the Pistol Packin' Mama that fateful day and
the copilot of Oscar's old crew was on the Lady the day the Lady was
shot down. 15 enemy planes—won't Oscar be happy when he finds out
what his beloved Lady did?

Ollie[21]

The Sophisticated Lady had made the news back in the States as indicated
by Ollie in having received a newspaper clipping of its final mission. It was

quite a thrilling story: Pilot Gil Bradley and the crew of Pistol Packin' Mama took the Sophisticated Lady with Air Force Hughes (Bob Bird's copilot) as his substitute copilot. The Lady was one of twenty-four B-24s of the 449th Bomb Group that participated in another raid on the Messerschmitt factory at Regensburg, Germany, on February 25, three days after Oscar's crew went down.

Bradley recalled that as they approached Regensburg, "The air space literally filled with aircraft, both American bombers and German fighters."[22] Flak was extremely heavy. B-24s, smoking, flaming, and disintegrating, began plunging earthward. Flak hit the Lady and knocked out the number two engine, reducing its speed and causing it to fall back. Bombers in this condition were like gazelles separated from the herd, easy prey for predators (enemy fighters). The Lady was alone except for another B-24, the Heavenly Body, flown by Bradley's best friend, Lt. Ed Drinan. Drinan queried his crew, "Shall we stay behind to help defend Sophisticated Lady?"[23] They unanimously agreed. For a bomber to leave its formation was against standing orders. Despite Heavenly Body's additional guns, the Lady staggered and slowed under the German onslaught. Smelling blood, the German fighters moved in for the kill. They lined up, awaiting their turn to make attack runs and came at the Lady from front and rear. Pilots Bradley and Hughes held a steady course despite 20 mm shells smashing into the nose and cockpit. The gunners heroically battled the Luftwaffe fighters, sending a number down. Under constant attack, the Lady's hydraulic, electrical, and communications system were shot out. When a third engine was blasted out by German bullets and shells, the crew had no choice but to bail out. The Sophisticated Lady, fighting to the end, then plunged into the snow-covered Yugoslavian Alps. One of Bradley's crew was killed during the fight, waist gunner S.Sgt. Paul S. Biggart. All the others survived the fight and bailout. They were rescued by Tito's Yugoslavian partisans, who led the American fliers on an epic, frigid, and grueling thirty-nine-day journey, moving at night to avoid detection, through snowy and rugged mountains to get to an airfield where an American transport aircraft picked them up. They were returned six weeks after their bailout to the Fifteenth Air Force Headquarters in Bari, Italy. Each member of Bradley's crew was awarded the Distinguished Flying Cross. The crew was credited with destroying fifteen enemy fighters in the fight over Regensburg. Ed Drinan received the Silver Star for his selfless and heroic efforts to save Bradley's crew and aircraft.[24]

Ollie opens the above letter with some good news for Harold: he had a good cotton crop on his farm. What was especially good about this was that cotton prices reached a sixteen-year high in 1944.[25] Farming during the war, like business in general, was doing very well.

While the farm was looking good, Oscar's situation was not. In the following chapter we will see that the progress of the war would have a dramatic effect on Oscar and the other prisoners at Stalag Luft VI.

Chapter 10

Oscar by Ship and by Train and Stalag Moves: July 1944–April 1945

I n 1944 the Germans were pressed by the Soviet Army along the entire eastern front. As summer approached, during the Soviet's Baltic Offensive, it appeared likely that the Soviets would advance to the Baltic Sea. Operation Bagration, a highly important Soviet offensive to retake Belorussia and East Prussia, began in June 1944. This was two weeks after D-Day, the Allied landings at Normandy. By October the Soviet army was on East Prussia's border and thus close to Heydekrug. Although Bagration was a signal victory for the Soviets, they were not able to defeat the Germans in East Prussia until the eve of V-E Day (victory in Europe) in April 1945.[1]

The Germans were taking no chances of losing their POWs, however, as Oscar relates:

> The advancing Russians forced us to move in July. The sun shone nearly all day and night. At this time, the Germans offered freedom to any prisoner who would join them to fight the oncoming Russians, to become members of the Wehrmacht and help save the world from Communism. Nearly everyone laughed at the idea, and our leaders urged us not to defect. We had no commissioned officers in this camp except for some doctors or medical personnel, dentists, etc. I did have to have an aching tooth pulled by a dentist from New Zealand—how

he got to be taken prisoner, I'll never know. I didn't even wonder about it at the time. His equipment was primitive and he had no anesthetic; it was horribly painful and he was sympathetic, but I wasn't in the mood to hear his story and I don't suppose he was in the mood to tell it. He was a good man doing what he could for us, and we were lucky to have him and other doctors from Britain and other Allied countries.

Anyway, there was no real authority to forbid one from joining the Wehrmacht, but I don't think any Americans did. Some British and others who had been prisoners for so long took their offer, but I don't suppose anyone knows what happened to them. They enjoyed freedom of a sort for a short time, I guess.

My little family[2] and I decided to take things as they came. We were confident that the Allies would win before we died of old age anyway. The invasion of D-Day gave us new hope for a short waiting period. We could hear the Russian guns not too far away as we gathered our meager supplies and prepared to move out.

Oscar and the other POWs certainly would be able to hear the Russian guns. Heydekrug was within hearing distance of the artillery barrage that initiated Operation Bagration. This barrage was one of the biggest, most intense ever.

Oscar continues:

We walked many miles—about thirty—to an unnamed seaport where we were loaded, bag and baggage, into the empty hold of a coal freighter, more than a thousand men right down in the bottom. It seemed the tiny square of light of the open hatch above was at least a hundred feet, but down we went on two steel ladders, side by side. It took hours to get us all in. The air was heavy with coal dust, and we'd never been more crowded, even on the worst train ride. I'd never been on a ship. I thought I'd get seasick, but I didn't. Some did and some died. I lost track of time again and water was in short supply, lowered to us in buckets on ropes and waste hauled out in the same buckets probably. It was the worst time of all, I think. A nightmare, unreal.

The only clue to our location was the name of the freighter's home-port, Memel, a port of the Soviet Union on the Baltic Sea. Some days later we arrived at Stettin, about 300 miles southwest of Memel and about 100 miles north of Berlin. In Stettin harbor we saw dozens of German submarines. Stettin was one of Germany's main U-boat bases.

We were taken by train, an enjoyable trip by comparison to our cruise, about 90 miles east of Stettin to Stalag Luft IV where we moved into another new camp five or six miles from the city [Gross Tychow].

The ship that moved Oscar and other POWs was the merchant ship *Masuren*, and it awaited the prisoners at the port of Memel (now Klaipėda, Lithuania) a distance of about eighty miles from Heydekrug. The *Masuren* had formerly been a Soviet freighter, a rusty old coal boat, with the hammer and sickle still on the smokestack.[3] Another prisoner, Hy Hatton, recalled that "it was impossible to reach food, sleeping was out of the question and there was no means for relief. We were aboard that freighter for 56 hours."[4] There were about nine hundred men packed into the hold.[5]

Much has been written and spoken about the "hell ships" that Japan used to transport prisoners in absolutely inhumane circumstances from one location to another, including to Japan, where they were placed in POW camps essentially to serve as slave laborers. These ships certainly deserved the name. Oscar's experience aboard the coal freighter was a similar experience, although his trip from Memel to Stettin was clearly not as long as the Japanese hell ship transit from the Philippines to Japan. Nevertheless, the trip on the *Masuren* was hell for the POWs that endured it.

Stalag Luft IV turned out to be a rougher experience than Stalag Luft VI at Heydekrug. Luft IV, near the town of Gross Tychow in northwestern Poland and about two hundred miles from Berlin, had been partially built by April 1944. The three thousand prisoners that came from Stalag Luft VI, of whom Oscar was a part, arrived in July. The prisoners' "welcome" to Stalag Luft IV was a particularly harsh experience, as Oscar describes:

We walked with our packs and possessions on our backs, but not fast enough to suit our new camp commandant, a short, red-faced, well-dressed Luftwaffe major who worked himself into a rage as he rode in his staff car behind the column of prisoners. My little group was near the tail end, and we were being escorted by guards and many dogs on both sides and in the rear. I could hear the major's monologue. I don't know all the words he said, but he had nothing nice to say about POWs. He finally exploded and ordered the guards to double-time march us the rest of the distance. I guess we were pretty slow, but after a four or five day Baltic sea cruise, who could enjoy a five-mile hike with full packs? Luckily, I didn't have much to carry but others who had prospered at Heydebrug [Heydekrug] and were loaded just had to drop it when the dogs came in.

I saw one man break his beautiful guitar over a dog's head to escape being bitten, and the road was cluttered with discarded goods of all kinds. These things weren't returned to us either. It just shows one shouldn't be too ambitious or greedy.

I didn't have much, so I lost nothing, but by the time we went through the gate of our new home, I was exhausted. A few more died on the road. Many passed out in the heat, but I don't think anyone was shot or otherwise deliberately killed.

It was a beautiful summer afternoon and under other conditions could have been an enjoyable walk. The countryside was very scenic with evergreen trees and summer flowers. Maybe I did lose another pound from my skinny body. We were really thirsty when we got to the water.

While Oscar describes his experiences in a low-key tone, other prisoners were much more descriptive. The "red-faced" German officer was Capt. Hauptmann Pickard. He was an entirely different type of camp commandant than the one at Stalag Luft VI, Colonel Von Hoerman, who one prisoner recalled was a very "fine Prussian gentleman officer. Very stern, very strict, but very fair. He abided by the rules of the Geneva Convention."[6]

Pickard, however, was a fine Nazi. He had raised the ire of the German guards with an inflammatory speech against the POWs to include calling them "gangster airmen" who received bonus pay when they bombed women and children.[7] The prisoners were pleasantly surprised to receive two Red Cross parcels per man before the march began. However, with their personal baggage brought from Heydekrug, this would be quite a load. The train station was, as Oscar says, five or six miles from the prison camp. The prisoners moved too slowly for Hauptmann. He ordered the guards to fix bayonets, fired his pistol in the air, then commanded, as Oscar relates, that the POWs run. It was a hot July day. The prisoners were already dehydrated and hungry due to the ship and rail transit from Heydekrug. Many were shackled together at the wrists and ankles. Others still wore their heavy winter coats, thinking ahead to the harsh winter. They did their best to comply, to run, but loaded down, it was a tough go. They tossed personal effects and even Red Cross goods. These items, including the Red Cross food, were never returned to the prisoners. When a man fell out or collapsed, the German guards prodded them with bayonets that produced light but painful puncture wounds. The guard dogs attacked. As the guards prodded them along, they shouted names of German cities that had been bombed in Allied air raids, "Eine fur Hamburg, Eine fur Koln!"[8] Upon arrival, the POWs were forced to wait outside in the sun, without water for hours and, in some cases, over a day. The wait was for a strip search ordered by the camp commandant before they were turned in to the camp.[9]

The International Committee of the Red Cross inspected the camp in October 1944. It found that there were almost 7,100 Americans in the camp and over 1,500 prisoners from England and Commonwealth nations. The Red Cross reported that the camp was overcrowded; a sleeping area for 16 men had 24 packed in. Each barracks had only a two-hole latrine with urinals for 240 men. An open-air outside latrine also was available, with barrels that collected the waste, but they were not emptied often enough, a job reserved for Russian prisoners. Rarely was clothing issued, and there was no means for showering. Prisoners suffered from body lice and fleas. Medical care was scarce, although the committee did find the prisoners' health to be generally good and medical supplies sufficient. Overall, the committee declared that Stalag Luft IV was a "bad camp, although the situation, the accommodation and the food, do not differ from those in other camps."[10]

There was always a lack of food. Red Cross parcels were often pilfered or plundered by German guards. Prisoners were given a ration of watery vegetable soup daily, an ounce of meat, and an occasional bit of cheese, jam, or sugar. Calorie intake was about 1,200 per man, per day. Remarking on the shortage of food, one prisoner said, "You woke up hungry, you went to bed hungry, you were hungry all day long."[11]

Oscar continues:

> After a week or so we settled into our new home, and it was really nice if we could just have had a bit more food. It's hard to enjoy beautiful scenery looking through barbed wire while you're hungry.

Kriegsgefangenenpost [from Stalag IV]
Dear Mom & Everybody
August 6, 1944

How're y'all? I hope everybody's okay. Everything here is still under control, just about the same old story. Nothing to do and nowhere to go. I think I'd be much happier at home. Everybody is getting rather short-tempered and kinda hard to get along with. But, I guess they can't be blamed for that. . . . Doggone, I'd sure like to hear from somebody. It seems like ages since I had mail. How's the farm coming along? Pickin' cotton yet? You goin' to school O. M. [Ollie Mae]? How are you Mary? And Jim, you're okay I s'pose? You gettin' any fatter Wiley? Sure wish I were there. Well so long till next time. Goodnite and I'll dream of home.

Love from Oscar[12]

A month later he jubilantly reported that he had finally received the mail he desperately longed for. The letters from home took almost sixty days to get to him. He happily reported:

Kriegsgefangenenpost
Germany, 9/6/44

Dear Mom & Everybody—Happy day—Got two letters from you yesterday, one of June 11 & one June 14. I'm sure glad to know everybody is okay, but it seems I missed a couple of chapters somewhere in the story.

Love from Oscar[13]

Then one day a blessed event: he had mail and bounty from home:

Kriegsgefangenenpost

Dear Mom & Everybody—How're y'all? Everybody here is okay; considering. The crew is all happy, everyone now has a parcel of some sort from home. Even I and man, I sure do appreciate it and send my thanks to all concerned. I got the 60 Luckies and the May personal

box. The cigarettes are all good, but worms got into everything eata-
ble in the other. Not bad after you pick 'em out though. Everything
else is okay and that new tooth brush and the Pepsodent sure work
good together.

I'd sure like to be there now. I guess it's winter there too by
now. Is the cotton picker situation gonna be bad this year? Hope the
cotton is makin' good as I think. I'd sure like to see all of you. You &
Wiley & O. M. & Mary & Jim (all grown up now). Jr. & H [Harold]
in their "hot rock," uniforms, Jerry & Ethel & all the kids. Well I can
still dream. Goodbye now, I think about all of you a lot. Love to all,
from - Oscar.[14]

The date Oscar wrote this letter was not apparent. It is estimated that it
is at least a month after the preceding one, which would be no earlier than
October 1944. He comments on winter in New Mexico, which normally does
not arrive before October. Therefore, it took at least five months for the pack-
age to make it to Oscar. This explains the worm-eaten food contents. He ate
it anyway, after picking out the worms.

This letter expresses Oscar's longing for family and farm. In almost
every letter he asks about his siblings. His comments about Junior and Harold,
who by now were both officers and pilots, and their "hot rocks" uniforms, is
interesting.[15] It is said in a brotherly joking manner and not in a bad spirit.
But it also denotes a sense of getting behind. He is concerned that his career
and personal advancement were waylaid by his prisoner status. Note also
the "black sheep" comment in the letter of June 6, 1944 (above). This feeling was expressed to his son Mack later that his time as a POW was wasted
time. This, in addition to their combat trauma, was additional fallout POWs
suffered for a long time.

Oscar continues:

The new buildings here were of wooden frame construction, wooden
floors about 2 feet off the ground. The buildings were divided into
separate rooms for sixteen men. Again, our family moved in together.
We were indestructible and inseparable.

Somehow our information about the outside world situation was
improved. I suppose because primitive secret radios were closer to
main broadcasting stations. We got daily news of the situation and
were greatly encouraged by the reported progress of the Allied forces.

We weren't any better fed, but it was summer, and morale was high. We knew the war couldn't last much longer. But it did.

We'd been there about a month when the commandant lost his temper again. His cat disappeared, and he was sure some prisoner had taken the cat for food. I never ate any cat, but I think I could have. It was surely equal to dog. I don't know what happened to the cat, and the major's week-long investigation didn't solve the mystery. Many were questioned and some served time in solitary confinement but nothing really serious came of it.

The invasion on D-Day took place shortly before we moved, and our hopes for a short war soared, but summer faded into fall then winter came again, and even though general conditions here were better, we were still hungry most of the time and morale took a downturn.

During the summer, there was an outbreak of escape fever and the engineering of several escape tunnels started along with many individual attempts to cut through the wire at night. The only tunnel that ever surfaced outside the fence was completed by the German guards from the outside. Several prisoners were trapped in the tunnel and disciplined with long sentences of solitary, but I think none were shot. I was apathetic about escape, maybe just lazy, but the odds against success just seemed too great. It was very discouraging. We were still short of food, and it seemed that the only thing to do was take it day by day.

In some Stalags the German guards would allow tunnels to be dug until they were almost finished, then, as in the case Oscar describes, the guards would dig a tunnel from the outside toward the tunnel the prisoners were working on. When the guards broke through, they arrested the POWs and punishment followed—probably time in solitary. The Germans reasoned that by letting the prisoners dig, the prisoners would be kept busy and thereby not plot other escapes.[16]

These buildings were harder to keep warm than the brick buildings of Heydekrug. Christmas was a cheerful time for the Germans. They had broken out in their counteroffensive in the Battle of the Bulge, and they gave us extra food on Christmas Day and let us stay outside the buildings all night. The Germans were generous with frequent reports of the Battle of the Bulge where the Wehrmacht had surrounded [Brigadier] General Terry McAuliffe and his forces at Bastogne, Belgium and were demanding his surrender. His classic reply was, "Nuts!" and he was saved by General [George S.] Patton's double-timing Third Army moving in record time to break the back of the last major action of the German forces. By then everyone knew the end was certain to Germany's surrender and the end was finally in sight.

We were squeezed out of Stalag IV in February [1945]. About half of us were put on a train to Nuremberg. The distance of 250 miles took a week or more to go through Berlin and many bombing raids occurred both day and night. Some of the night bombings we had seen from our camp at Tychow, but none as close as these and the raids on Nuremberg after we arrived there. We dug our own trenches and bomb shelters, and the ancient army post served as our prison there.

The prisoners not shipped by train took to the road on foot, and we never saw them again until we all got together at Moosburg. Their trip was disastrous. Many men were lost from exposure and starvation. The winter was cold, and they hiked from Stalag Luft IV to Moosburg in much colder weather than ours of ninety or 100 miles from Nuremberg to Moosburg [this occurred later and will be described in ch. 15]. Again, I was lucky to be on the train. My whole family was except Blake and Whistler. Blake made it but Whistler didn't. We don't know what happened to him except that he decided to leave the organized march and take off on his own. [This implies that Whistler had rejoined the group after healing from two broken ankles in the parachute landing.] Some got home more quickly this way, but most were lost.

In February 1945 Oscar and his fellow POWs in Stalag Luft IV in Poland again heard Russian artillery and flashes on the eastern horizon. Again, they were moved west. Oscar was among those who were moved by train to Nuremberg, Germany, departing Tychow on February 2, 1945. A train bearing the sick and injured had departed a few days earlier. While many of the Stalag Luft IV internees (about 1,500) were shuttled west by train, including Oscar, many more (almost 6,000) ended up walking westward. Evidently this included Blake and Whistler. How it was determined which prisoners got train rides and who walked is not known. Oscar and his "family" were extremely fortunate to be on this train. Those that endured what has come to be known as the death march suffered horribly. The winter of 1945 in Europe was one of the worst ever, with intense cold and heavy snow. The suffering of those who were forced to walk for long distances was therefore extreme. They were exposed to the German winter conditions, and their misery was exacerbated by their already poor physical condition, near starvation, and rampant sickness. An unknown number died on these marches, all headed toward the final prison camp at Moosburg. The march spanned eighty-six

---

days and covered an estimated six hundred miles. Of particular note is that despite the extreme suffering in the most inhumane conditions, the march is often noted as a time when the Allied prisoners displayed, in an extraordinary fashion, great care and sacrifice for one another.[17]

The POW camp at Nuremberg, Stalag XIII-D, like other prison camps, had been the homes of POWs from the various nations the Germans had captured in previous battles. Stalag XIII-D was located on what had been the parade grounds of the massive Nazi rallies often seen in news reels of the period. The camp's population grew enormously in 1944–1945 as prisoners arrived from other camps farther east that were in the way of advancing Russians. After the war Stalag XIII-D was used to imprison fifteen thousand former Nazi SS members.[18]

Oscar recalls:

We saw some very spectacular fireworks of the night bombing raids after we reached Nuremberg with several near misses of bombs, but the greatest danger was from the falling fragments of flak and of falling aircraft. I'm sure the location of our camp was known, and we were never in the actual target area, but mistakes can be made. Our closest call was when a night raiding [De Havilland DH 98] Mosquito bomber was shot down and crashed, burning into one of the guard towers. But the greatest show was when the radar scout plane marked out the target area with half dozen or so bright parachute flares that lit up the area almost as bright as day. Then the lumbering heavy bombers moved in with the blockbuster bombs that made their own special sound as they fell to their target. Then the earthquake of their blast, the night fighters racing in, and their tracer fire mixing with that from the bombers made every known geometric pattern in even brighter color. It was such a show we almost forgot to be afraid.

The only big daylight bombing we saw was the day we were put on the road to march from Nuremberg to Moosburg, although we only knew at the time that we were moving south. Our destination was unknown probably even to the Germans.

It was a fairly nice day in late March and as we left the city, B-24s and B-17s moved across in what seemed like thousands.[19] There were many fighters, too—nearly all Allied—and they left the high-altitude bombers to go to treetop level for strafing of targets missed by the bombs.

A group of P-47 Thunderbolt American fighters mistook our strag-
gling column for German troops and made several passes firing their
deadly .50 caliber guns into our midst before we could be identified.
I was terrified and dived into the bush beside the road, expecting to
be hit by the next shell. Several men were hit and two were killed,
but again I was lucky and came through with only a few fragments of
something barely penetrating the skin on my back. I didn't even know
about it until later. It was painless.[20]

We were soon identified as American POWs and from then on, we
were under almost constant surveillance of American fighter planes,
usually a pair of P-51s. They checked on our progress and I'm sure
Allied headquarters knew where we were at all times. The German
guards became more and more friendly and went out of their way to
arrange shelter from the weather at night, usually in a farmer's barn,
and we shared rations of potatoes with the farmers' hogs. The civilians
were mostly friendly, too, sharing a little of their short supply of food.
They knew the end was near.

The hike from Nuremberg to Moosburg was quite a distance, about a
hundred miles. The weather conditions were not extreme, and as Oscar notes,
the guards had become friendlier, no doubt sensing that the war was ending
and they were on the losing side. Despite the long distance, hunger, and exposure to the weather, the prisoners were optimistic. American fighter aircraft
daily overhead shepherding them along were a source of spiritual uplift,
"angels on our shoulders."[21] The Mustang fighters were a sign that things
were going to end well, and soon.

Oscar was nearing the end of his confinement and, as this was occurring in April 1945, the war was drawing to a conclusion. We have yet,
however, to tell of Harold and Wiley's experiences as they moved through
training and into combat. We must reset to March 1944, when Oscar was
only one month into his POW experience, Wiley was finishing up his basic
flight training, and Harold was starting to train on the B-25. While Oscar
was dealing with Stalag life during most of 1944 and into 1945, this is what
his two brothers in uniform were experiencing. In the next chapter Wiley's
flight training is related to the point that he is ready for deployment to a
combat theater. Harold's journey and the family home front is related in the
chapter following.

Chapter 11

Bombers and Fighters, Harold and Wiley Jr. Flight Training: March–November 1944

We left Wiley Jr. in March 1944 (ch. 5). He had finished his basic stage of flight training while Harold had completed advanced flight training, returned home, and married Jean McKinstry. Harold and Jean headed to Columbia, South Carolina, where Harold joined a transition squadron that trained pilots in how to fly the twin-engine North American B-25 Mitchell bomber. Upon completion of basic, Wiley Jr. was assigned to Eagle Pass Army Airfield, where he began advanced flight training.

Eagle Pass was in far south Texas, adjacent to the Mexican border. It had been built to support the war effort and opened in April 1942. Cadets in advanced training flew the beloved North American AT-6 Texan aircraft. The AT-6 was popular as an advanced trainer with the navy and with Britain and its Commonwealth nations. More than fifteen thousand Texans were built. It continued service after the war. In the Korean War its two-man crew—pilot and forward observer or air controller—directed artillery fire or air strikes on enemy positions.

The Texan was a step up in power, performance, and complexity. It had retractable landing gear and a six-hundred-horsepower engine, the Pratt & Whitney R-1340 Wasp reciprocal engine. It was faster than the

BT-13 (208 miles per hour compared to 180) and had the look and feel of a tactical fighter.

Advanced training consisted of formation, navigation (day and night), instruments, and aerobatics. Cadets also practiced in Link simulators. In formation training future pilots flew in the tight three-plane V to build proficiency. Five feet between wingtips was the standard distance to maintain in formation flying. More often they flew a tactical, two-plane formation, leader and wingman. Larger formations of up to twelve aircraft were flown to practice "air discipline, precise, and accurate position holding."[1] Most training was done at midaltitude, five thousand to ten thousand feet, although in advanced at least one low-level flight was mad, and if oxygen equipment was available, a flight above fifteen thousand feet was made. Aerobatics—practicing sophisticated flight maneuvers—became centrally important. This sharpened dogfighting skills, air-to-air combat against enemy fighters. Navigation was an important skill for fighter pilots because unlike with bomber crews, which had a dedicated navigator, a fighter pilot was on his own for navigation. Actual military training diminished in advanced, although a rigorous physical training regime persisted, and there were still inspections, marching, and training in military courtesies and customs. The emphasis, of course, remained on flying.

In the advanced stage, the curriculum required about sixty to seventy hours to complete. Gunnery training followed graduation. Wiley Jr. flew the P-40 fighter for his gunnery training. In gunnery cadets practiced strafing, firing at ground and air targets, in anticipation of air combat. Shooting skeet prepared cadets for gunnery. The air target was a long sleeve pulled through the air by another aircraft. Pilots made gun runs on the sleeve. Each pilot's bullets were marked with a certain color, thus showing which bullet holes in the target belonged to which pilot. This allowed hits to be counted. Pilots who flew aggressively and did well in gunnery were selected to be combat fighter pilots. Wiley Jr. did well. On some gunnery flights, he scored over 50 percent hits on the sleeve. He thereby was designated a fighter pilot.

Advanced training was dangerous for all cadets, but especially fighter pilots, who were killed at the rate of seventy per 100,000 hours of flight. This was an incredibly high rate when one considers that in today's military, the fatality rate per 100,000 hours is less than three. This was not ignored by high command. Cadets were threatened with severe disciplinary actions for violating procedures and deliberately flying in a dangerous manner. This, of course, addressed the main cause of accidents: pilot error. Pilots were threatened with court-martial and/or dismissal from the service for violations of flight procedures. Death benefits for families of pilots who were killed as a result of violating flight regulations were also threatened to be withheld.

Upon arrival at the Eagle Pass base, Wiley Jr. wrote home.

March 1944
Dear Mom,

Well I'm now in advanced. Just can't realize it tho. We are going to fly AT-6s. They're really nice planes. We have a few P-40s here too. They look small compared to the AT-6.

I'm really gonna like this place here. The officers treat us nice and the food is ok. We even have grass around the barracks. I've only been here one day so I don't know much about this place. We get gunnery in Link trainers here I think. Some fun. We have to come back here after graduation and fly the P-40s for a month-take gunnery and stuff.

Heck Mom, I really don't know much to say. Say, I guess Harold is home now, eh? [Yes, he was home and marrying Jean.] Boy, I bet he's really glad too isn't he. I'll be if I don't wash out here. I have exactly 151 hrs & 50 min. of [flight] time all logged now. And 70 more here so that makes about 220 hrs. Not bad considering that it hasn't cost anything. I'll probably get instructor. In fact, I'm asking for it. You really learn to fly then. Well Mom, guess I'd better stop now. Tell Harold to have a big time. Oh yes, we had an 8 hr. layover in San Antonio. Lots of fun.

Your loving son,
Wiley[2]

The next month, April 1944, he wrote:

Dearest Mother

Look Mom, will you kick me real good if I get my wings. I know I haven't written in two weeks, and I know that you're angry with me. I'm really worried tho. It's quite a strain here—I mean washing out. I may get it any day now, who knows. I almost got it Sat. Damned near ground looped. You will pardon my language I hope, but it makes me mad to think that I almost did it. Oh, you should have seen our air review Sat. P-40s firing and buzzing along with a [P-]51 and a [P-]47, of course our AT-6s which came in along the ramp about 30 feet off. But, you should have seen our P-51. Oh it is a honey. It came in about 10 ft off, and at least 300 mph. Oh, it is a honey. I'm really in love with it. The main features are its "lines," (Ha) and its wide landing gear. Well, if I get thru here, I get one I hope.

With all my love, I remain, your loving son,

Wiley Jr[3]

Just a few days later he wrote:

Dearest Mom,

How's my sweetheart doin? OK I hope. And how is everybody? Gosh Mom, but I'm sorry I don't write more often; seems like I never get around to it.

Oh say did I tell you that we've finished ground school? Yep we're all thru now. All we do is get up in time for breakfast, and not then if we don't feel like it. Then we have P.T. [physical training] at 10:30. That's all there is to it. Next week we start night flying, and finish that week. I have about 40 hrs. now and 35 to go. We have had about 6 hrs. of formation. We have 6 x 12 ship formations. And tomorrow we go on a rendezvous over a certain town. Just like combat you know. We also get a night X-C [cross country]. It's pretty long too.

I've finished my 500 rounds of skeet. Had a fair score too. You know Mom, they washed out 6 "Joes" yesterday. Tough stuff. Hope they don't get me. These ships [T-6 Texans] are really nice to fly, but too easy to ground loop. I almost gnd looped last Sat; had a flat tail wheel and a flat strut. Every time it hit a bump the tail came up. Boy I was sweatin blood.

Well enough of my troubles. Oh yes, we have 500 ex-cadets or rather students. They work on the line here. They'll never get to fly nor anyone else. They're slowin down.

Say how are things at home? And how's the farming coming? Well Mom wish me luck.

Your loving son,
Wiley Jr.[4]

The next month Wiley again wrote his mother.

May 1944
Dearest Mom,

Got your letter, and needless to say, was very glad to hear that things are going o.k. Say, I guess I lost that last letter I got from Oscar. He hasn't written since so I don't know how he is. He's ok tho, I know. [Oscar was in fact okay but was a prisoner, and at this time was in Heydekrug in East Prussia.] He may have been shot down or had a forced landing somewhere. Forced landings are very common among bombers. Course now in the single engine fighters, you have a real ship that can take anything & more. If something goes wrong, you just bailout or make a forced landing somewhere. There's little chance of getting hurt in one, cause you have your shoulder harness & safety belt.

Say Mom will you send me Harold's address. I lost his letter someplace. And just think, only 12 more days until graduation [this was to be on May 23, 1944]. . . . I may go to instructors school. I really want P-40s. Then P-51s & 47s. Nice eh? They're just like an AT-6 only faster. Well Mom guess I better close now. If you hear from Oscar let me know. And don't worry any cause we are all ok.

Your loving son,
Wiley
P.S. – I'll be home about the last of June for 15 days.[5]

This is an interesting letter in that Wiley still does not know of Oscar's captivity and status as a POW, when a month earlier, Ollie had official news that Oscar had in fact been captured and had notified Harold and Annie and Ed Allison. It is also interesting in that Wiley expresses a lot of confidence in the survivability of fighter-type aircraft.

May 1944   5 days till grad
Dearest Mom,

Well Mom guess I'll make it if everything goes ok the last 5 days. By the way I'm not a flight officer.[6] Seems like I have a pretty fair record so far. In fact I was recommended for a good conduct ribbon.

Course it doesn't mean anything really, but it's nice to know you're doing o.k.

I told you we were going to be here 4 more weeks didn't I? Yeah, we have to get gunnery & P-40 time (10 hrs). Then we get 15 days & travel time [leave]. P-40s are pretty hard to fly it seems. Lot of airplane there you know. By the way, have you heard from Oscar lately? I sure haven't. But, don't worry, he's o.k.

Your loving son,
Wiley [7]

The Curtis P-40 Warhawk was one of the Allies' main fighters. More of them were built for the Allies than any other fighter except the P-51 and P-47. It is sometimes pictured as having a shark's mouth painted on the cowling. It had a 1,740-horsepower engine and its top speed was about 340 miles per hour (later models were faster). It remained in operation until the war's end. Although its high-altitude performance was less than German fighters, it nevertheless was a capable fighter. Over two hundred Allied pilots became aces (shooting down five or more enemy aircraft) in the Warhawk. It flew predominately in North Africa, India, Burma, China, and Eastern Europe, where high-altitude flight was not so important, as in protecting high-flying bombers.[8]

[ca. May 1944]
Dearest Mother,

Didn't fly today Mom. I'm feelin pretty bad. Flew last night tho, and finished night formation. I was element leader. I had a pretty good wingman too. Made a good landing last night. You know I'm really glad that I got to fly P-40s after all. They're the hardest to fly, but they make a nice trainer.

Well they're having a stag party at the Officers Club so I guess I'd better go and watch the gambling. They really have some big games too. Oh yes, I guess we get paid Sat. and I have about $70 left. Not bad eh?

Your lovin' son,
Wiley[9]

Junior graduated flight training May 23, 1944. At that point he was a commissioned officer and designated a pilot. A major goal had been achieved. He now proudly wore the gold bars of a second lieutenant and silver AAF pilot wings, the top of the AAF culture. He remained, however, at Eagle Pass and continued to fly the P-40 fighter.

June 1944
Dearest Mom,

Gosh Mom, I guess you thot I'd never write. We've been pretty busy finishing our time in the [P-]40s. I finished today. Tomorrow I start gunnery. I doubt if I'll have as much time as I have had. We get to fire 3,000 rounds of .30 caliber ammunition. We haven't had any accidents due to pilot error yet. I think there was one forced landing. He came in wheels up in the mesquite. Didn't hurt the plane much at all and didn't even scratch the guy. Yes, we have a fine record so far. Hope the other squadron does as good as we have. And I hope we shoot as good a score as they did in gunnery. We have the best scores of any transition school in the central command.

Your loving son,
Wiley Jr.[10]

As his training at Eagle Pass neared completion, he wrote:

Dearest Mom,

Thanks a million for the gas, but aren't you a little short? But I guess you have quite a few "T" stamps [gasoline rationing stamps].
    Well Mom I guess we leave here the 8th [July] then to Tallahassee. From here to a P.O.E. [point of embarkation]. However we may get a leave. Not much chance tho, but if I do I'll let you know. I have around 140 hours now. Guess I'm high man in our squadron. Things are going OK here. The weather is pretty changeable tho now.
    I'm glad to leave here in a way cause this school gets pretty old at times. We've had a good time flying the last week. Lots of buzzing on the deck and stuff like that.
    Well Mom I'm sorry that I haven't written any sooner. Oh yes Mom, a very happy birthday

All my love to the sweetest Mother in the world.

Your son,
Wiley[11]

Wiley Jr. left Eagle Pass in late June 1944. He was allowed some days' leave en route to his next duty station, which was at Perry Army Air Base in Perry, Florida. He went home for a few days and spent the time with family and friends. This visit was poignantly remembered by his parents and siblings. He arrived at Dale Mabry Airfield near Tallahassee in mid-July. Within a couple of weeks he went to the subfield at Perry, Florida, about fifty miles southeast of Tallahassee. Here, flight training in the P-40 was conducted. He wrote home upon arrival at Tallahassee:

July 1944
Dear Mom,

Got here [Tallahassee] o.k., and it's a nice place here. A nice clean town. Lots of trees too. We've been here 5 days and it's rained 7 times. So you can tell about the climate. Sure are lots of girls here. Just like Chickasha College you know. Boy was it hot today. Whew, I bet I've sweated a gallon, maybe more. Say, it hasn't rained today. How about that? Oh yes, we had a parade this morning. Nothing to it tho, except that it was awful hot.

We are to be here about 2 more weeks, and then go to a school where we fly [Perry]. We'll get about 100 hrs in the damned P-40 and maybe P-51, if we're lucky you know.

Well please forgive me for not writing sooner. I lost track of my bag in Dallas so I didn't write. And I hardly had time after I left Dallas. I didn't even have a meal for 4 days.

Love,
Wiley Jr. [12]

A couple of weeks later he wrote from Perry, an isolated little southern town of about 2,700 residents:

August 1944
Dearest Mother,

Mom, I'm so sorry about not writing to you. I really have no excuse I guess. However, I did want to wait till I got to my new station before I wrote.

And what a place this is. It's really awful. It's just a small place out in the swamps, and I really mean swamps. Only it's just one large one. Oh there's plenty of vegetation. We have a lot of pines, which are almost drowned out. And we have a very abundant crop of bed bugs. As yet I haven't had any trouble, but some of the other fellows have. They haven't gotten around to me yet. But we do have nice food here and a swell club. And I'm here with "Gus" [Richard N. Gustke] and the rest of the boys from Eagle Pass. Gus has his car down here now. He has a '39 Ford convertible. Nice car eh? You know Mom, I sure wish I had a car, or much better a motorcycle. You see, I figure I ought to have my fun here in the states. But I just hate to throw all that money away. Of course if I had a motorcycle I could ship it home.

Well, how are things at home now? Is the cotton and feed doin OK? Boy, I really hope so. And how did the wheat make out? Say, I'll bet that new "M" is really a swell job, eh?[13]

Well I guess I'll say good nite to the sweetest little Mother in the whole world.

Your loving son,
Wiley Jr.[14]

Wiley Jr. provides his impression of Perry. He mentions fellow cadet and good friend Gus. This was Richard N. Gustke from Battle Creek, Michigan. They remained together and deployed to the Eighth Air Force in England, were in the same fighter squadron, and then went into combat. A month later, still at Perry, he wrote:

Dearest Mom,

I was so glad to get the card Mom, it was very nice. I've been pretty busy. We are now flying all day. I have almost 50 hrs., and tonight we start night flying. We're to get 3 hrs. of it. There's really nothing that happens here Mom, I mean anything you'd like to hear.

How are things at home these days? Everybody ok? Hey I guess Ollie Mae has left for school hasn't she? My how time do fly. Seems like I was home only yesterday.

Guess we will be here one more month, and then back to Tallahassee. For a week or so. Don't guess I'll get a leave.

I'm gonna try to see Harold and Jean someday. It's been a long time since I saw Harold, or Jean either for that matter.

Well sweetheart guess this is all for now.

Your loving son,
Wiley Jr.

P.S. I'm not a very good bombardier. I dropped 3 bombs in the Gulf instead of in the box. It just goes to show how much a fighter pilot has to know. Ha, ha. Don't tell Harold[15]

While Perry Airfield might not have had the most exciting social life, serious flight training was conducted there. This was the last stop before a fighter pilot headed to Europe and combat. After arriving at Perry, Junior obtained another 143 hours in the Warhawk. Although the P-40 was not the aircraft he flew in combat, it was a real fighter and therefore valuable for preparing him to fly the P-51.

His overall flight time obtained in training was 401 hours. This gave him and his contemporaries a significant advantage over enemy pilots. At this time the Luftwaffe had been ravaged by five years of steady combat and was a bare nub of the fearsome force it had been earlier. The typical replacement German fighter pilot at this time, late in the war, only had about a fourth of the flight hours that American pilots received in training.[16]

His official training record shows how fighter pilots were prepared for combat. The main categories of flight were transition, formation, acrobatics, navigation, gunnery, night flying, bombing, instrument flying, combat (or dogfighting), combined training, and miscellaneous. In formation flying he flew twenty-one hours, and interestingly, half of the formation time was at low level, below five hundred feet. This was indicative of the type of missions fighter pilots were currently flying, lots of low-level strafing. He got fifteen hours of navigation, mostly dead reckoning—estimating one's position based on speed, distance, and time traveled. Electronic navigational aids were sparse at the time. Over forty-five hours were spent on gunnery training. Ten hours of this was ground gunnery, strafing, and combat flying. Twenty hours were practiced with a camera gun—that is, filming the pilot's aiming point so as to critique his firing runs without using live ammunition. Live ammunition was used also. Wiley Jr. fired over five thousand rounds of .50-caliber bullets at a towed banner, of which 21 percent were hits. He flew six hours at night, four of which were in formation. He dropped twenty-eight bombs, all in low level or skip bombing practice but, interestingly, none in dive bombing. He flew almost seven hours of air combat, or dogfighting, and eight hours in combined training above eight thousand feet. He flew thirty-nine missions in the miscellaneous category. Sixteen of these were "homing" missions, or practicing what passed for a precision approach in those days. This was listening to radio signals as one flew toward the radio transmitter at an airfield. If he was on course (i.e., headed directly toward the station), the pilot heard a steady tone. If he drifted left or right of the prescribed course, he heard a morse code *A* (right of course) or *N* (left of course). The trick was staying on course as one flew closer to the station and the "beam" got narrower. This was a difficult procedure but essential for finding a runway in bad weather or at night. It was called "flying the beam."[17]

Wiley Jr. and other replacement pilots also got a good dose of ground training in subjects considered essential for operating in the European war zone. This classroom instruction included signal communications (six hours), chemical warfare (six hours), combat intelligence (six hours), camouflage (four hours), navigation (six hours), meteorology (three hours), medical training (ten hours), frostbite (two hours), altitude indoctrination (four hours), wordsmanship (one hour), seamanship (one hour), ditching (one hour), parachute (one hour), and propeller (one hour). Ground training, in total, was sixty-six hours.

Flight training and ground training was not all. There were also subjects and procedures that the AAF deemed necessary for being a combat fighter pilot. These included aircraft maintenance (eighteen hours; Wiley got twenty-four). The aircraft maintenance portion of his training was not just classroom academics; it was hands-on. Wiley serviced a fighter aircraft with fuel, oil, coolant, and oxygen. He inspected, cleaned, and replaced the oil screen, changed a tire, inspected and inflated the oleo strut, inspected and changed the distributor head, and tested and changed the battery. Wiley Jr. was no doubt comfortable doing aircraft maintenance after growing up on his father's farm. Tractor and equipment maintenance were daily duties. His other training included armament, gunnery training aids, gunnery ground school, gun camera assessment, aircraft recognition, Link trainer, current events, briefing criteria, physical training, and skeet shooting.[18]

After training at Perry airfield, he and his contemporaries were well trained, but as we will see, not ready for combat. He shipped out—literally— for England in November 1945.

He wrote a descriptive letter to little brother Jim, now 15 years old, as he neared completion of his training at Perry:

Hi ya Bud,

Say that was a swell letter from you the other day. And was I glad to hear from you. I know I've waited a long time to answer, but we've been pretty busy finishing up our 120 schedule. I now have 130 hrs here, and then the 10 that I got in Eagle Pass. I now have one more Bomb to drop, and then I'll be thru. Guess I'm pretty lucky to get that much, when you take into consideration the time that fellows got two years ago.

I think we leave here Nov. 6th. Not sure yet tho. I'm sort of tired of this going to school but I'm still in the states. I sure don't want to go, but it's my duty to so I guess I will. Ha, Ha—I'm anxious to go really. And it won't be long.

Do you have a cute little gal, eh? Well, my girl is in Pensacola now teaching school.

Well ole sack, write your ole bud more often. I'd sure like to come home and buzz the house a couple of times in a [P-]40. So long for now.

Love,
Wiley[19]

Little is known about Wiley's girlfriend in Pensacola: how they came to meet, if they stayed in touch as he deployed to war, or whatever happened to her. Although Pensacola is in Florida, it was still a good distance away—two hundred miles. One wonders who she was and how they met. It is ironic that he should have a girlfriend in Pensacola. After all it was, and is, a navy / marine corps town—the Home of Naval Aviation.

Wiley completed his flight training and was ready for deployment to a combat theater as the pivotal year 1944 drew to a close. In the next chapter, Harold's B-25 flight training will be portrayed. In addition, letters from home will provide the reader with a look at the home front farming situation in the midst of all-out war.

Chapter 12

Farming on the Home Front and Harold, Training to the End: March 1944–September 1945

L et us catch up with Harold. We left him in March 1944 when he had married Jean in Hagerman, New Mexico. They had set out for his next duty station in Columbia, South Carolina. Harold and Jean got a letter from Ollie soon after their arrival in Columbia:

Wed. nite, April 12, 1944

Dear Harold and Jean, I got your letter today, honey, and of course I was glad. I got some good news today about Oscar, too, dear. A telegram saying he was a German prisoner. Oh, God, dear children, that sure was good to read. I sat 3 or 4 minutes before I could open it. I wondered what was inside that envelope. I am still nervous as I can be. Now I'll get to see my sweet boy again. I'll get a letter soon they said, telling me about it and I'll write the day I get it and let you know.

We are all okay, still farmin'. I have so many letters to write tonite, dears, telling them about Oscar, so I'll say I love you both and I'm thinking of you. Good nite.

Mom[1]

A month later they got a letter from Wiley Sr.:
[May 1944]

Dexter, NM
Dear Harold and Jean,

I want to thank you for the Father's Day present. They are the nicest things I have ever had. I keep thinking about how happy you two are and how lucky you were to get married at the time you did. Going off to war is the most trying time in a man's life, and if he is lucky enough to marry the girl he loves, that love is likely to stay with him always, and I think it is the same with the girl.

Well it looks as if the war with Germany may soon be over unless they have something up their sleeve.

Harold I would sure like to have you here to take over while I harvest my wheat over on the plains. The wheat is very good, about fifty percent better than I thought it would be. I have bought another old truck and Jim and I are going to do the hauling.

Thanks again for the presents, and give Jean that kiss that I wanted to give her at the wedding. Wiley

P.S.—Mama is making me save paper.[2]

This rare letter from stepfather Wiley is affectionate and fatherly in his counsel to the newlyweds. He is also upbeat about his wheat crop on his farm near Tulia, Texas, in the panhandle. Not only did it produce more than expected, but the price of wheat that farmers received was also steadily increasing.[3] That he could buy another truck indicates that his farm was prospering and reflected the nationwide trend of increased profits. That he purchased an old truck reminds one that during the war, factories that formerly turned out trucks were now turning out tanks, jeeps, bombers, and fighters. Youngest son Jim, at this time 14 years old and a steady worker, was going to share the grain hauling duties with his father.

Ollie again wrote Harold and Jean:

Fri. A.M. July 28th, 1944
Dear Children:

I got your letter, Jean, last Wed. no. It was Mon. and I got the picture Wed. and how glad I was to get both. Oh, the picture is so good of you and Harold. I just love it. But there is one thing that hurt me. Harold, Gerald looked so sad and he wants one so bad. Could you please send him one? Course, I know you can't send all the kids one and we don't expect it, but Gerald has a home and he likes to show off his brothers. Please don't tell him I told you 'cause he wouldn't like it if he knew I have said what I have, but he was so hurt. He is working hard right now, baling hay day and nite, you might say. They were all so "all in" yesterday, and it was so hot, they just had to sleep all PM.

Boy, oh boy, you sure got some fine cotton on your place this year and its sure good cotton growing weather, so hot and no wind, just like it is in S.C. Daddy got a new "M" last week and took it and his big plow over to Tulia and got a guy to plow his wheat land. His wheat averaged about 15 bushels per acre. Not very good, but they didn't get much rain at Tulia.

I got one letter from Jr. since he left. He said he had been there [Tallahassee] 5 days and it had rained 7 times and said he'd bet he had sweated a gallon that day, so I guess its hot everywhere. Said he wouldn't be there but 2 more weeks. Don't know where he'll go then. I haven't heard from Oscar any more and I'm sure worried. [At this time Oscar was being moved from Stalag Luft VI in East Prussia to Stalag Luft IV, which entailed the hell ship voyage and the rough treatment upon arrival at Stalag Luft IV.] I sent him his 2nd personal box the 19th and I've sent him cigarettes 3 times. I doubt if he ever gets any of it though. I imagine they have moved that camp since the Russians started their last drive and are getting so close to East Prussia. Gerald and daddy thinks they will just go off and leave them. 'Course no one here knows.

The pilot's mother has never heard from Bob [Bird]. I am writing to all the moms and they are a sweet bunch of moms, too. Mrs. Syzmanski sent me her picture and Mrs. Leaf sent me a clipping of the wonderful job the "Lady" did on Feb. 25th.

Well darlings, I'll have to quit if I get this off this AM. Oh, yeah, we have the mail coming right by the house now, or did I tell you? Sure handy and saves gas and rubber. Bye now my dears.

Bushels of love.
Mom
P.S.—Jean you can just call me mom like Harold does and daddy said just call him Dad or Wiley or anything you want to. But I kinda like mom.[4]

Ollie's letter sheds some light on life on the home front as well as Ollie's persistent motherly concern for her sons—in this case Gerald and Oscar.

Although Gerald was a mature, married, and successful man, Ollie was still sensitive of his feelings. This was the same feelings that probably spurred Ollie to have Gerald move to Texas when he was fifteen and at odds with his stepfather.

Gerald no doubt felt a bit out of the action with his brothers off fighting while he remained at home. Military service then, especially, was glorified and highly esteemed. The nation was at war against two powerful, aggressive, and threatening enemies. People believed that the military was literally keeping the wolf at bay. To not be in uniform and participating in this high, noble cause might cause a man to feel stigmatized and self-conscious. As noted earlier, Gerald had tried to get into the army but was disqualified as being too old, with a family, and farming. Farming for his brothers who were in uniform denoted a significant contribution toward winning the war. As Ollie observes, he and the others worked literally night and day managing and working the farm.

Ollie also notes the good cotton crop that, like the wheat, was bringing a good price. A sizeable profit could be expected. Of course, the good crop could be ruined by a bad hailstorm, which happened all too frequently. The purchase of a new Farmall M tractor was truly an indication that things were looking good financially for Wiley. New tractors were hard to obtain during the war as industry was turned to producing war goods. Farm production, however, was recognized as essential for victory, which allowed some farm equipment to be manufactured. The Farmall M tractor was truly modern. It was rated at thirty-eight horsepower and could pull three plows through furrows. The cost in 1944 was $1,400, or $40,000 in 2022 dollars.[5]

Ollie mentions her dismay at not hearing from Oscar. She is up on the war news and was especially concerned with affairs in northern and eastern Europe, where Oscar was imprisoned. She was right in believing the camp would be moved. At the time she wrote this letter, Oscar had already been displaced to Stalag Luft IV at Gross Tychow, Poland. Older brother Gerald, recall, was farming Harold and Oscar's land as well as his own, and also helping Wiley with his farm. In the following letter to Harold and Jean,

Gerald and his wife, Ethel, give an informational account of farming and child-rearing:

Oct 26, 1944
Dear Harold and Jean,

We got your letter today and for once maybe I'll get an answer off before I lose the letter. At least I'll get it started tonight. Been baling [hay] today and may get tired and go to bed before I get thru but here I am a while. We're on the last cutting now, as you know, got ours about all cut but none of it baled yet. Baling for Mr. Young today and came a shower about sundown. So guess I'll sleep late in the morning. Hay is sure coming slow, as it always does this time of year. This makes 5 cuttings for the new hay and 4 for the others.

We got the cotton picked over once, finished Tuesday this week. Went over it in 8 days and got 33 bales. Sure had a nice crew after the first two days. They all said it was the easiest cotton in the country to pick and they quit other fields to come here. Guess we got about 20 or 25 more bales if it all opens. Sure made good cotton. I sold the first 17 bales for an average of 24.44 cents per pound. A little over $125 a bale.

And what do you know? We finally got a new tractor! Yessir. With lights, starter, power takeoff, belt pulley and power lift. Sure is a honey. Haven't got to use it much except on the bales and hauling cotton but I sure am proud of it. Archie says we can get all the plow tools we'll want but very little hay machinery for next year.

I built us another trailer just like the one we had. Had a devil of a time getting any tires for it. Didn't want new ones and couldn't get certificates for new ones anyway. Got permits for good 3 but the only ones I could find were priced as high as new tires and all had been patched up and so I just scouted out the tire shops for junk tires and had 'em vulcanized. Cost about three to four dollars a piece that way.

Sure would like a case of that anti-freeze if it's any good. I'd like to put some in the new tractor and also my car and the pickup. Had to use alcohol last year and the prospects don't seem any better now. I guess it would take about six gallons for all three outfits.

The kids are all okay and mean as ever if not worse. Jimmy got put up to the third grade this year, or did I tell you? Pee-Wee's [Winston] doing good in the first. We, or rather Ethel is, keeping one of the school teacher's little girl. She's a year-and-a-half and sure is cute. Her dad is in the Army and Ethel keeps her during school hours. She calls Ethel "mama" and me "daddy."

Jerry [Gerald][6]

It is harvest time and Gerald is pleased with the cotton crop. He has had the picking crew go through the cotton fields once, then when more of the bolls opened, they went through it again. In total he is hoping to have up to fifty-eight bales of cotton. The price was good at over 24 cents per pound. This was above the national average for 1944, 20.73 cents. Again, the war years had been good to farmers as the price of cotton in 1940 was only 9.89 cents.[7] The Allison brothers (Gerald, Harold, and Oscar) had picked a good time to get into farming.

Gerald also mentions baling hay for a Mr. Young. We are not sure of the economic arrangements here, but there is a good chance that Gerald was doing this out of neighborliness. The shortage of farm equipment and laborers in many cases caused farmers to share equipment and extend a helping hand to other farmers when the situation demanded. We can be sure that Gerald, Wiley, and son Jim remained very busy during the war years.

Gerald is ecstatic about the new M tractor, which is understandable. Again, new tractors were scarce in the war years. A modern, powerful tractor greatly increased efficiency and productivity. He mentions its modern features: lights and a push-button starter—no more cranking the engine. The power takeoff was a mechanism that transferred tractor engine power to the implement being pulled. This tractor belonged to the Allison brothers and served them well for many years in the future. This highlights the mechanization trend that occurred in World War II. Farmers were able to farm much more land with fewer workers. This had the long-range result of increasing farm size and decreasing the farm population and was another factor fueling urbanization.

Farmers and others had to do a great deal of improvising in the war years. Antifreeze (ethylene glycol) had come into widespread use in the 1920s. In World War II, however, military vehicles had priority thus the shortage of antifreeze on the home front, so farmers improvised. Alcohol was a suitable substitute but, unlike antifreeze, it was not an effective coolant. Worse yet was alcohol's corrosive effect on engines.[8]

Finally, Gerald mentions his children, Jimmy and Winston (Pee-Wee). Not mentioned was his daughter, Sherry, who was three. He notes that they are doing well, and they continued to do so. Jimmy eventually became an aerospace engineer, Winston an accountant, and Sherry the mother of two and a corporate secretary.

Enclosed in the same letter was a letter from Ethel:

Dear kids,

I thought I would add a line this time. Didn't you mention something about sending us a picture of the two of you? I want you to know I would like to have it. I have your picture framed, Harold, and also Oscar's and Junior's and all sitting in the front room so I can show them to everybody but I think yours would look better if Jean were with you, don't you? One of these days I am going to drag Jerry [Gerald] up and have our picture made. I've been trying for 8 years now but I think maybe I'll make it before he is completely bald and I have false teeth. He is very stubborn about doing things he don't want to.

You were worrying about Oscar forgetting Sherry Lynn's name. Don't you remember he was already in the Army when she was born and he never even saw her very many times. I think he's okay. Of course we'd all like to see him home and maybe we will before too long.

A person can't even get their laundry done here anymore. And if you could it would break you up. I really have been worked to death since school started trying to keep the boys clean and I have to take them to school and go after them. Also I've been canning a lot. And I've become a member of the "Canteen club" and am on the hospitality committee for PTA. And am third grade room mother. It sure keeps me busy. I had to weigh cotton a few days while Bill and Jerry [Gerald] were baling. I don't know what we'll do next year since our hay balers are in the Army. Maybe I'll have to bale hay too or maybe Jim can help next year. He is learning to drive the tractor. He and the others too are all getting so big you wouldn't know them.

Well Harold, I hope you get another furlough soon, and Jean, you'll come to see us even if Harold doesn't get to come, won't you?

Bye now and write to us,
Ethel and all[9]

Ethel's letter provides some insight into how the war affected mothers. She notes that she had difficulty getting laundry done. We presume that she had before sent the family clothes out to be washed and ironed. This source of hired help was no longer readily available and, if it was, it was prohibitively expensive. This again highlights the labor shortage on the home front and how people who had worked at menial jobs before now were probably making much better money elsewhere. In Gerald's letter preceding, he notes that Ethel is taking care of a teacher's child. With the father in the army and the mother teaching, Ethel filled in. Ethel probably assumed this responsibility as an act of neighborly concern and a shared effort to win the war on the home front. Such acts of service and sacrifice at the individual level marked American society during these years.

Ethel had her own family to care for. Keeping the boys Jimmy and Winston clean (clothes washed) was a concern and understandable in that her house had no indoor plumbing. She also served on the PTA (Parent Teacher Association) hospitality committee and was a room mother for Jimmy's class. She also notes that she served with the Canteen Club. She is referring to a club that the local citizens operated for servicemen stationed at the Roswell air base. Such activities were common and often were offshoots from the USO. The driving idea of the USO and other clubs was to provide wholesome entertainment for the military personnel so that they were less likely to engage in less tasteful activities such as drunkenness, prostitution, and the like. It was also a way for locals to support the war effort and build morale among the military.

The Grizzle girls, Ollie Mae and Mary, now (in 1944) 18 and 16, respectively, might have also participated in the local USO activities. Local young women were encouraged—indeed bus transportation was arranged for them—to attend USO functions, closely monitored dances, or holiday-related events to meet and socialize with soldiers.[10]

Ethel was a very busy woman. She also helped out with the farm, although she did not do physical labor. Here she notes that she is weighing cotton. This means pulling trailer loads of cotton to the cotton gin where they were weighed before ginning, which was the process that pulled cotton lint free of the boll husks and seeds. She mentions Jim, the Grizzle's youngest son, now 15 years old, as being a prime candidate to operate sophisticated farm equipment.

The letters from Gerald and Ethel were heartily appreciated by Harold and Jean, now stationed in Columbia, South Carolina. Harold was certainly happy to hear that Gerald had their farm operating well and profitably. This allowed him to focus fully on his next task, which was learning to fly the North American B-25 Mitchell medium bomber.

Assigned to the Columbia replacement training unit (329th AAF Base Unit Squadron S), he underwent transition training to serve as a copilot in the B-25. The B-25 proved to be one of the war's best bombers. It was reliable and, compared to its sister medium bomber, the B-26, was refreshingly easy to fly. It was already famous when Harold began his transition in July 1944. This was a result of the (General) Doolittle raiders flying B-25s to bomb Tokyo, Japan, on April 18, 1942—one of the war's boldest and most daring raids. It was significant not because of the destruction it wrought, which was relatively little (there were only sixteen bombers, each carrying about a two-thousand-pound bomb load), but because it was an immense morale builder for the nation. To hit the enemy's most prominent city, its capital, in broad daylight was phenomenal. Furthermore, it occurred at the war's darkest period, early 1942. This was shortly after the Pearl Harbor attack and before the pivotal battle of Midway in June 1942.[11]

About ten thousand B-25s were built, and they flew in all theaters of the war. The Marine Corps also flew B-25s, designated PBJs.[12] The B-25 was built to provide air support for infantrymen. For this purpose, it was well equipped. Some versions of the Mitchell carried a 75 mm cannon in the nose. Others had a proliferation of .50-caliber machine guns. In some variants fourteen forward-firing machine guns were installed to provide a veritable storm of .50-caliber bullets.[13] The B-25 was also versatile. It flew a number of different missions beyond just providing air support; indeed, most of its missions were not direct air support. These included high-level, strategic bombing, reconnaissance, antisubmarine patrols, and low-level skip bombing that sent bombs bouncing across the water into enemy ships.

Harold began flying in July 1944. His first flights were in BT-13s. Having not flown since March, he needed to get reacquainted with the fundamentals of flying. He also flew sixteen simulator hours in a Link trainer. His first flights in the B-25J were in August. He made three flights that month, slightly over eight hours, all copilot time.

The next two months included many more training flights, including one in the B-25G. This variant had a 75 mm cannon in the nose. He recalled that when the cannon was fired, "it really shook the whole airplane." Harold's job as copilot was backing up the pilot. The B-25 pilot's manual described the copilot's duties: "The copilot is the pilot's executive officer, his chief assistant, understudy, and strong right arm. He must be familiar enough with every one of the pilot's duties, both as chief pilot and aircraft commander to take over and act in the pilot's place at any time."[14] As Oscar said above (ch. 4), "the copilot had more to do than the pilot it seemed." Copilots monitored the engine and systems gauges and adjusted throttles and propellers. This allowed the pilot to focus on flying the airplane.

By the end of October, Harold had completed his transition training. He had acquired sixty-two hours of flight time in the B-25. He was assigned to a B-25 combat crew, and they were directed to Hunter Army Airfield in Savannah, Georgia, where they picked up a factory-fresh B-25.[15] Harold and crew departed Hunter headed for the port of embarkation at Sacramento, California. Having successfully completed army flight training, Harold and his B-25 crew were combat ready and eager to deal a blow to the enemy.

At Sacramento, on a predeployment physical, Harold was found to have a hernia. While repairing it was relatively simple, the recovery time took weeks. He was pulled out of his crew and replaced. Harold was highly disappointed. He would not be with his crew when they sallied forth into combat, for which he had trained for two years.[16]

Harold remained in the hospital for two months. Jean had traveled to Sacramento to be with him. Sacramento was packed with military personnel, and Jean had an extremely difficult time finding a place to live. This was a common occurrence in military towns. Bases had been built so rapidly that, unlike today, there was no housing for military families. It was almost an assumption that men going to war would leave their wives back home with family. In many, many instances, this was not the case. Husband and wife wanted to be together.

Jean desired to be with Harold as he went from base to base, but hundreds of other wives had the same idea. This exacerbated the difficulty of finding a place to rent. In Sacramento Jean finally found a place, a screened-in porch. Privacy was allowed with canvas overlaying the screen. Her room was furnished with a bed and a small chest of drawers. She shared the porch with two other young women in the same predicament.[17] She was not in Sacramento long. Once out of the hospital in mid-February, Harold was sent across the country to the Third Air Force Personnel Depot in Plant Park, Tampa, Florida, to await reassignment. Jean eventually followed him there.

Despite his wish to remain in B-25s or, better yet, the A-26 Invader, Harold was ordered to transition training for the B-17. Training started on March 29. He was not in Tampa long as he (with Jean) transferred to the Army Air Field in Alexandria, Louisiana. He remained there through June 1945. He was then transferred to Dyersburg, Tennessee, to continue his training. Jean followed him to each of these places. In each town they had to undertake a search to find a place to live.

The war was coming to an end. Victory in Europe had already occurred on May 8, 1945. Harold's last training flight in the B-17 was on August 10, 1945, the day before a B-29 had dropped an atomic bomb on Nagasaki. Four days before that, Hiroshima had been devastated by the first atom bomb. On September 2, 1945, Japan surrendered, thereby ending World War II. Harold flew his last military flight on September 7, 1945, in an AT-7, multiengine training aircraft. In all he logged almost 185 flight hours as copilot in the B-17G.[18]

Harold was extremely proud of his World War II experience. He was pleased to have served his country and become an officer and pilot in the AAF. He was, however, tremendously disappointed that he never got to strike a blow for victory. Although not in combat, he was not necessarily safe from harm. The AAF lost 65,164 aircraft to all causes during the war. But incredibly, 21,583, or almost 33 percent, were lost within the United States, mostly to training accidents.[19] World War II military flying was a terribly dangerous business in and out of combat.

But combat was most dangerous. As the war was winding down in Europe at the end of 1944, the Germans surprised the Allies with a dramatic and powerful offensive that drove a deep wedge or bulge into the Allied lines. This was the Battle of the Bulge—a bold move on the Germans' part. For a time it appeared that they might succeed. Although the Allies won out, it was a close call. It put the Allies on notice that the Germans had lots of combat power still at hand and were determined to fight to the end. In the next chapter, Wiley goes into combat with the Eighth Air Force against a determined and dangerous Luftwaffe.

Chapter 13

Wiley Jr. into Combat with the Eighth Air Force: December 1944–February 1945

Wiley left the replacement training unit at Perry, Florida, on November 8, 1944, and shipped out to England as a replacement fighter pilot. There he was assigned to the 350th Fighter Squadron (350th FS) of the 353rd Fighter Group (353rd FG), called the Slybirds of the 3rd Air Division of the Eighth Air Force.

The 353rd FG had arrived in England and joined the Eighth Air Force in August 1943 and played a part in all the major air campaigns from that time to the end of the war in Europe. When Wiley Jr. joined the 350th Fighter Squadron, it was a veteran and battle-tested squadron. Its pilots had varying levels of experience, from the old hands with lots of combat hours and battle savvy to brand new replacements like Wiley Jr.

The 353rd's combat record was impressive, its pilots claiming 786.5 enemy aircraft destroyed both in the air and on the ground. Its losses were 104 men killed in air combat or in operational accidents. Thirty-five of its pilots became prisoners of war.[1]

Junior wrote the following early on after his arrival in England:

[Undated, ca mid-December 1944]
Dearest [Mom] and Folks,

Can you imagine me getting here without some mishap, or even getting sick? The ride wasn't bad at all. Of course, it was a little rough one night.

You should see this beautiful country here. And I mean beautiful. England is a very picturesque country you know. And it's just like the stories you read. All of those old stone houses; as good now as ever, with their numerous chimneys and shuttered windows. The hills are very, very pretty, with the green grass and hedges, and stone fences. It's a pretty country alright, but it's pretty foggy now.

Love to all,
Wiley Jr[2]

A few days later, he wrote home again:

Somewhere in England
December 20, 1944
Dearest Mom,

Well I finally made it to my Sq. [squadron]. It's really a swell deal here. Pretty cold tho. I got the ship I wanted, and it's the newest out. Gus and I are still together, so I guess we will be the rest of the way. We haven't flown any yet, but I think we check out Sat. I guess you got my first letter, we only stayed there four days. Got here on the 18th. We're doing pretty good here. Good food. Got a bad cold tho.

Love, Wiley[3]

Wiley reports making it to his squadron, the 350th. He was accompanied by five other new pilots: Ray C. Gordon, Bernard Greenfield, John Guthrie, Howard Hakonen, and Richard N. Gustke. "It is clearly apparent that the AAF did things alphabetically!"[4] Wiley is positively impressed with the base and its facilities at Raydon, a small village in Suffolk County in East Anglia, sixty miles north of London (geographically, this was that portion of England that bumped out eastward and thereby was closer to Europe). Most of the sixty-plus Eighth Air Force bases were in East Anglia. Due east from Raydon two hundred miles lay German-occupied Holland. German antiaircraft artillery was positioned on the coasts. Pilots flying into Europe knew they had hit the Holland coast when German flak exploded around their formation and "welcomed" them to Nazi-occupied Europe.

Unlike brother Oscar's experience at Grottaglie, Raydon was a well-developed and modern base. Originally built as a bomber base, it had three concrete runways. This was at a time when some fighter units flew from grass fields. It had two large hangars, a well-appointed officers' club, and squadron-ready rooms and suitable lodging for pilots. Pilots lived in Nissen huts—tin, half-cylindrical shaped structures like Quonset huts. Eight pilots lived in each and had bunks along both sides of the hut. The huts were comfortable except were poorly heated and therefore cold. They had a single coal-burning stove in the center with a flue that went up through the roof. The farther from the stove, the colder it got. Americans often remarked it was always damp and cold in England.[5]

He also mentioned that the food was good. At Raydon the mess hall was in a larger Nissen hut. In fact, just about every facility at Raydon, and other American bases, were Nissen huts of varying sizes to accommodate whatever activity was inside. Breakfast consisted of toast, fruit juice, coffee, and rolls, and a luxury provided for combat pilots: fresh eggs. Other meals were not so special and featured Spam, Brussels sprouts, mutton, and powdered milk. Full-on feasts were provided on special holidays.[6]

Wiley, like most pilots, probably spent a lot of his free time at the officers' club, morbidly known as the Auger Inn (in pilot slang, to auger in meant a high-speed, nose-down, nonsurvivable crash into the ground), where officers congregated. Drinks, comfortable chairs, and reading material were available and occasionally stage shows were presented. A PX, a movie theater—the Thunderbolt Theater—and a chapel were available for the Raydon men, all in Nissen huts. The Red Cross hosted dances on base, and local young ladies attended and danced with the Americans.[7] The local English folk were friendly and generally welcomed the GIs. Pilots often visited nearby pubs for meals and drinks. There were no substantial towns close by; the closest village was five miles. The well-paid Americans could "drink a pub dry and eliminate its supply of fish and chips in minutes."[8] Pilots who had a day or two off could travel to London or nearby cities such as Ipswich or Colchester. We are not certain that Wiley did so in the short time, three months, that he was at Raydon.

But this was all of secondary importance. Operational flying was the highest priority, and the first order of business for Wiley and the other replacement pilots was preparing to fly combat. And this required more training. Wiley and presumably the others had not yet flown the Mustang. They certainly had not experienced combat. Fighter groups relied on their veteran pilots to teach the replacement pilots the essentials.

This training was done by an Operational Training Unit (OTU), nick-named Uncle Ben's (after Col. Ben Rimerman, the 353rd group commander) Finishing School, or Clobber College.[9] Wiley flew the Mustang for the first time on Christmas Day 1944. That he flew on Christmas indicates that training and operations never stopped. Every day was a workday.[10] His first combat mission was on February 20, 1945, just about a month after he joined the squadron. It was during this month that he went through the OTU course. The OTU taught the essentials for flying in combat: formations, takeoff and landing procedures, radio use, and most importantly, how to fly the P-51 proficiently. Junior did have extensive flight time in the P-40, but every fighter was different, with a different cockpit layout and different flight characteristics. During the month before he flew a combat mission, Wiley Jr. made twenty-six noncombat flights in a P-51. He also learned a lot through official lectures and, perhaps most importantly, in unofficial discussions with combat veteran pilots.

Wiley wrote that he "got the ship [he] wanted." This was the North American P-51 Mustang fighter. He had called it "a honey" of an airplane when he saw it at Eagle Pass. The P-51 was arguably the best fighter of the war. Besides being possibly the most visually appealing aircraft ever built, it was a great air combat fighter. It performed well against the main German fighters, Messerschmitts, and Focke-Wulfs. Perhaps its greatest contribution to victory was its "legs." P-51s were able to escort bombers deep into Germany and thereby protect them from German fighters the entire way. It had twice the range of its predecessor, the P-47 Thunderbolt, which, with an external fuel tank, could go eight hundred miles.[11] Bomber losses were thus significantly reduced. The appearance of enemy fighters brought terror to bomber crews, not unlike an enemy soldier who appears suddenly on the lip of a foxhole. For the gunners on the bombers, it was an all-out fight to the death as their .50-caliber machine guns hammered at the German fighters that seemed to appear out of nowhere, charging, wing guns and nose cannons winking as they spewed deadly shells. The appearance of P-51s, or any Allied fighter for that matter, in the midst of this fight brought cheering and ecstatic relief. The enemy fighters, now the hunted, withheld their attacks on the bombers out of concern for their own survival. The Mustang therefore represented a significant strategic asset. Bombing raids now were bigger and could rang almost freely over Germany.

General Doolittle had given up command of the Fifteenth Air Force in January 1944 and taken command of the Eighth Air Force. He changed the mission of his fighters from escorting bombers, which they still did, to also allowing them to aggressively go after German fighters. Before, fighter pilots were required to stick close to the bombers. With the bombers lumbering into Germany to attack critical targets, now they also served as bait to lure up German fighters. Then they were exposed to capable Allied fighters flown by well-trained and aggressive pilots. Unleashing the fighters destroyed the German fighter force as they were attacked in the air and on the ground.[12] Fighters became an offensive force in their own right, destroying not only enemy aircraft but also ground targets of any military value, especially trains and other components of the German transportation systems.

Beyond its strategic importance, the Mustang was a fighter pilot's genuine delight. It was relatively easy to fly compared to other fighters. It had wide landing gear, as Wiley noted in his letter earlier, a great attribute. This prevented "ground loops"—when something causes an airplane to be whipped around horizontally. At fault could be a crosswind, poor braking action, a pothole, ice, or muddy patches. An aircraft with narrow main wheels like the P-40 was easy to ground loop, whereas the P-51's wide separation between the main wheels provided much more stability.

Wiley was assigned the latest model of the Mustang, the P-51K. The K model was manufactured in Texas at North American Aviation's

Dallas facility. Whereas the bulk of P-51s were built in Inglewood, California, the need to boost production of the Mustang had caused North American to turn its Dallas plant to making P-51s. There was little difference between the K and the more common D except the propeller. The Hamilton-Standard propeller on the Ds was replaced with an Aeroproducts prop on the K. This prop was a four-blade, eleven-foot diameter hollow steel propeller, two inches shorter than the Hamilton-Standard. Performance was slightly inferior, and pilots blamed it on the prop, which they said reacted slower. Otherwise, the K had the latest British-made Packard-Rolls Royce engine, the V-1650-7, a magnificent engine by all standards.[13]

The 353rd Fighter Group painted their Mustangs' cowlings a distinctive black and yellow checkerboard pattern. The 350th Fighter Squadron's fighters were denoted with big *LH* letters painted on the fuselage. We are not sure that Wiley, only a few days after arriving at the 353rd, received his own aircraft, although he implies it in his letter from December 20, 1944: "I got the ship I wanted." Author Graham Cross, who wrote the definitive history of the 353rd, noted that, generally, new pilots did not get an aircraft assigned to them until later, when they had established themselves as combat-competent pilots.[14] Supporting the idea that he did get a P-51 assigned to him early on is the fact that the 353rd Fighter Group had ninety-seven Mustangs on hand in December 1944. This is more than they had had in any month previously. Regardless of when Junior got his own Mustang, he named it G-Nat.[15]

When Wiley Jr. joined the Eighth Air Force's 350th Fighter Squadron in December 1944, the Allies controlled the air over Germany. This did not mean the German air force was obliterated. It still had teeth, and vigilance was required when flying into German-occupied territory. German fighters still attacked. They husbanded their resources, however, not taking unnecessary chances, attacking when conditions were in their favor and when their favorite targets, bombers, were available and vulnerable. The Germans, ever innovative, had also fielded the first jet fighters. Although these were relatively few in number, their superior flight characteristics presented a real danger to American and British fighters and bombers.

Attacking ground targets with low-level strafing put Allied fighters in range of enemy antiaircraft guns and small-arms fire from German troops.

Weather was a serious danger. Bad weather made navigation extremely tenuous. Electronic navigation aids were primitive and generally limited to radio homing signals.

The sorties into Germany were necessarily long. The Mustangs escorted American bombers all the way to their targets deep into Germany. Missions could exceed six hundred miles distant from Raydon and incur over six hours of flight time. This was a long time in a small cockpit on a hard seat cushion. On some missions, once released from bomber escort, fighters dropped low and searched for targets to strafe anything that helped the Nazis keep fighting.

Most of the missions were flown by the entire squadron of sixteen aircraft, divided into flights of four aircraft. These flights were split into two elements. The two-aircraft element was the basic tactical formation. It consisted of a leader designated by a color, such as Green Three, and wingman. Flights maintained a "fingers four" formation, suggesting the fingers of a hand. Separation between fighters was 50 to 150 feet. When entering enemy country, the formation became a loose line abreast. There was more separation between aircraft, between one thousand to three thousand feet. Pilots could freely scan the sky for enemy aircraft without worrying about maintaining a close formation.[16]

The process of preparing for a combat mission was complex. For early morning missions, pilots were rousted awake by another squadron officer. After a hearty breakfast, the pilots headed for the mission brief in a large room with rows of chairs or benches. Upon entering the briefing hall, pilots saw a map on a large board at the front that marked the target for the day's mission. First to mount the stage in front of the map was the intelligence officer, who detailed the mission, route of flight, rendezvous points, and flak and enemy fighter locations, and gave escape and evasion possibilities if one were shot down.[17]

Next came the weather officer's brief. He gave the weather forecast for the route of flight, the target, and home base. He also included information on altitudes at which aircraft left telltale vapor trails. Vapor trails were like signboards pointing to where aircraft were flying, a great help to enemy flak gunners and fighter pilots. The squadron leader then outlined the mission and essential information for actually flying it. This included details on forming up, routes to be flown, headings and altitudes of the bombers' route of flight, and comments on antiaircraft positions. The antiaircraft sites were the big worry, not enemy fighters. The fighter pilots hoped for a chance to bag an enemy aircraft in air combat. The last presenter might be the chaplain, who offered a prayer for protection and God's blessing of the mission.[18]

After the briefing, which might take anywhere from fifteen to forty-five minutes, the pilots walked to the squadron ready rooms. The ready room was the hub of information for the pilots. It was a place pilots hung out when not flying or waiting to fly. Before a mission pilots might get last-minute instructions or information about the upcoming mission or a pep talk from the squadron leader.[19]

As takeoff time drew near, pilots went to the flight equipment shop, where each received their flight gear. They slipped into A-4 coveralls over which they pulled on an A-2 leather jacket or a B-15 fur-collared jacket. Over this they put on a Mae West life preserver.[20] They wore GI shoes or boots and a flight helmet and goggles. Wiley also wore a piece of flight gear new to the AAF, a G-suit. Introduced at the 353rd in October 1944, the G-suit zipped over the pilot's legs from waist to ankles. It had bladders sewn inside and connected to a port at the cockpit floor, and were automatically inflated when a pilot pulled Gs.[21] The inflated bladders pressed against the belly and legs and kept the blood from flowing down into his legs. This kept blood in the brain and thus prevented blackouts. Interestingly, a news release appearing in the Roswell newspaper reported that Wiley Jr. was happy with the G-suit.[22] He was not the only one. Fighter pilots in the 353rd remarked how the G-suit gave them an advantage over German pilots in dogfights by allowing them to maintain consciousness in high-G maneuvering. Finally, pilots slipped a parachute backpack on and a dinghy seat cushion. The dinghy was a small raft that inflated automatically when it hit the water after bailout.[23] Now weighing forty pounds heavier, pilots then waddled to jeeps that carried them to the flight line.[24]

Wiley flew his first combat mission on January 20, 1945. It lasted slightly over five hours. The target for the bombers the 353rd escorted was Mannheim, Germany, an important link in Germany's rail network. Mannheim sat on the Rhine River in southern Germany and would be an important crossing point for the US Sixth Army when the time came to plunge into the heart of Germany. Maj. Leslie Seppala led the 350th Fighter Squadron's contingent of seventeen Mustangs. Two weeks later Major Seppala would be shot down by small-arms fire as he strafed a ground target. He spent the remainder of the war as a POW. Coincidentally, Seppala was in the same POW camp as Oscar at Nuremberg and again at Moosburg.

The weather was bad somewhere along the way. Wiley logged one hour of instrument time. This would have been taxing. He had not flown on instruments since November 2, 1944. This was a long time without practice in this difficult procedure and especially difficult on his first combat mission when everything was new and challenging.[25] Instrument flying was essential for operations in Europe. The winter weather was awful. Despite the obvious need, instrument flight training was an area of training and preparedness that the AAF shorted their pilots, and it resulted in numerous accidents and deaths.[26] Wiley, however, managed the flight well and returned safely to Raydon.

He now knew of the physical demands of flying fighters in combat: "Strapped tightly into a small cockpit above hundreds of gallons of explosive fuel, on oxygen with a mask that could make you gag, constantly watching to maintain position in the Group. It was tiring. Alone the whole time, no one to share the burdens of flying or to talk to. The pilot must be ready always to break up an attack on the bombers even at the cost of his own life. Constant head turning, watching for the enemy, made even the toughest neck tired." Tom Lorance recalled, "I would get so stiff. (Upon return), I couldn't straighten out when I got out of the plane. And because the oxygen was dehydrated to keep it from freezing in the lines you would get home so dry you couldn't spit and your lungs would ache."[27]

Wiley flew another combat mission on February 3. It was cut short, however. He had to return to base after flying two hours and fifteen minutes. We do not know what caused the abort, but there were any number of reasons. Most were caused by a mechanical problem with the aircraft. Indeed, the 353rd Fighter Group suffered a spate of mechanical malfunctions just as Wiley was checking in during December and January. Engine and cooling system malfunctions were common. Compounding this was the miserable weather. There were a series of accidents. Three pilots were killed in takeoff accidents in January, and another was killed in a crash landing near the base.

Mechanical failures forced three belly landings. Another four were damaged by flak, and two were damaged in takeoff accidents. Not exactly a warm welcome for Wiley and the other new pilots.[28]

Wiley missed a big show by aborting on the February 3 mission. The target was Berlin, the Nazi capital. The weather was good and the one thousand B-17s that the 353rd was escorting (along with other fighter groups) gave it a good going-over. It was a costly strike. Twenty-one of the Fortresses were brought down by the "murderous flak." Railway facilities and important government buildings, the nerve center of Nazidom such as Hitler's headquarters at the Reich chancellery, Air Ministry, Foreign Office, Ministry of Propaganda, and Gestapo headquarters all were blasted by American bombs. The escorting P-51s were "entirely effective" at keeping German fighters off the B-17s. Once the bombers cleared, some P-51s dropped down and strafed whatever targets the pilots found.[29]

Watching the bombers approach a target elicited strong emotions and tons of respect from fighter pilots for the bomber crews. P-51 pilot Maj. Wayne K. "Blick" Blickenstaff described how he felt watching the bombers approach Kassel: "As usual, the flak was heavy at the target, and we [the fighter pilots] had to dawdle around the edges and watch that terrible, lurid, movie-like scene of the bombers plowing into that black hellhole and then, coming out, chaotically, all bruised and beaten-up, limping like a flock of geese caught in a volley of buckshot. There was always that tinge of guilt. If they didn't lose more than ten bombers, they were lucky. And it was not easy to forget that each plane carried ten men."[30]

Wiley wrote home shortly after he turned 21 years old (January 24, 1945):

Feb 1, 1945
Dearest Mother,

Got your "V" mail dated the 14th Jan. It was awfully sweet that you write on my birthday. I was thinking of you, home and everybody that day. Especially you and Pop. Course it doesn't seem any different since you're 21, and I guess there isn't much difference. Ha.

Well I just got back from the club about 20 min. ago. Had to build a fire. It's nice & warm now. Oh yes—today I installed a loudspeaker in the barracks. Had to get it in town. Cost quite a bit but the boys helped me. It cost 42 shillings.

We have the worst weather here. Ten minutes ago rain, and now, it's clear. Almost. It won't be in 30 min.

Well Mom guess this is all for now. I guess Oscar is ok now. Mail is awfully slow. Even Air mail goes by boat. Good nite to the most wonderful Mother in the world.

Your loving son, W. Jr.[31]

Weather socked in the Eighth Air Force for a few days, then on the ninth Wiley flew another combat mission. It, too, was just over five hours in duration. Capt. (soon-to-be Maj.) Walker "Daniel" Boone led the squadron. The target was Magdeburg, Germany. Four of the 350th's pilots aborted prior to reaching the target. Magdeburg, in north-central Germany, produced a lot of synthetic oil for the Nazi machine and was bombed repeatedly throughout the war. Bombers hit it again on the ninth, escorted by the 350th Fighter Squadron, Wiley included.

Wiley did not fly a combat sortie again until February 20. In the interim he flew three test hops, on the eleventh, twelfth, and eighteenth, and a Link trainer session on the thirteenth. Test hops were required when significant mechanical work had been performed on an aircraft. Wiley often flew training sorties on days he did not fly a combat mission.[32] Life in a combat squadron was not easy. Every day was a workday, even if a combat mission was not flown. Fellow fighter pilot Bob Strobel commented that only about 50 percent of his total flights were combat flights. He also remarked, "Piloting a fighter airplane . . . is hard work. Coping with the rigors of combat flying was only half the story. The other half was devoted to keeping the pilots and their airplanes in top operational condition. This was done by 'local' flying, flying every day, flying more times than on combat missions."[33]

The two missions on February 20 and 21 are significant for the family. Both these missions were to Nuremberg. Oscar was in Stalag XIII-D at Nuremberg and comments on the night bombing that he witnessed (ch. 10). Since they were night raids, they were British strikes. He does not comment on daylight raids (American), although Nuremberg, a principal producer of military vehicles and equipment, received a good pounding day and night at this time.

These missions were escorts, guarding bombers that hit Nuremberg, which was "crammed with supply trains." The Eighth Air Force bombers dropped 3,800 tons on the city during these two days' missions.[34] On the twenty-first, the 350th Fighter Squadron, led by the experienced Lt. Col. Bill Bailey, who was actually the commanding officer of sister squadron, the 352nd, strafed and destroyed a locomotive and an oil car. They also shot up a military barracks.[35] In strafing, Wiley and the other pilots would have flown low and fast, at about fifty feet off the ground and three hundred miles per hour. It would have been a poignant experience for both Wiley and Oscar if they had known how close they were to each other physically and realized this would be the last time they would be close.

Chapter 14

Wiley Jr., Deadly Dogfights: February 1945–March 1945

A lthough bad weather restricted flying during the first half of the month, in the second half of February the 350th flew at an intense combat tempo. Wiley flew almost forty-seven hours that month. All but ten hours were after the eighteenth. The recent setback to the Allies in December 1944 due to the German Ardennes Offensive, or Battle of the Bulge, caused Allied leaders to despair that possibly the Germans were much more powerful than previously considered. Therefore, in the new year, 1945, an all-out air attack was laid out. Called Operation Clarion, it aimed to bring the war to the cities, towns, and countryside and hit places that had not previously experienced Allied airpower. The hope was that this would thoroughly cripple transportation and communications in Germany. Fighter squadrons did their part by strafing and bombing these facilities, as well as attacking German aircraft wherever they could be found, in the air or on the ground. Fighter pilots were admonished to be aggressive, as if they needed to be told. They eagerly, and ruthlessly, executed this mission.[1]

Clarion began for the fighters on February 22, 1945. This was exactly one year after the onset of Big Week and the day that Oscar's bomber had been shot down. About nine thousand aircraft flew missions that day. Wiley was one of them. The mission was five hours and forty minutes long. The priority was destroying the German transportation systems. The 350th did their part. Launching with a force of twenty Mustangs and led by perhaps the 350th's best fighter pilot, Major Blickenstaff, they strafed trains, trucks, barges, and other facilities and equipment at Brandenburg, Germany. They encountered four ME-262s. Blickenstaff, after fruitlessly trying to chase one down, cut the corner on another and, giving it lots of lead, nailed it. This was his fifth kill, making him an ace.[2]

The 350th's score was impressive: eight locomotives destroyed, fifty freight cars, four trucks, an oil car, a trailer, a switch tower, a marker beacon, and two barges shot up and left damaged.[3] The 353rd Group as a whole claimed seventeen locomotives destroyed. Thirteen Eighth Air Force Fighters were shot down, one of them being 1st Lt. John Balason of the 350th. Seven Eighth Air Force bombers went down.[4]

Harold wrote Wiley Jr. a letter in February from Tampa, Florida. He had recovered from his hernia surgery and was awaiting assignment to his next flying duties:

Well, son the meter reader ain't reading any meters even right now, but he's sure sweatin' out some orders. [Harold is jesting about his own situation. Evidently copilots were kidded about being "meter readers" because one of their main cockpit jobs was monitoring the vast array of cockpit dials and gauges.] Boy, I don't know what will happen to me now. I hope I go back to [B-]25s but don't know for sure. I just got your letter of Jan. 2 and an earlier one received in NY the 18th of Dec. I guess they've been all over hell and back catching up with me. You can see I'm in Tampa now and it is a beautiful town. Wish I'd been here about four months ago when you were here in these parts.

Boy, you really forged ahead of me didn't you? I can't bring myself to criticize the 51. I know it is a hell of a nice-looking plane & probably a good one as single engines go. I'm definitely a twin-engine man. MOS [military occupational specialty]1051 and I'd sure like to get an A-26 some way, but no chance.[5]

I bet you have some missions by now son and I hope you get to shoot up a lot of stuff. You're a real fighter pilot. Don't take any unnecessary chances and keep your head out.

Your lovin' bud,
Harold[6]

Harold's last admonition was critical information. A fighter pilot's survival depended on his awareness of what was happening around him, especially behind him. "Put your head on a swivel" was the watchword. Many, many aircraft were shot down when an enemy fighter approached unseen from the rear. In many cases a fighter pilot never saw the aircraft that shot him down.

On February 26 Wiley flew his longest mission, a six-hour and twenty minute mission escorting bombers to Berlin. There were 1,102 bombers in the bomber stream. Wiley remarked that "strings of bombers lined up on the target in perfect formation." Flying at twenty-five thousand feet, Wiley reported that he could see the flashes of the Russian artillery along the east bank of the Oder River opposite Berlin.[7] The flight was relatively uneventful. No German fighters rose to challenge the air raid on their capital.[8]

The next day, February 27, Wiley flew in a mission that proved to be one of the 350th's best of the war. The primary mission was escorting bombers to the Leipzig area, almost six hundred miles from Raydon. As the bombers withdrew, heading for home, the seventeen Mustangs of the 350th, under the leadership of Major Boone, were cleared to go hunting for "targets of opportunity."[9] The P-51s dropped to about six thousand feet, skimming the top of a cloud layer below them. Through a hole in the undercast, Boone saw two German aircraft, well camouflaged, on a grass field near Röhrensee, Germany. He dove his Mustang down to investigate and determine the level of German defenses guarding the field. Flying low and fast over the field, he saw that the airfield was flush with German aircraft of all sorts. In this initial pass, he strafed the field and flamed three aircraft. He saw no antiaircraft fire. He called the squadron down and soon his pilots were full into the attack. They set up a figure 8 weave, flying two hundred to four hundred feet over the field and dropping below the treetops on strafing runs. Wiley Jr. was the wingman of Capt. Herbert Kolb. Kolb was Blue Flight's leader (the squadron identified each flight of four aircraft with a color and the aircraft in the flight with a number. Blue One was Kolk, Blue Two his wingman, Blue Three the next element leader, and Blue Four the wingman of Blue Three). Kolb had followed Boone down in the initial attack, and Wiley, as wingman (Blue Two), was close behind and therefore one of the earliest to attack the German airfield. Kolb made multiple passes. Firing 1,440 rounds of .50-caliber ammunition, he destroyed three FW-190s and damaged five other aircraft. Wiley did some shooting himself, 880 rounds' worth. He made eight passes and fired on five different aircraft. He shot up an FW-190 and left it smoking. He made two passes on an ME-410, a German two-engine fighter, and as he roared over, he saw it had been set ablaze. He and Kolb then attacked another aircraft and damaged it.[10]

Wiley's good friend, Richard Gustke, was Boone's wingman. He had a banner day. In strafing attacks he destroyed a JU-88 bomber and an ME-410 fighter. He also shared in the destruction of an FW-190 and damaged four other aircraft.[11] Flight Officer Gustke turned out to be an excellent fighter pilot and finished the war with 12.5 aircraft destroyed, all ground kills.[12]

Mission leader Boone called an end to the death and destruction, telling his pilots to save some ammunition. They were deep in enemy territory and had to fight their way out. His pilots had other ideas, though. Boone recalled, "The Kids had not satisfied their thirst and paid no attention. That was good enough for me. I made four more attacks damaging three or four more twin-engine and single-engine planes."[13]

Wiley received official credit for the destruction of the ME-410 and partial credit for the aircraft he and Kolb destroyed.[14] The squadron that day destroyed thirty-eight German aircraft—a magnificent accomplishment. Remarkably, no ground fire was observed and not one 350th Mustang was hit by enemy fire. This mission gave a needed boost to the 350th's morale. Since it began flying combat missions in October 1942, it had seemed "snake bit": "Just bad luck and difficult circumstances seemed to haunt the squadron." They were shaded by the 353rd Group's other two squadrons, the 352nd and 351st. The missions on February 27 and 28 changed that. They had outperformed and outproduced their sister squadrons.[15]

This was Wiley's sixth flight in the last week of February. Each of them was a long combat mission into Germany. He wrote his littlest sister, Mary, the next day:

Feb. 28
Hi ya Sis,

Well, how's the gal these days? I dare say you're ok. Working hard?
Boy, I am so tired I could drop in my tracks. I flew a long mission today
and again tomorrow. I'll try to send you something one of these days.
Tell Mom I haven't gotten any packages as yet. Right now I'm at the
Officers Club listening to some sour program. Think I'll go to the late
show—just thot I'd drop a short line. Thanks very much for the letter
Sis. Write more often, Please.

Your lovin' bud,
Wiley[16]

A day later, he wrote his mother by V-mail:

March 1, 1945

Got your letter yesterday Mom. I'm sure glad you got my Valentines.
I was wondering if you would get it. Well I've got 52 hours now and
1 enemy aircraft to my credit. On the ground though, and 1 shared.[17]
Gus got two the same day. It was really lots of fun too. How are things
at home these days? If everything goes OK I'll be home in July or Aug
I hope. Well Mom dearest I've got to write to Jerry [Gerald] I guess.
So I'll say good night.

Love to all,
W. Jr.[18]

Harold wrote to Wiley and gave him a rundown on his situation and also
encouragement:

March 3, [1945]
Tampa
Dear bud Jr.

Well hows my boy? Hope your doing fine as usual. I got a letter from
Mom telling that you were accumulating some missions. That's fine
bud—hope you accumulate a lot more and come home poco pronto.

How do you like the [P-]51 now? I guess you've got it tamed and stump-broke & everything else by now. What do you think about [B-]17s? I hope you don't hate 'em as bad as I do that would be too much ill will towards the wonderful ole critters. I guess I'm in 'em now. I don't mind it so much as I thought I would. Course they're not as neat & nice as a [B-]25 but they fly and get you there & back that's enough ain't it?

How do you, the old master, like the English gals? Don't say good as American ones. You just have to get to know them and make 'em know you. That's what it says here in the Readers Digest. I guess you have all the same magazines & stuff to read you always had, no? How is the coal situation & cigs [cigarettes] now? Boy they don't let us have many smokes. They save 'em all for the permanent party guys and we have to take Herbert Tarreytons & Chelseas & things like that.

Boy is it getting hot around here about now. We're in khakis but it doesn't help much. There just ain't enough wind for me an old New Mexico boy. I like a nice little breeze of about ten or fifteen mph all the time.

Mom hasn't heard any more from Oscar since Oct I believe. I sure wish we knew how he is doing. [Oscar was in the Stalag at Nuremberg.] I still have the feeling he is OK most of the time. I hope he doesn't have to undergo so many hardships as we read about. It sure makes me killing mad when I read some of those stories. And they're true no doubt but I can't believe anything like that is happening to Oscar.

Jean isn't down here yet and I haven't heard from her in some time so I guess she is either trying to get here or trying to find somebody to come with her.

Are you still with your buddy over there? I've lost everyone I ever knew except thru letters and I don't hear from them very often that way. I did get a letter from ole Al Brown. He's in Italy and has ten missions. I wish I had even one. All of them will be coming home when I start across.

Well son don't let those limeys get you down and write the dope to

Your lovin' bud,
Harold[19]

There was no slack in combat operations for the 350th Fighter Squadron or any other Eighth Air Force fighter squadron in March. The Allied ground forces were pushing toward the Rhine and anticipating crossing it and moving into the industrial German heartland of the Ruhr

Valley. The Allied air forces continued to pound German cities, industry, trains, and their marshalling yards, trucks, bridges, oil production, and especially airfields. Anything that would assist the Allied armies to accomplish their mission and thereby bring utter defeat to the Nazi war machine came under the Eighth Air Force's hammer blows. The Luftwaffe was virtually defeated and could mount little opposition to the swarms of Allied aircraft that flew daily into Germany. Nevertheless, German fighters occasionally did appear. The German air force now had the daunting jet fighter, the ME-262. It was considerably faster than P-51s and when they had the opportunity— not that easy considering the thick fighter screen around the bombers—could inflict considerable damage. In March they downed thirty Eighth Air Force bombers. Their numbers, however, were never enough to seriously impede the air offensive. In March the Allies sniffed victory in the air. "The strategic air offensive had only a few more weeks to go before victory."[20]

As the air offensive against Germany reached a crescendo in March 1945, Wiley Jr., along with the 350th Fighter Squadron, flew at a high tempo.[21] The 353rd Fighter Group flew twenty-three missions in twenty-one days of flying. In the six encounters with enemy aircraft, the 353rd destroyed sixty of them but suffered the loss of twenty of their own. Three pilots were killed in action and the rest, minus one who bailed out over England, were prisoners of war.[22] Although Germany would surrender in less than two months, March 1945 was nevertheless a deadly month for the 353rd Fighter Group, one of the deadliest of the war.[23]

In the first three weeks of the month, Wiley flew twelve combat missions, which gave him sixty-five hours of combat flight time.[24] In several instances on bomber escorts, ME-262s were encountered. The 350th also flew strafing missions. Like a pack of wolve fighters ranged throughout Germany searching for any worthy target, bridges, marshalling yards, and all transportation assets were attacked. Traffic in and out of the Ruhr Valley was to be stopped by the time the Allies crossed the Rhine.

Wiley Jr. flew a mission to Berlin on March 18. It was a massive raid. Fourteen fighter groups escorted 1,250 bombers. The heavies dropped over three thousand tons on the German capital, hitting transportation and industrial targets. But the price for that bombing was high. Twenty-four bombers and five fighters were lost, mainly to German jets. There might have been as many as thirty-six of the German jets that ripped into the bomber formations. Flak was also heavy and damaged fully one-half of the bombers, sixteen of which were so badly damaged they had to land behind Russian lines, which were just east of Berlin. Wiley flew the next day also. The one-thousand-bomber force the fighters escorted had targets around Leipzig. The jets came up again and this time shot down three B-17s.[25]

The twenty-fourth of March was the beginning of the "victory drive" into Germany. Operations Varsity and Plunder were the code names for breaching the Rhine. Varsity was an airborne assault, while Plunder was the assault on land that breached the Rhine.[26] The Eighth Air Force surged sorties in support. Over 1,700 bomber sorties were flown, and a screen of fighters guarded the Rhine crossing points. Although the Luftwaffe was expected to fiercely oppose the Rhine assault, only about two hundred German aircraft launched to oppose the crossings.[27] One large group of German fighters attempted to oppose the landing and attack Allied troops and positions, but they were intercepted by the 350th Fighter Squadron. The squadron had been assigned to support the 2nd Air Division (B-24s) on their bombing mission to the Leipzig area.[28]

"Nuthouse," the US fighter control agency, directed the nineteen Mustangs of the 350th Fighter Squadron to take off at 1310 and patrol west of Kassel.[29] Wiley (Green Three) and his wingman, 2nd Lt. John P. Onkey (Green Four), were flying in the tail end position of the entire squadron formation. Flying at six thousand to seven thousand feet, the 350th pilots encountered a fifteen-plane group of ME-109s at coequal altitude. Down low, below five thousand and possibly on the deck at less than one thousand feet, were fifteen FW-190s with belly fuel tanks. The German fighters belonged to Jagdgeschwader 300 (JG-300). They had taken off from Löbnitz and were flying west toward Bottrop. This was a small village just east of the Rhine, at a point Allied forces planned to cross into the Ruhrland.[30]

The dogfight occurred over and near the picturesque village of Sattenhausen, about twenty-five miles east of Kassel and nestled in beautiful rolling farmland, intersected with streams and forestland. Lt. Col. Wayne K.

Blickenstaff (he had been promoted in early March), the 350th's flight leader, started the fierce fight by slicing down and alongside an FW-190. A big white cross on its fuselage identified it positively as a German aircraft. He shot it down. The fight was on as the formations broke apart with Messerschmitts, Focke-Wulfs, and Mustangs flying in all directions.

A savage dogfight ensued, much of it practically on the treetops. This doubled the danger because pilots of crippled aircraft would have little time to bail out. Wildlife and livestock ran madly about in the forest and farmers' fields. Burning aircraft plunged to the ground. In the fight Mustang pilots shot down twenty-nine of the German fighters. Lieutenant Colonel Blickenstaff and Maj. Robert Elder shot down five apiece and obtained the rare status of "ace in a day."[31] It was a highly noteworthy accomplishment for the squadron, the most successful air-to-air combat for the squadron of the war. Although outnumbered by the enemy fighters, the 350th pilots almost wiped out the entire force of German fighters, which were intent on attacking Allied troops crossing the Rhine. How many lives were saved one can only guess.[32]

The price, however, was high. It was especially high for the Grizzle-Allison family of East Plains, New Mexico. Five Mustangs were shot down, and two pilots were killed. One of them was a Lt. John H. Hopkins. The other was 2nd Lt. Wiley Grizzle Jr.[33]

Wiley was Green Three, the second element leader in the Green four-plane division. He and wingman Onkey were at the tail end of the nineteen-plane formation. When the dogfight began, Wiley called, "I'm going on my own." Wiley probably saw the attack on the low flying Focke-Wulfs, picked one out, and dove down to shoot it down. The Messerschmitt pilots above were vigilant. They did their job in attacking the Mustangs that attacked the Focke-Wulfs. A Messerschmitt most likely attacked Wiley's Mustang from the rear and fired into it, setting the Mustang afire and killing or wounding Wiley. Being at a low altitude, and at a high speed, there was little room for recovery. Wiley's G-Nat plowed into the German earth and exploded in a field just outside the village of Sattenhausen.[34]

Before Wiley was shot down, an ME-109 attacked wingman Onkey (it might have been the same German pilot that got Wiley). Onkey described what happened:

> By the time we were going down and dropping our tanks I was hit, so that kind of took me out of the action. I tried to call Grizzle on the radio to tell him I was no longer with him, but my radio was shot out. I had several holes in the canopy and in the wing root. What I was trying to do was get out and bail out. I had a fire behind me in the radio compartment area and I couldn't get the canopy off. I knew I had to set it down, so I headed for the line as fast as I could go and on the way out I had a German plane come right out in front of me; it was a 109 and I had to turn to avoid hitting him, and as I did I gave a burst into him with starboard guns. You could see them hit into the plane from the angle of my turn. Proceeding on the way out the fire didn't seem to be getting a whole lot worse. The plane was flying all right although I didn't have many instruments left. I saw a plane in front of me so I fired on that. At about that time my plane started putting out smoke. I couldn't see where I was going and I didn't want to turn over, so went straight up ahead, chopped the throttle and brought the plane down to the ground. There was a real hard crash and it came back up in the air and came in a second time and it was all broken up. I knew I was hurt pretty good. I stood up on the seat and pushed the canopy open and came out of the airplane like a cork out of a champagne bottle. I was restrained by the air hose to the bladder on the G suit, so I pulled that out. I jumped down on the ground and ran away from the plane as fast as I could because it was burning pretty good. I rolled under a fence and at that time the plane blew up. After a lengthy procedure I was finally captured by the Germans.[35]

Wiley, by being selected to lead a two-plane element, indicated he was making good progress as a fighter pilot. Yet he was still a novice; this was his eighteenth combat mission. It was Onkey's thirteenth. They were both new to air combat, an environment that was extremely challenging and deadly. There were still some good German fighter pilots. The few veteran pilots who had survived to this point in the war had to be good.

Wiley took aggressive action. He did not hesitate to attack the 190s below when flight leader Blickenstaff identified them as German. He pickled his external fuel tanks,[36] a standard procedure before a high-G dogfight, and, with his wingman, headed down. He radioed to the other pilots: "I'm going on my own." This statement suggests that Wiley had identified a German fighter that he planned to engage—probably, like Blickenstaff, a low-flying Focke-Wulf. Wiley and Onkey were, as noted, "tail-end Charlies" in the formation. That means there were no American planes behind them, which left them in a vulnerable position. Wiley was depending on Onkey to clear his "six" behind him, where it was difficult to see, especially if one were focused forward as Wiley would have been. Onkey, however, was already under attack himself and had an inoperable radio.[37] The German fighter moved in behind G-Nat, probably unseen by Wiley, and fired into his Mustang. Two Mustangs were seen going down in the vicinity; one was likely Wiley's.[38] It probably all happened in seconds.

His mother had written a letter to Wiley on March 8 that he never got to read:

Thurs nite Mar 8

Hello honey, how's my boy tonite? I do hope he's okay & everything is alright. Honey, I'm <u>still</u> enjoying my valentine, there never was anything sweeter or prettier. Its as pretty as it was Feb. 14, oh, I love it honey, & the boy who sent it to me. We are all okay. Farming as hard as we can. Daddy is still over in Muleshoe, farming. Gerald began putting fertilizer on cotton land, here on the home place this afternoon. Alfred is here, now, working. He helps Gerald feed the lambs & anything else he can do. He irrigated some last week for Gerald, watered his oats. I saw Mrs Wier Tues. & she & Thomas are fine. Said Charles & Ellery were still okay. Did I tell you C.A. is on Iwo Jima? Yeah, right in the thick of it and I guess you are too darling & I'm praying that everything is alright. Honey did you <u>ever</u> get your pipe? I wonder if you get all the letters I write, I write twice a week. Got a letter from Ollie Mae Wed. & she had had a letter from you, she told me what you wrote her. Also got a letter from Ethel Kreps in S.C. & she had gotten a letter from Oscar dated Nov. 10. Said he was cheerful & that he had received a picture of her that I had sent him. Said he believed he'd be a rovin' hobo when he got home & never stop more than a week in one place, just to be convinced he was really free.

I guess Jean got to Florida & Harold last Mon. I haven't heard from either of them.

Here are some basketball clippings, thought might interest you. How is Gus? Is he in your squadron? I hope he's okay.

Well darling, there's no news to write, all the boys gone to war, you know. So, I'll be thinking of you & loving you & praying you will be alright. I miss you honey. Good nite sweetheart.

Mom[39]

The next Ollie heard of Wiley was from the War Department. This is a follow-up to the War Department's initial telegram:

12 April 1945
Dear Mrs. Grizzle,

This letter is to confirm my recent telegram in which you were regretfully informed that your son, Second Lieutenant Wiley Grizzle, Jr. 02056952, has been reported missing in action over Germany since 24 March 1945.

I realized the distress caused by failure to receive more information or details; therefore, I wish to assure you that in the event additional information is received any time, it will be transmitted to you without delay. If no information is received in the meantime, I will communicate with you again three months from the date of this letter. It is the policy of the Commanding General of the Army Air Forces, upon receipt of the "Missing Air Crew Report," to convey to you any details that might be contained in the report.

Inquiries relative to allowances, effects, and allotments should be addressed to the agencies indicated in the enclosed Bulletin of Information.

Permit me to extend to you my heartfelt sympathy during this period of uncertainty.

Sincerely yours,
J.A. Ulio, Major General, The Adjutant General[40]

Wiley Jr. was listed as Missing in Action because no one, except possibly the German pilot that shot him down, had seen Wiley's Mustang actually crash, and this German airman was probably killed in the dogfight. Only three of the German pilots survived the fight. Even Wiley Jr.'s wingman, Onkey, distracted by his own peril, had lost sight of Wiley.[41]

Of course the news of Wiley's disappearance caused great distress to his mother. She wrote the following to her son in June after receiving the War Department telegram and letters that reported him missing:

Sun June 10 [1945]

My Darling boy: Oh, honey, won't I ever hear from you? It has been so long, but I hope & pray you are well & everything is alright. Maybe soon now, I'll hear you are okay, & will be coming home. Oscar was liberated April 29th & arrived in New Jersey last Sun. & he's in Ft. Bliss now, will be there about another week. I can hardly believe even yet, he's really in the U.S. Harold is still in Alexandria, La. Daddy & Jim are farming at Muleshoe & batching. Everything here is about the same. Ollie Mae is home now. Cotton looks good, & wheat at Muleshoe is fine daddy says. Darling with all my heart I pray everything is alright & honey I'm thinking of you every minute, almost, & honey, I love you so much.

Bye now,
Mom[42]

While Wiley was in deadly combat, about 180 miles south, Oscar remained a POW at Nuremberg. The war in Germany was on the very cusp of ending in victory for the Allies. It was such a tragedy that Wiley did not live to celebrate this great event. Things were brighter, however, for Oscar, as Ollie's letter above relates. In the following chapter we will see what the final days of interment were like for him.

Chapter 15

Oscar, Liberation and Home: April 1945–1949

We had left Oscar in April 1945 as the prisoner of war camp at Nuremberg was evacuated, the POWs again moving out of the path of the American Seventh Army that was bearing down on Nuremberg. With the other POWs evacuating Nuremberg, Oscar walked toward Moosburg (Stalag VII), a sprawling compound near Munich. Here, Allied prisoners were concentrated as the other Stalags were near to being overrun by Allied armies. About one hundred thousand men were interred there when Oscar was there in April and May 1945. Virtually all the Allied nationalities were represented: Americans, British, Canadians, South Africans, Russians, Indians, and Asians.[1] While the guards might have been friendlier at this point of the war, the conditions that awaited Oscar's arrival at Stalag VII were appalling. Frank Murphy, one POW, described them:

> The brutal central European winter now drawing to a close had kept us cooped up in our dirty, damp, dark, unheated, overcrowded barracks where over 400 men were assigned to buildings built to house 180. Outside the buildings large tents had been erected wherever there was enough space to set them up. Our cheerless barbed wire encircled world was comprised exclusively of austere, dilapidated buildings, grungy

tents, mud, and clusters of gaunt, emaciated men in shoddy, worn out clothing occupying every inch of unused space they could find.

We had one cold-water spigot in each building; they were our only source of water for every purpose. The fortunate ones among us slept on triple-deck wooden bunks on gunnysack mattresses filled with excelsior and infested with fleas, lice, and bedbugs—the unlucky ones slept on floors, tables, or outside on the ground inside crowded tents.

We were all covered with insect bites and always hungry—there was never enough food. Our daily food ration consisted of two or three slices of heavy German black bread, which we believed was made from a combination of flour and sawdust, each morning, plain boiled potatoes or turnips, and a bowl of a vile, ill-tasting, watery soup made from dehydrated vegetables, which we called green-death, at midday; and one or two more slices of black bread in the evening.

We had no sanitary facilities inside our barracks; our latrines were unheated, unlit, unspeakably foul-smelling separate structures that were nothing more than large outhouses with a narrow passageway and a long row of bench seating against a back wall. The bench seating contained a series of about twenty holes, spaced about eighteen inches apart. Beneath the seating was a sickening, stinking, open slit trench. Every hole was continually in use and there were always long lines of men waiting their turn. Misery, diarrhea and dysentery were rampant. There was nothing to read and no room to walk. We could only sit and wait for the war to end.[2]

Oscar continues:

On April 12, 1945, we were halted and the announcement was made to us that President Roosevelt had died. The Germans had respected him. About this time maybe a little before we walked across the bridge over the Danube River at Ingolstadt. It is big and beautiful but as Spike Jones said, in his popular recording, "The Danube Isn't Blue, It's Green."[3] By the time we got to Moosburg, the Americans were almost in charge. Here was gathered the largest part of the Allied POWs in any one place. Officers and enlisted men together, even our first group commander, Colonel Alkire was there. He was a senior officer there. He had been at an officers' camp at another place in Germany before being brought to Moosburg. He heated water for his coffee just as everyone else did if he could find the fuel. Our squadron adjutant was there boiling his water for coffee or tea just as we did. Rank meant nothing for the last few days there before General Patton's armored forces took charge.

Our German captors didn't wait for them, they left in secret sometime before [their arrival]. Regulations were very lax, and prisoners roamed at will inside the outer fences. Thousands of men of all Allied nations were there waiting for the day of liberation.

It came on the morning of April 29, 1945 when General Patton's armored forces moved in and took over.[4] There was a little resistance, but our guards had disappeared. The American tanks moved into position and started shelling artillery positions. Close behind were the infantrymen. The battle lasted only a couple of hours, but some of the stir-crazy prisoners climbed the fence and into the guard towers for a better view of the battle, and a few didn't live to be liberated. They were killed as innocent bystanders and spectators. Personally, I found the deepest depression in camp and stayed there until I was sure it was all over. I even missed General Patton's personal appearance in a white Packard convertible with four beautiful Red Cross girls.[5] I did come out when the Red Cross brought in the coffee and donuts, and I was there for the American K and C rations and the white bread baked before night by the U.S. Army bakers. It was a great day. All the officers dressed in their best uniforms, and it was really picturesque, especially the Scotsmen in their kilts crawling through the wire and showing their olive drab GI panties—very unfeminine.

The next day was spent in getting everybody back into prison so some organization for evacuation could be made. Some prisoners left the camp and went into town to loot stores and wineshops and cellars. They were uncontrollable. Some of these nuts who went into the city the day before were never found. It was really shameful. The percentage, however, was small.

Oscar's fellow POW, Frank Murphy, elaborated on the escapades of the liberated POWs:

Meanwhile liberated kriegies were pouring through the fences of the camp and roaming the Bavarian countryside around Moosburg "liberating" stocks of food, spirits, and souvenirs. Many of them went as far as Munich in their foraging.

By night, the [14th Armored] Division was established along the Isar, and behind it were unbelievable scenes—miles long columns of German prisoners being marched to the rear, a light tank in front of the column and a light tank in the rear—each with its lights on full blast—and the fields with 2000 Germans in a bunch, being guarded under lights, while among them lay the burned out German vehicles caught in the fight that morning, the German dead lying in grotesque positions as Graves Registration Officers moved among them preparing for burial—all the bloody incredible litter of a battlefield just passed, under the bright lights of overwatching vehicles.

And through the streets roamed streams of Allied prisoners, newly freed and not quite sure what they wanted to do, but they wanted to do something. They broke into liquor—schnapps and champagne and cognac and wine—in cellars and kitchens and wine shops and warehouses. They got into food—chickens and pigs and lambs and geese, potatoes and eggs and ham and bread. . . .

Ex-POWs and ex-slave laborers, ex-concentration camp inmates, soldiers and civilians, men and women, young and old, from every nation in Europe, drunk or sober, crying or laughing, they roamed the streets that night and reeled along the sidewalks, singing, shouting, kissing, wearing tall silk hats gotten from God knows where, carrying stoves, geese, pictures, cross-bows, and sabers.

Through that seething jam the American Army was trying to move back more German prisoners of war, columns four men wide and half a mile long. British ex-prisoners of war rode bicycles through the towns—freed prisoners took most of the bicycles and motorcycles and autos with which Germany was so well supplied. Slave laborers, men and women stood by every road, making a "V" with their fingers and grinning and throwing flowers.

"Endlisch frei, endlich frei," said one, a private first class of the French army introduced himself and gravely said: "It is very fine that our governments understand each other, and our generals and ministers, but I would like to tell all the American privates first class that I am eternally indebted to them and eternally grateful."[6]

Oscar continues:

I guess it's understandable that a great number of men like that would have a few who would lose control and just go berserk like a herd of cattle breaking out of a corral, half-starved and crazed with years of confinement and abuse. I guess the amazing thing was that so many kept their cool and waited for the organization of the U.S. Army to evacuate the survivors.

They were efficient and within a very few days we were de-loused and cleaned-up, shaved and showered, with clean clothing and plenty of food that made living worthwhile again.

In a few days we were flown out on C-47 transport planes and for the first time in my life, I got airsick. We were told we could take no food with us and although I wasn't hungry, I insisted on eating everything I had—it was just too much.

We were taken to Camp Lucky Strike in France, and we didn't know why we were cheered as we traveled from the airfield by truck by crowds lining the road all the way. We learned when we got to Lucky Strike that Germany had surrendered that morning. It was VE Day, May 7, 1945. The French were wild with joy. They had waited almost six years for this day.

Camp Lucky Strike was one of ten camps in Europe, all named after cigarette brands, by which troops were organized and processed for return to the United States. Camp Lucky Strike was the largest and accommodated 58,000 troops. It was also the primary camp for handling released POWs and designated recovered American military personnel. Most POWs were already at Moosburg, Stalag VII-A, and like Oscar were trucked from the Stalag to Strasbourg, then flown by AAF C-47s to Camp Lucky Strike, near the port city of La Havre, France.[7]

The ex-POWs received treatment to ensure they were in good health before returning to the States. They got an appropriate diet and fresh uniforms and were examined and treated for ailments of all sorts: malnutrition, typhus, respiratory infections, and vermin. The Red Cross was in evidence handing out donuts. But because of rampant digestive problems among the men, donuts were limited to one a day. The POWs, though, experts at barter after their interment, often found ways to get substantially more than the allotted one, which was not conducive to healing their digestion issues.[8]

Some recovered quickly of any and all ailments within days and were dispatched to the United States. Others took weeks to recover, and some did not ever recover either physically or mentally. While Camp Lucky Strike's aim was to return the men to good health and ease their suffering, there were daunting aspects to their stay. One was to be debriefed regarding their last mission, their capture, and their prisoner experience. Such intense questioning might resurrect painful memories of lost comrades, violent and bloody air combat, and maltreatment of themselves or fellow prisoners. The paperwork involved with their preparation for embarkation to the United States earned Camp Lucky Strike the nickname "Mount Paper Trail."[9]

Oscar continues:

All POWs went through a physical examination and most spent a few
days there, then went on to La Havre to go home by troop ship. A few
of us were kept a little longer. I was there about three weeks in a field
hospital before moving out.

We boarded the USS *Lejeune* (AP 74)[10] at La Havre, crossed the
English Channel to Southampton, England, and waited a day or two
for a convoy to be formed then we were on the high sea to home.
My second sea cruise was very pleasant compared to the first on the
German freighter. We were crowded but each man had his own bunk,
and I think they fed us six times a day. It was great.

Eleven days from Southampton we steamed into New York harbor.
I saw the Statue of Liberty and I was really proud to be an American.
We were ferried to Camp Kilmer, New Jersey and processed and
divided into groups to go to different parts of the U.S.A.[11] In about
three days we were aboard a troop train going to Ft. Bliss, El Paso with
$200 and nothing to spend it on.

In El Paso we were allowed to call home. I learned my younger
brother had been killed in action in his P-51 over Germany just days
before VE Day.

After about a week at Ft. Bliss, I got my teeth all fixed up with a
bridge of new front teeth, then I took a bus to home for a 30-day furlough.
Home was about 200 miles from Ft. Bliss, and I was met at the bus station
by my mom and Pappy. I hadn't considered it before finding out that my
brother had been killed, but I started wondering then and I still wonder how
to classify myself. I know my brother is a hero of the great war, but what
am I? The more I write of this, the more I wonder, and now I'm trying to
finish this story as quickly as I can. It's an awkward feeling for me now.
I'd never given much thought to this aspect of the situation before.

Oscar had a hard time reconciling his POW experience. He believed it was
wasted time and nothing had occurred in his fifteen-month interment that
advanced him professionally or personally. He was exposed to the worst aspects
of mankind in how the POWs had been treated. He had entered the army to
strike a blow for freedom but found himself at the mercy of those very individuals he had wanted to kill or destroy. It left him scarred and embittered.

I had a thirty day furlough and by the time it was over, the two atomic
bombs had been dropped on Japan. On Hiroshima, August 6, 1945 and
August 9, 1945 on Nagasaki.

I left home August 13, 1945 to go to Santa Monica, California for re-assignment to duty in the Pacific.

I was in Phoenix, Arizona, on August 14, 1945 after driving all night in the cool, and was asleep in an air-conditioned motel preparing to finish my trip to California the next day. About two o'clock that afternoon I was awakened by enough noise to be the warning of an air raid. I couldn't imagine what could be happening.

I went outside and the people had gone crazy—it was VJ Day. I was advised by the military police to get inside somewhere. Servicemen were being mobbed like Frank Sinatra then or like Elvis Presley later. I went back to the motel and waited a few hours. The temperature outside was 119 degrees. I remember well. It was really a hot situation.

At about dark I stole out of town and got into Santa Monica the next afternoon. People had cooled off some, but it was bumper to bumper traffic for miles in Los Angeles. I just happened to get into the line of traffic that took hours to get me to the luxury hotel, El Miramar, at Santa Monica beach, where my quarters would be for a couple of weeks before being sent back to Ft. Bliss for discharge.

It was a wonderful two weeks. Everyone was celebrating the end of the greatest war of all time. I was ready though to get back to Ft. Bliss for two or three days for discharge and then home about mid-September. My older brother [Harold] wasn't far behind me.

Oscar, after being discharged from the army reunited with his family. They were engaged in farming now in Muleshoe, Texas, and he was helping out.

July 8, 1945
Dear Annie & Ed,

Oscar has been helping Gerald combine & haul oats last week, they just finished today. Oscar seems to be happy working on the farm again.

Ollie[12]

Oscar stayed with Gerald and Ethel and their three little children—Jimmy, Winston, and Sherry—for a few weeks. He helped with Gerald and Ethel's farming enterprise. They, and eventually almost the entire Grizzle-Allison clan, moved to Muleshoe, about ninety miles northeast of Roswell, shortly after the war. Wiley Grizzle had discovered this land. It was in native grass and had abundant water under the surface. It was a farming boomtown. Wiley had bought a large amount of land and sold farms to his children. Farmwork, being close by family, and Gerald's and Ethel's three young kids were wonderful therapy for Oscar after his war experience, which understandably included considerable trauma.[13]

Wiley encouraged Oscar to go to college. He chose New Mexico College A&M (in 1960, New Mexico State University) in Las Cruces, New Mexico. Younger brother Jim was a student there at the time. Sammy McKinstry, the oldest daughter of Sam and Loveta McKinstry, lived in Las Cruces with her aunt, Eva West, and worked as a telephone operator. She had married Aubrey Hewatt of Roswell before the war. They had three children, Nan, Susan, and Mack. Hewatt (he preferred to be known by his last name) went through pilot training in the AAF and became, like Wiley Jr., a P-51 pilot. He ended up flying with the 4th Fighter Group (334th Fighter Squadron) of the Eighth Air Force. The 4th was one of the premier fighter groups of the AAF. He flew eighteen combat missions (coincidentally, the same number as Wiley Jr.), and shared a kill of a German training aircraft with another pilot. Despite his skill as a fighter pilot, on May 28, 1944, he was shot down by a BF-109 Messerschmitt fighter near Magdeburg, Germany, and captured. In the latter part of his captivity, he and other pilots managed to escape. After the war Hewatt, who suffered from some war trauma, decided to divorce Sammy; he had found another woman to marry.[14]

Oscar and Sammy were old friends, having grown up together as neighbors and gone to school in Hagerman together. Oscar paid a visit to Sammy and struck up a romantic relationship. On one occasion Jim and Oscar returned late to college after a visit home. The dorms were closed, so they stayed at Sammy's and Aunt Eva's house. The next morning, Oscar asked Sammy, "Why don't we get married?" She replied, "Well, I need to marry one of you, as the neighbors will wonder with two men spending the night with me!" Within a few days, on January 2, 1948, Oscar and Sammy married. The ceremony was at Harold and Jean's house in East Grand Plains, New Mexico, "brothers marrying sisters."[15]

Sammy's children—Nan, 7; Susan, 5; and Mack, 3—were part of the ceremony, and Jean recalled were "so cute." Susan recalled the wedding,

"We [meaning the three children as well as Sammy] married Oscar. We loved Oscar!" They were happy to have him for a daddy. He was a good father, reliable, understanding, and loyal. He and Sammy had a child in December 1949, Sam Oscar. Susan attested that the three stepchildren were never treated differently than Sam; there were no favorites.[16] Indeed, as I grew up close to Oscar's family, no one ever called Nan, Susan, or Mack a stepchild, stepdaughter, or stepson. There were no "steps" in Oscar's family. Oscar, who had shepherded his B-24 crew, his "family," through the war and Stalags, once again had a family to shepherd.

In the meantime, Ollie persisted in finding out Wiley Jr.'s fate. He was still considered missing in action by the War Department. She agonized over the fact that no one really saw what happened to Wiley, the actually crash; there were just no remains and thus no confirmation that he was actually dead. She refused to believe he had been killed and held out hope that he was alive.

Ollie wrote to government officials trying to determine Wiley's fate. The War Department reported only that he was still missing in action and they were trying to determine his exact status. She also tried to track down other pilots who were with Junior on that fateful day of March 24, 1945. John Onkey responded with a kind letter, undated, but in an envelope postmarked March, 11, 1946. As Oscar's wingman, he, of all people, should have more information on what happened. Onkey was out of the service now and studying at Yale University. He responded to her letter:

Sunday
Dear Mrs. Grizzle,

I am back at school now after a vacation at home. Your letters were waiting for me there but I did not get around to answering them because my mother was very sick and I was kept pretty busy.

I was flying on your son's wing on March 24th and I was hit by flak and bellied in not far from the fight. I was taken prisoner and when I reached the army post nearby, the German Intelligence Officer told me that five of our ships were shot down. He said that two of us were killed. Carl Larsen, Jack May, and I were the only boys who survived as far as I have been able to find out. I heard no other word about "Griz" than this.

I debated writing this to you as I did not actually see anything happen to your son and what I know comes from the Germans. However, I know you want to find out all you can and I have told you the facts as I know them. I have waited this long to write to you hoping I would hear that Wiley was O.K.

I bunked next to him for a month and a half and we were good friends. We had good times together and I respected his pilot ability only second to his good naturedness. Everyone liked "Griz" and hope that somehow you hear good news. If there is anything else I can tell you, please let me know.

Sincerely,
John P. Onkey[17]

It is not clear why Onkey states in this letter that he was hit by flak. This differs from the official reports in that none of the pilots reported flak in the area. Onkey does not mention flak in his interview done in 1991 with the historian Graham Cross.[18] This letter, I believe, was the source of disinformation I heard growing up, that Junior had been shot down by flak. Perhaps Onkey bore a sense of guilt for the loss of his leader, which was unjustified in that he, as he states to Cross, was under attack himself. Also, a dogfight is tremendously dynamic; things happen suddenly and require an immediate response upon which lies life or death.

Then in early March 1946, almost a year after Wiley Jr. had been lost, the War Department confirmed his death in combat:

WAR DEPARTMENT
THE ADJUTANT GENERAL'S OFFICE
WASHINGTON, D.C.   13 March 1946
Dear Mrs. Grizzle:

It is with profound regret that I confirm the recent telegram informing you of the death of your son, Second Lieutenant Wiley Grizzle, Jr. 02056952, Air Corps, who was previously reported missing in action on 24 March 1945 over Germany.

An official message has now been received which states that he was killed in action on the date he was previously reported missing in action. You may rest assured that, without any further request on your part, you will be advised promptly if any additional information concerning your loved one is received

I realize the anxiety you have suffered since he was first reported missing in action and deeply regret the sorrow this later report brings you. May the knowledge that he made the supreme sacrifice for his home and country be a source of sustaining comfort.

My sympathy is with you in this time of great sorrow.

Sincerely yours,
Edward F. Witsell, Major General[19]

Ollie wrote back to Onkey upon hearing this bad news. Onkey responded with this letter:

Monday
Dear Mrs. Grizzle,

I'm glad you have found out about Wiley although the blow must have been hard. I am sure that the report is correct from what I know. Lt. Clark was correct in saying he saw me hit at high speed for I did so and as very lucky to get out of it.

It was Wiley's second mission that day because I flew with him in the morning if I remember correctly. We strafed some trucks and came back to the base and had a sandwich while our ships were being refueled and reloaded. Griz and I were the second element in Lt. Clark's flight, with Jr. as my element leader. He was still in the air and had not been hit when I left him. I left him when I was hit by flak that started a fire in the cockpit. I tried to call Wiley but my radio was shot out. That was the last I actually saw of him. I saw a couple of ships that I thought were 51s go down in flames and I was told that one of four boys had crashed in flames not far from the spot where I went down. Civilians told me this. This ship could have been Wiley's. I don't know. The Germans told me that two of us had been killed in the battle but did not mention any names or place of burial.

I was a prisoner of Stalag Luft I in Barth, Germany. I was also interrogated in Pinneberg, near Hamburg. I was on an airfield from which some of the planes that were in the fight had flown—Gottingen, Germany. I spent the first night about three or four miles from the scene of the fight in a cellar.

The time was about 3 PM and the place, as near as I can figure was between Duderstadt and Helligenstadt (N.W. of Kassel). [These towns are not northwest of Kassel, but northeast and close to where the fight occurred, near Sattenhausen, and where Wiley crashed.] I haven't written Jack Clark [Wiley and Onkey's flight lead] but I intend to. I am sorry I have no other information for you than this and I don't imagine that the War Dept knows any more than I do. I hope that some German records will be uncovered to disclose more about Wiley.

If I can be of any more assistance, please let me know, Mrs. Grizzle. Sincerely, John Onkey[20]

Since none of the other pilots who were in that last mission with Wiley actually saw his crash, there was no definite proof. Maybe he had survived the crash, like Onkey, and then was captured but never released. Who knows what might have happened in the turmoil and flux occurring at the end of the war. There was always a possibility that he was alive. Ollie's fierce love did not allow her to be at peace until a body was produced.

After receiving Major General Witsell's letter from the War Department announcing the death of Wiley Jr., Ollie wrote back the following month:

Dexter, N. Mex.
April 24, 1946
Dear Major General,

You ask me not to write concerning my son, Lt. Wiley Grizzle, Jr. who you reported killed in action Mar. 24, 1945. But please tell me what the message was, reporting his death.

How did he die, where did he die and where is he buried or has his body ever been found?

If they told you anything about it, please let us know, won't you?

It is so terrible, not knowing anything. Are they still trying to find missing boys? Thank you sir, very much for anything you can tell me.

Yours sincerely,
Ollie B. Grizzle[21]

She, in a way, spoke for all the mothers and fathers who lost sons in combat. They knew little of the circumstances. She received a response from the general, mailed on May 7, 1946, almost immediately upon the receipt of the above letter.

Dear Mrs. Grizzle,

Your desire to receive additional information regarding the circumstances surrounding the death of your son is most understandable. . . .
Our commanders in the zones of occupation immediately upon entering their areas begin a search for information concerning personnel
who have been reported missing. This is done by interrogation of
the inhabitants, examination of captured enemy records, and careful
search of all parts of the surrounding terrain. . . . I am directing the
Commanding General, European Theater, to furnish the information
upon which the report of death was based and upon receipt of this
information, you will be notified promptly.

Sincerely yours,
Edward F. Witsell
Major General
The Adjutant General of the Army[22]

She also received a letter from the army's quartermaster general, who wrote
on May 17, 1946. Major General Witsell evidently forwarded Ollie's letter
to his office (adjutant general). Whereas Witsell addressed the circumstances
by which Wiley was killed, the quartermaster's office was responsible for
the army's efforts to recover bodies or remains. The US government and the
army (as well as other services) are to be commended for undertaking this
massive effort. First Lieutenant William E. Reid of the quartermaster's office
wrote in part:

I regret that I must inform you that information concerning the burial
of the remains of your son has not yet been received in this office.
However, our Graves Registration Forces in the field are making a
complete and thorough search of all areas over which our men fought.
All available information such as enemy reports of death and burial,
either captured or transmitted through the International Red Cross,
results of interrogation of returned Prisoners of War, statements made
by natives of the localities being searched, and reports submitted by
Commanding Officers and fellow soldiers who were in the vicinity at
the time of the fatality, are being used to implement their efforts.[23]

Indeed, a graves registration team did investigate the crash site five months
later, in October 1946 (they, no doubt, were very busy investigating other

cases of missing soldiers at this time). One is impressed with the thoroughness of their search efforts, part of which was interviewing locals from the Sattenhausen area. From their comments one understands what the dogfight looked like from the ground.

A German civilian, August Seebode, observed the dogfight. He testified:

> During the air skirmish, there was a total of about 8 planes shot down near Sattenhausen. One of them was of American nationality. The American plane crashed east of the small stream about 88 meters from the village. The plane burned in the air before the crash, and probably exploded, since the different parts of the plane crashed separately. The plane also burned on the ground. One day later I went to the scene of the crash. All I saw were completely burned plane parts. The motor was buried deep in the earth. I didn't see any parts of the pilot's body.[24]

Another Sattenhausen villager, Heinrich Buermann, a painter, told the American investigators:

> I was on the road leading out of the village to the west. I saw two planes crash. The German plane in a southeast direction from the village, and the other plane in a northeast direction from the village. The pilot of the German plane escaped by bailing out with his parachute and was badly injured. He stated that he had been in an air battle with an American. He died the next day from his wounds. In the afternoon [of the air battle] I was at the scene of the crash of the American plane. I couldn't see anything of a human body, I imagine that the pilot of the plane had no opportunity to bail out since the plane collapsed in the air already, and I suppose that he completely burned under the wreckage.[25]

This statement harmonizes with the previous statement by Seebode. It also, however, raises the possibility that Wiley battled with a German plane and possibility shot it down, but in the process was himself shot down.

Another villager, Paul Krope, a forest laborer, provided information that was not in the previous two: "When I arrived at Sattenhausen, I went immediately to the scene of the crash of the other American plane, the plane was not burning any more, and among the wreckage of the plane I could see a part of a human arm and a part of the teeth. According to what my father-in-law told me later, he buried these parts temporarily at the scene of the crash. He can't remember anymore today the exact place of burial."[26]

Although there was little to identify the aircraft, it had burned completely, and the engine was buried deep. Important pieces of information were at the crash site that could identify it as Wiley's aircraft: the six machine guns. These guns were solid iron and neither burned nor were destroyed in the crash. The numbers matched the serial numbers of the guns in G-Nat.

There was little evidence to identify the pilot. There were no clothing or personal items. This suggested a violent crash and an all-consuming fire, possibly occurring even before ground impact. No remains were discovered at this time by the army's investigators. The team concluded that the body had been destroyed in the fiery crash.

Army soldiers from another graves registration company, however, investigated the crash site ten days later and did find remains (bones). They were forwarded to the American cemetery at Neuville en Condroz, Belgium. The central identification point there, a forensics lab, concluded there was nothing in the bones, which consisted of pieces of seven ribs and one-third of the left clavicle, to allow positive identification. There were no teeth. The status of the remains was marked "Unknown."[27]

The army concluded, however, that since the remains had been found at the crash site, which was certainly Wiley's plane, then the remains must be Wiley. The arm and jaw pieces that the German civilian said his father-in-law buried were not retrieved. The German said, however, that he did not remember where he buried them. Nevertheless, the remains were placed in a coffin and buried at Neuville en Condroz in a respectful and reverent ceremony on December 21, 1946. Officiating were two chaplains, one Protestant, the other Catholic. A wooden cross marked the grave. On Wiley's left and right were two unknown servicemen.

Even with this information, Ollie held out hope for Junior's return. For a time she refused to believe that he was ever really dead. Or perhaps it was a means of grieving, but she wrote Christmas cards to Wiley Jr. in 1945, 1946, and 1947.

To "Junie," somewhere, Christmas, 1945:

To you darling where-ever you are, this sad Christmas of 1945.
I'm thinking of you sweetheart, all of the time. How I want you,
nobody knows. I'd gladly give the rest of my life just to know you
are safe & well. Nearly bedtime for you, so goodnite my darling boy,
happy dreams.

Mom

To "Junie" wherever you are Christmas 1946:

I am thinking of you my darling boy this Christmas Eve of 1946, &
wishing you were here & hoping & praying you will come back
sometime. It's so sad without you. Tomorrow I'll miss you so much
when dinner is ready & you won't be there. Good nite sweetheart &
wherever you are I hope you have the nicest Christmas you can
possibly have.

Mom

To "Junie," Somewhere Christmas 1947:

Another Christmas darling boy, and you haven't come back, but I still
have hopes that you will, sometime, I don't know how I can stand it
if ever I do have to give up hopes of you coming back. It will be sad
tomorrow, at dinner, I do miss you so, at dinner especially. I love you,
so very much "Junie," & wherever you are honey boy, I hope your
Christmas of 1947 will be as happy, as is possible for it to be.

Mom[28]

Two years later, as part of the World War II Return of the Dead Program,
the family requested that Wiley's remains be returned to Roswell for burial.
His casket was disinterred at the Belgium cemetery and shipped to the United
States. He was reburied June 5, 1949, in Roswell's South Park cemetery.[29]
His family was all there. Gerald, Harold, Oscar, Jim, Ollie Mae, and Mary
all attended with their families. They were all married by this time except

Jim, who married Verona Wagner of Muleshoe the next year. It was a deeply mournful experience for them all. Gerald's son Larry, 3 years old, remembered standing in the front seat of the family car between Gerald and Ethel. As a military detachment fired a twenty-one-gun salute, Gerald "buried his face in his hands and wept uncontrollably."[30] The others in the family had similarly powerful emotions. Ollie and Wiley, too, of course. I do not know if Ollie ever gave up her hope of seeing her son again or just shifted it to an eternal hope of seeing him in the hereafter.

It certainly may be true that the greatest suffering in war is by the mothers of servicemen and women lost in combat. Their agony may never cease. Wiley Grizzle passed away in 1973. Ollie Grizzle followed three years later. She was 92.

Epilogue

T hings moved rapidly after the end of the war. In 1946 the Allison Brothers established a farming partnership on two sections of land, 1,280 acres in Muleshoe. Here, Gerald and Ethel, Harold and Jean, and Oscar and Sammy lived, worked, and raised their families that included fourteen children. Harold and Oscar's wartime experience in the AAF was always a part of their life. Attendance at air shows at Cannon Air Force Base near Clovis, New Mexico; Reese Air Force Base, near Lubbock, Texas; or Amarillo Air Force Base were a common event. They took their male children, Mack, Sam, Fred, Jack, and Jim Allison. They relived their military flying experiences and educated their boys on military aviation, and the boys got to see real warbirds up close. What a thrill!

In 1973 the pilot of Oscar's B-24, Bob Bird, returned to Austria with his wife, Ann.[1] His intent was to find the place where he had landed after bailing out of Pistol Packin' Mama, any remains of the plane, and the Austrian village where he was first taken after being captured. With the assistance of Austrian officials, he found the town. It was Koglhof, and the townspeople were genuinely friendly. The Birds' visit there stirred a lot of interest, and people gathered to meet them. Bob had always wanted to return and visit the town that had been peaceful and friendly after the airborne fight. One farmer showed him where the plane had crashed, and Bob was able to locate where he had landed after parachuting from Mama. Bob was concerned that Pistol Packin' Mama might have damaged or destroyed a castle when it crashed. He saw the castle from where he had parachuted down in the distance and the smoke from his burning B-24. It turns out this was the Schloss Frondsberg castle. Locals, however, assured him that the B-24 actually crashed a distance behind the castle, along a footpath to a farmhouse. The castle still stood. Fuel from the bomber, however, did splash over a farmhouse, set it ablaze, and actually destroyed it. Apparently, no one was home, so there were no injuries. Farmers produced pieces of the aircraft, a fuel selector valve from the cockpit, and pieces of corrugated metal. Bob was actually able to bring enough of the pieces of the B-24 home to give each crewmember a small piece. Oscar displayed his piece of Pistol Packin' Mama proudly in his office at his home on the Allison Brothers farm near Muleshoe. Another farmer reported that two of the machine guns from the bomber had also been found when work was done widening the path where the crash occurred.

As with the Austrians who "captured" Oscar, the Koglhof villagers were friendly and concerned with the well-being of the American airmen. The village where Oscar was taken after being first arrested was not Koglhof but must have been nearby. Some of the villagers present recalled having cared for the badly injured Manning until medical personnel arrived. With all that he had witnessed and seen, Bob was convinced this was where he had landed, where he had been brought after being captured that day in 1944. The villagers encouraged the Birds to one day return.

The Birds did return to Austria. In 1982 they again went to Koglhof to renew friendships with the townspeople. The local media interviewed Bird during his stay in Austria, and the interview was written up and published in several Austrian newspapers. Due to this publicity, Bob received a book that documented the history of the German 27th Fighter Wing (Jagdgeschwader [JAG]-27). This book included a German pilot's account of shooting down a Liberator and being shot down himself by the same Liberator, then meeting an American B-24 crew on a train the next day. Of course this was Bird's crew (see ch. 8 for more on this story).[2]

The little village of Koglhof subsequently invited the Birds back for a four-day celebration as village guests to occur in 1984. They also invited Helmut Beckmann and his wife. The Birds were there, accompanied by bombardier Deane Manning and his wife. Helmut Beckmann and his wife, Gerda, also came to Koglhof. Beckmann, the Birds reported, was fortunate to have survived the war. He had shot down fifteen American aircraft during the war. His shootdown by Dixon was only one of seven times he had been shot down. The Birds reported that the celebration exceeded their "wildest imaginings."[3]

A number of prominent VIPs welcomed the former foes. These included officials from Koglhof, the town band, fire department, and police. Officials from nearby towns and the province of Styria were there, as well as Austrian air force representatives. From four hundred to five hundred people attended an event in which speeches were made. Then Bob, Deane, and Helmut stood before the crowd and shook hands. Bob found the Beckmanns were extremely likable, and they became friends. The Austrians claimed that this was the first meeting of this type, former enemies coming together in goodwill and reconciliation, that had occurred in Austria and possibly in Europe. The three aviators were then presented with Austrian Pilot Badges, the first to ever have been given to Americans. A wreath was laid on the town's war memorial, and an exhibition in the town hall was opened that displayed pieces of Pistol Packin' Mama, the most prominent being a machine gun.[4]

The next day, the celebration continued with an outdoor Mass in which Bob was presented with a rude cross made from bomb fragments recovered from the Monte Cassino Abbey in Italy. A picnic followed in which the band, folk dancers, and singing groups entertained the diners. The guests of honor were then treated to a carriage ride into the country where the Pistol Packin' Mama had crashed and where Bob and Deane had landed. "It was a fairy tale come true," Ann attested. In the days after, Bob and Ann drove to Dortmund, Germany, to attend a reunion of Beckmann's fighter wing JG-27 at Beckmann's invitation. There he was a guest of Beckmann. There was goodwill all around, and Bird presented a 449th Bomb Group plaque to JG-27.[5]

This author has found that the Austrians generally treated the downed airmen well. This attitude continues to the present in that efforts are made to commemorate Allied airmen who crashed in Austria. Leading this effort is Christian Arzberger, an Austrian gentleman who works with village leaders and other officials to include Austrian government and military officials, the Austrian Catholic church, the American embassy in Vienna, and families of the bomber crews to erect impressive memorials in villages nearest where the bombers crashed. The celebrations are similar to what Bob Bird and his wife experienced in Koglhof. Thus far, eleven markers have been dedicated.[6]

The three Allison brothers—Gerald, Harold, and Oscar—settled down to farming and raising their children on land about nine miles east of Muleshoe. They were community leaders. They remained close and their children grew up playing with one another. My cousins were my first best friends, and we remain friends today. It was a tight-knit, prosperous, and secure setting for their families. Encouraged by their wives, the brothers developed a strong faith. They rarely worked on Sunday. Despite the hardships of farming in West Texas, they were optimistic but realistic. They worked hard just as they had grown up doing. Their farms prospered.

They lived close to one another and met near daily at one or another's homes. Gerald's son Larry recalled discussing farming. They also "sat around the kitchen table, having a cup of 'mud' or 'Joe.' The stories would begin, and I remember sitting nearby and listening to the philosophies, the passions, and the humor of these guys who had grown up in such difficult circumstances. Such verbal events were referred to as the exercise of "cracking wise" and they sparred with each other in a battle of witticisms."[7] When the other siblings were present, those who lived distantly, the coffee-drinking sessions included little brother Jim Grizzle, George Didlake (Ollie Mae's husband), and Andy Andreas (Mary's husband). I remember one such occasion at Gerald and Ethel's kitchen; they had the lights dimmed and were showing film from Junior's pilot training. The film, taken from a "gun camera" in Junior's airplane (probably a P-40), filmed his firing passes at a towed airborne banner. Junior was not forgotten.

Oscar passed away on January 1, 1982. Gerald died four months later, April 1982, and Harold followed on June 11, 1991. On each occasion, the family mourned.

Oscar's experience in combat and in captivity had an extra dimension. The memories lived on in him. In the hospital and near death, in deep but fitful sleep, he dreamed and would sleep talk. Those memories returned. He called out names of his fellow crewmen, his combat family: "Skeets—Leafski—Jackson!" They were flying again, on a mission. Many of the memories were good, and some were incredibly dark. As he said in his memoir, "Some stories, especially true stories, are better left untold. I will write about the things that I choose to remember and keep trying to forget those that I've been trying to forget since the beginning of 1944 AD." But he never forgot them—until his death in January 1982. The mission was over. He was home and at peace.

Endnotes

Preface

1. The name *Roswell* is going to remind some readers of the UFO incident that occurred near there in 1947. None of my relatives ever spoke of this incident, except after the fact, after the major publicity occurred.
2. "Farming in the U.S.," *American Experience*, PBS, accessed August 30, 2023, https://www.pbs.org/wgbh/americanexperience/features/troublesome-farm-ing-us/#:~:text=1940%20The%20downward%20spiral%20in%20the%20number%20of,population%20to%20less%20than%203%20percent%20by%201981.

Notes for Chapter 1

1. Harold Kilmer, "Pecos Valley History," De Baca County, *NMGenWeb Project*, accessed March 12, 2022, https://debaca.nmgenweb.us/resources/pecos_valley.html.
2. Helen Curry, "The Beginning," in *Meeting the Train: Hagerman, New Mexico and Its Pioneers*, ed. William Farrington, comp. Hagerman Historical Society (Santa Fe: Sleeping Fox Enterprises, 1975), 17.
3. Curry, "Beginning," 16–17, 21.
4. The Homestead Act of 1862 was the federal legislation that allowed this. In order to settle the west, the government offered 160 acres of land to settlers who could remain on the land for five years. Robert Fink, "Homestead Act of 1862," accessed September 4, 2022, *Britannica*, https://www.britannica.com/topic/Homestead-Act.
5. Jo Grizzle Johnson, email to author, March 17, 2022.
6. Veta Jean Allison, *Love Lifted Me* (San Antonio: Litho Press, 2012), 45.
7. Johnson email, March 18, 2022.
8. "Overview of Fresh and Brackish Water Quality—Roswell Artesian Basin," accessed March 22, 2022, *New Mexico Bureau of Geology and Mineral Resources*, https://geoinfo.nmt.edu/resources/water/projects/bwa/roswell/home.html.
9. Farrington, *Meeting the Train*, 229–30.
10. Larry Allison, Gerald's third son, was especially helpful in providing context and elaboration on Gerald's situation at this point.
11. This information derives from conversations and emails with Larry Allison.
12. Johnson email, March 17, 2022.
13. Allison, *Love Lifted Me*, 45–46, 51.
14. Allison, *Love Lifted Me*, 56–57.
15. Allison, *Love Lifted Me*, 11; Farrington, *Meeting the Train*, 177–78.
16. Allison, *Love Lifted Me*, 50.
17. Allison, *Love Lifted Me*, 53.

18. Allison, *Love Lifted Me*, 41.
19. Allison, *Love Lifted Me*, 60.
20. Larry Allison commentary. This summary of Gerald and Ethel's activities is enhanced by a collection of letters between Gerald and Ethel, dated 1935–1937, and provided courtesy of Christy Wylie, daughter of Robert Allison, Gerald's and Ethel's youngest child.
21. Per letters between Gerald and Ethel, dated 1935–1937.
22. *Hagerman Messenger* newspaper. The weekly editions of this newspaper (1928–1938) were searched by the author, who discovered that it published an incredible amount of information on local families.
23. Bill Ganzel, "Farming in the 1930s," *Wessels Living History Farm*, accessed March 31, 2022, https://livinghistoryfarm.org/farming-in-the-1930s/.
24. University of Nebraska–Lincoln, "Agriculture," *Great Plains in World War II*, accessed March 29, 2022, http://plainshumanities.unl.edu/homefront/agriculture.html.
25. William White, "Economic History of Tractors in the United States," *Economic History Association*, accessed March 30, 2022, https://eh.net/encyclopedia/economic-history-of-tractors-in-the-united-states/.
26. White, "Economic History of Tractors."
27. "Farmall B," *Tractor Data,* accessed March 31, 2022, https://www.tractordata.com/farm-tractors/000/2/8/286-farmall-b.html.
28. Cindy Grizzle Pennington, email to author, March 17, 1922.

Notes for Chapter 2

1. Barnstormers were pilots, often ex-military, who flew from town to town in their own airplanes, usually a World War I biplane, and put on flight demonstrations for the locals. The barnstormer event was extremely popular in this time when people were fascinated with flight and drew crowds to a field or pasture where the aircraft took off and landed. The pilots often offered to take individuals on a short flight for free or for a small fee. John Fleischman, "The Barnstormer," *Smithsonian*, August 2021, https://www.smithsonianmag.com/air-space-magazine/barnstormer-1-180978267/.
2. "Civilian Pilot Training," *National Museum of the US Air Force*, accessed December 8, 2020, https://www.nationalmuseum.af.mil/Visit/Museum-Exhibits/Fact-Sheets/Display/Article/196137/civilian-pilot-training-program/.
3. Here Oscar is referring to American young men who flew with the Royal Air Force during the Battle of Britain (1940) in what was called the Eagle Squadron. He also is referring to General Chennault's American Volunteer Group, popularly known as the Flying Tigers—a mercenary fighter organization in the hire of Chiang Kai-Shek, the nationalist leader of China against the Japanese, who had invaded China in 1937.
4. 1-A was a draft status that indicated that the individual thus classified was totally eligible for drafting, physically and mentally; he had no deferments available to him.

5. "Over the Hill in October," *Ohio History Central*, accessed August 15, 2020, https://ohiohistorycentral.org/w/Over_the_Hill_in_October?rec=534.

6. By the end of 1940, Germany had overrun and seized part of Poland; the other part of Poland was seized by Stalin's Soviet army.

7. Elaine M. Marconi, "Robert Goddard: A Man and His Rocket," *NASA*, accessed August 17, 2020, https://www.nasa.gov/missions/research/f_goddard.html.

8. "Dr. Robert H. Goddard: The Father of Modern Rocketry," *National Museum of the US Air Force*, accessed August 17, 2020, https://www.nationalmuseum.af.mil/Visit/Museum-Exhibits/Fact-Sheets/Display/Article/197697/dr-robert-h-goddard/.

9. The *New York Times* opinion piece appeared on January 13, 1920. Among its comments it asserted that professor Goddard "does not know the relation of action to reaction, and the need to have something better than a vacuum against which to react—to say that would be absurd. Of course he only seems to lack the knowledge ladled out daily in high schools." The *Times*'s apology appeared in the July 17, 1969, edition, the day after Apollo 11 was launched, headed for the moon. Kiona N. Smith, "The Correction Heard Round the World: When the *New York Times* Apologized to Robert Goddard," *Forbes*, July 19, 2018, https://www.forbes.com/sites/kionasmith/2018/07/19/the-correction-heard-round-the-world-when-the-new-york-times-apologized-to-robert-goddard/?sh=70d42c124543.

10. Matthew Wills, "Robert H. Goddard: The Forgotten Father of Modern Rocketry," *JSTOR Daily*, accessed August 30, 2023, https://daily.jstor.org/robert-h-goddard-the-forgotten-father-of-rocketry/.

11. "Dr. Robert H. Goddard: The Father of Modern Rocketry."

12. Marconi, "Robert Goddard."

13. "Charles A. Lindbergh: Interest in Rocketry," *Charles Lindbergh: An American Aviator*, accessed August 22, 2023, http://www.charleslindbergh.com/rocket/.

14. Charles Augustus Lindbergh, *The Wartime Journals of Charles A. Lindbergh* (New York: Harcourt, Brace, Jovanovich, 1970), 8n, 199, 206, 210, 212; "Charles A. Lindbergh: Interest in Rocketry."

15. "Charles Lindbergh in Combat, 1944," *Eyewitness to History*, accessed August 23, 2023, http://www.eyewitnesstohistory.com/lindbergh2.htm; Lindbergh, *Wartime Journals*, 888–89. Here Lindbergh details shooting down a Japanese aircraft while flying a P-38 when he visited an AAF unit in the South Pacific.

16. Running irrigation water refers to watering row crops out of a water-filled ditch with suction tubes. This was required to grow crops in the arid farming region of eastern New Mexico. It was very labor intensive.

17. Alfred Goldberg, "Allocation and Distribution of Aircraft," and Arthur R. Kooker, "Broadening the Basis of Procurement," in *The Army Air Forces in World War II*, ed. Frank W. Craven and James Lea Cate, 7 vols. (Washington, DC: Office of Air Force History, 1983), VI:423–27.

18. Frank Futrell, "The Development of Base Facilities," in Craven and Cate, *Army Air Forces*, VI:120.

19. Kooker, "Basic Military Training and Classification of Personnel," in Craven and Cate, *Army Air Forces*, VI:529–30.

20. Kooker, "Broadening the Basis of Procurement," in Craven and Cate, *Army Air Forces*, VI:427.
21. Futrell, "Development of Base Facilities," in Craven and Cate, *Army Air Forces*, VI:123–27.
22. The US Air Force began in 1907 with a complement of three lieutenants and was designated the Aeronautical Division of the US Army Signal Corps. In 1909 it obtained its first aircraft, a Wright A Flyer, built by the Wright brothers, for which the government paid $30,000.
23. Allan M. Winkler, *Home Front U.S.A.: Americans during World War II* (Wheeling, IL: Harlan Davidson, 2000), 44–45.
24. The AAF had civilian depots for aircraft maintenance also at Fairfield, Ohio; San Antonio, Texas; and Sacramento, California. These maintenance facilities conducted the sophisticated and complex work of maintaining aircraft, such as complete overhauls of aircraft, that military maintenance units were not equipped or manned to do.
25. Larry Allison, email to author, March 12, 2022, and phone call with author, March 14, 2022.
26. L. Allison, email to author, March 12, 2022.

Notes for Chapter 3

1. Kooker, "Basic Military Training," in Craven and Cate, *Army Air Forces*, VI:529.
2. Rebecca H. Cameron, *Training to Fly: Military Flight Training, 1907–1945* (Washington, DC: Air Force History and Museums Program, 1999), 388. Cameron writes that the AAF graduated 193,440 pilots between July 1939 and August 1945.
3. Bruce A. Ashcroft, *We Wanted Wings: A History of the Aviation Cadet Program* (Randolph Air Force Base, TX: HQ, AETC/HO, 2005), 33, 36–37.
4. John C. McManus, *Deadly Sky: The American Combat Airmen in World War II* (New York: NAL Caliber, 2016), 21.
5. Ashcroft, *We Wanted Wings*, 35.
6. Cameron, *Training to Fly*, 385.
7. Ashcroft, *We Wanted Wings*, 34–35.
8. Thomas H. Greer, "Individual Training of Flying Personnel," in Craven and Cate, *Army Air Forces*, VI:562–63.
9. Ashcroft, *We Wanted Wings*, 37; Craven and Cate, "Foreword," in Craven and Cate, *Army Air Forces*, VI:xxv.
10. Wiley Grizzle Jr. to Ollie Grizzle, postmarked March 25, 1943, in author's possession, provided by Georga Didlake Collins. Georga is the daughter of Ollie Mae (Ollie and Wiley's oldest daughter) and George Didlake.
11. Wiley Jr. to Ollie, postmarked April 29, 1943, in author's possession, provided by Collins.
12. Wiley Jr. to Ollie, postmarked April 4, 1943, and May 21, 1943, in author's possession, provided by Cindy Grizzle Pennington.

13. Wiley Jr. to Jim Grizzle, June 1943, copy of letter in author's possession, provided by Pennington.
14. Wiley Jr. to Ollie, postmarked June 26, 1943, copy of letter in author's possession, provided by Pennington.
15. Wiley Jr. to Ollie, postmarked July 6, 1943, copy of letter in author's possession, provided by Pennington.
16. Wiley Jr. to Ollie, postmarked July 14, 1943, copy of letter in author's possession, provided by Collins.
17. Brass referred to various metal badges and insignia indicating that one was now an aviation cadet, an important and meaningful step in the process of becoming an AAF officer. They had no rank as of yet, although administratively they were enlisted men. This allowed the AAF to induct and fence in a large pool of high-quality trainees and feed them into flight training as the system could handle them.
18. Ashcroft, *We Wanted Wings*, 35. Junior's comments here noting a 12 percent attrition during the classification process is just below the overall wartime average of 15 percent who were eliminated during classification process.
19. Wiley Jr. to Ollie, postmarked July 16, 1943, in author's possession, provided by Collins.
20. Ashcroft, *We Wanted Wings*, 40–42.
21. Wiley Jr. to Ollie, Aug 3, 1943, copy of letter in author's possession, provided by Pennington.
22. Wiley is referring here to reading a blinker light from an airfield control tower that was a backup, or secondary source of communication.
23. Wiley Jr. to Ollie, August 30, 1943, in author's possession.
24. Cameron, *Training to Fly*, 27. Wiley is referring to classes on sending and receiving Morse code, which aircraft of that day used as a backup communication and navigation system. Some regarded it as the most hated class in preflight academics.
25. Wiley Jr. to Ollie, postmarked September 24, 1943, in author's possession, provided by Collins.
26. Wiley Jr. to Ollie, postmarked October 5, 1943, in author's possession, provided by Collins.
27. Wiley Jr. to Ollie, October 22, 1943, copy in author's possession, provided by Pennington.
28. Wiley Jr. to Ollie, October 24,1943, copy in author's possession, provided by Pennington.

Notes for Chapter 4

1. McManus, *Deadly Sky*, 38.
2. Tom Faulkner, *Flying with the 15th Air Force: A B-24 Pilot's Missions from Italy during World War II* (Denton: University of North Texas Press, 2018), 61; McManus, *Deadly Sky*, 38; Greer, "Individual Training of Flying Personnel," in Craven and Cate, *Army Air Forces*, VI:596.

3. McManus, *Deadly Sky*, 101.

4. McManus, *Deadly Sky*, 147.

5. Greer, "Individual Training of Flying Personnel," in Craven and Cate, *Army Air Forces*, VI:589–95.

6. "The Eighth Air Force vs. The Luftwaffe," *National WWII Museum*, accessed August 23, 2023, https://www.nationalww2museum.org/war/articles/eighth-air-force-vs-luftwaffe.

7. Ollie Grizzle to Annie Allison, July 25, 1943, in author's possession, provided by Georga Didlake Collins.

8. The Consolidated Aircraft Corporation B-24 was accepted into USAAF service in 1941. More B-24s were built in World War II than any other US aircraft, with the AAF accepting 18,190. Alfred Goldberg, "AAF Aircraft of World War II," in Craven and Cate, *Army Air Forces*, VI:205–7.

9. Faulkner, *Flying with the 15th*, 52; McManus, *Deadly Sky*, 63–64.

10. The 449th Bomb Group's (this is the group that Oscar's crew would join for their combat tour in Italy) B-24s probably had the Sperry bombsight and the Norden might have been installed later. See 1st Lt. Damon A. Turner's "War Diary: 449th Bombardment Group," 449th Bomb Group (WWII), accessed September 6, 2020, https://449th.com/diaries/. This website is a valuable historical source. G. Glenn Henry, "Sperry S-1 Bomb Sight," *Glenn's Computer Museum*, accessed September 6, 2020, http://www.glennsmuseum.com/items/sperry_s1/. Here it notes that the Sperry was standard equipment for AAF bombers, especially B-24 units, until late 1943 when all contracts with Sperry were canceled and bombers afterward, we can assume, were fitted out with Norden sights.

11. The German .88 mm cannon might very well have been the most feared German weapon of the war for both ground troops and airmen. It was extremely accurate and fired its rounds at high velocity. Designed primarily as an antiaircraft weapon, it was thoroughly deadly in ground combat use also. It could "punch through four inches of tank armor from a mile away." The Germans produced thousands of these cannons and posted them around likely targets of Allied bombers. More than 50 percent of Allied aircraft losses over Germany were due to the 88s; indeed, over twenty-six thousand Allied aircraft received at least some damage from 88 shells. James S. Corum, "The Weapon GIs Hated the Most," *HistoryNet*, accessed March 12, 2021, https://www.historynet.com/weapon-gis-hated-worst.htm.

12. The B-26 had a bad reputation, nicknamed the Widow-Maker and Flying Prostitute (with small wings that seemed to indicate "no visible means of support"), earned when it suffered several crashes early in its operational life. It was a hot aircraft and had a high landing speed. In 1942, as accidents persisted, the AAF investigated the aircraft to determine if production should be continued. The investigation board recommended several changes to the design, most importantly the installation of a bigger wing. These changes were made and the B-26 continued to fly throughout the war in the Pacific and the European theaters and, along with its competent crews, served admirably and significantly

contributed to victory. Goldberg, "AAF Aircraft of World War II," in Craven and Cate, *Army Air Forces*, VI:199–201.

13. The author is not sure of the meaning or origins of this saying, "the whole ball of yarn." It was probably a popular slang or aphorism from this era, possibly meaning something similar to "the whole nine yards."

14. Another aspect of Oscar being nicknamed "Pete," for Pedro, was that Oscar had a very dark complexion.

15. "History of Muleshoe," *City of Muleshoe, Texas*, accessed August 11, 2021, https://www.city-of-muleshoe.com/HistoryofMuleshoe. Muleshoe was a small farming/ranching community just inside Texas, about forty miles east of Clovis.

16. "History of Muleshoe."

17. Most of the B-29s that flew in World War II were built at Wichita, Kansas. Boeing, the Glenn L. Martin Company, and Bell Aircraft all built B-29s at Wichita; about four thousand were built during the war. Edward Phillips, "Wichita Builds the B-29," *KingAir Magazine*, July 29, 2016, http://www.kingairmagazine.com/article/wichita-builds-the-b-29/.

18. The B-24H was an improved version of the B-24D. Over three thousand were built by Ford Motor Company at its Willow Run, Michigan, plant. The main improvement featured by the H was better defenses, especially against head-on attacks. A turret was installed in the nose (very much like the tail turret) that gave better visibility for the bombardier and included twin .50 caliber guns with a broader range of fire. Additionally, the tail turret was modified for better gunner flexibility and visibility. The waist windows where the gunners fired .50-caliber guns were offset so that during a fight the gunners were not constantly bumping into each other. The top turret was also modified to give the gunner better visibility. "Consolidated B-24 Liberator," *Military Factory*, accessed September 6, 2020, https://www.militaryfactory.com/aircraft/detail.asp?aircraft_id=80.

Notes for Chapter 5

1. Rodney Baker, "The Man Who Founded Frontier Airlines," FARPA Newsletter, 2009, https://fal-1.tripod.com/Ray_WilsonArt09-08FARPA.pdf.

2. Cameron, *Training to Fly*, 390.

3. Cameron, *Training to Fly*, 394–95.

4. Cameron, *Training to Fly*, 395.

5. Wiley Grizzle Jr. to Wiley Sr. and Ollie Grizzle, November 1943, copy in author's possession, provided by Cindy Grizzle Pennington.

6. Wiley Jr. to Ollie, postmarked December 6, 1943, in author's possession, provided by Georga Didlake Collins.

7. Wiley Jr. to Ollie, December 9, 1943, in author's possession, provided by Pennington.

8. "The Link Flight Trainer," ASME International, June 10, 2020, https://www.asme.org/wwwasmeorg/media/resourcefiles/aboutasme/who%20we%20are/engineering%20history/landmarks/210-link-c-3-flight-trainer.pdf.

9. Wiley Jr. to Ollie Mae and Mary Grizzle, postmarked December 20, 1943, in author's possession, provided by Collins.
10. The author was unable to determine what 180-degree stages were.
11. Wiley Jr. to Wiley Sr., December 18, 1943, copy in author's possession, provided by Pennington.
12. The base at Garden City was built in 1943 and closed in 1947 and was thereafter the Garden City municipal airport.
13. Cameron, *Training to Fly*, 399.
14. Cameron, *Training to Fly*, 399.
15. Fred H. Allison, "Majors Field and Greenville, Texas in World War II," (MA thesis, Texas A&M University–Commerce, 1995), 154–55.
16. Cameron, *Training to Fly*, 396.
17. Goldberg, "Allocation and Distribution," in Craven and Cate, *Army Air Forces*, VI:398–99.
18. Wiley Jr. to Ollie, February 3, 1944, copy in author's possession, provided by Pennington.
19. Wiley Jr. here is saying that you can do these sophisticated maneuvers only in fighters, not bombers like the B-24 and B-17. He is poking fun at his big brothers Harold and Oscar.
20. Wiley Jr. to Ollie, postmarked Feb. 26, 1944, in author's possession, provided by Collins. Wiley Jr. at the top of this letter had drawn a picture of a B-24 and wrote: "This is a [B-]24 which Oscar & Harold fly. A crate."
21. Cameron, *Training to Fly*, 400.
22. Cameron, *Training to Fly*, 402.
23. Cameron, *Training to Fly*, 405.
24. Harold L. Allison, AAF official personnel and training files, in author's possession.
25. This came from him and his wife, Jean McKinstry Allison, telling the author about his wartime experiences.
26. Cameron, *Training to Fly*, 410.
27. Allison, *Love Lifted Me*, 75.
28. Allison, *Love Lifted Me,* 92.
29. Allison, *Love Lifted Me*, 99–100.

Notes for Chapter 6

1. "Over the Cauldron of Ploesti: The American Air War in Romania," *National WWII Museum*, August 12, 2019, https://www.nationalww2museum.org/war/articles/over-cauldron-ploesti-american-air-war-romania.
2. Barrett Tillman, *The Forgotten Fifteenth: The Daring Airmen Who Crippled Hitler's War Machine* (Washington, DC: Regnery History, 2014), ix–iix.
3. Tillman, *Forgotten Fifteenth,* 1.
4. Tillman, *Forgotten Fifteenth*, 1.
5. They never did have another, but the crew members stayed in touch with one another. Of all the crew, Oscar stayed in touch with Skeets the most in the passing years.

6. Damon A. Turner, "War Diary: 449th Bombardment Group," 449th Bomb Group (WWII), accessed September 6, 2020, https://449th.com/diaries/.

7. Turner, "War Diary."

8. Faulkner, *Flying with the 15th*, 70.

9. This flight was about 1,450 miles, and with a cruise speed of about 210 miles per hour, it would have taken about seven hours for the Sophisticated Lady to make this trip.

10. Turner, "War Diary."

11. Tillman, *Forgotten Fifteenth*, 5.

12. Tilman, *Forgotten Fifteenth*, 3; Roger A. Freeman, *The Mighty Eighth: A History of the US Eighth Army Air Force* (Garden City, NY: Doubleday, 1978), 99.

13. Damon Turner, *Tucson to Grottaglie*, book I of *History of 449th Bomb Group, World War II* (Huntington Beach, CA: 449th Bomb Group Association, 1985), 2.

14. Turner, "War Diary." Taranto was the largest town near Grottaglie, thirteen miles away; John E. Fagg, "The Aviation Engineers in Africa and Europe," in Craven and Cate, *Army Air Forces*, VII:260.

15. Fagg, "Aviation Engineers," in Craven and Cate, *Army Air Forces*, VII:260.

16. Turner, "War Diary."

17. Albert F. Simpson, "Anzio," in Craven and Cate, *Army Air Forces*, III:346.

18. "Fiat G.50 Freccia," *Plane Encyclopedia*, accessed August 17, 2023, https://plane-encyclopedia.com/ww2/fiat-g-50-freccia/. The Fiat G.50 saw its first combat in the Spanish Civil War. After World War II started in 1939, Fiat G.50s served in almost all theaters alongside Luftwaffe units. Fiats also flew with the Finnish air force during the 1941 campaign against Russia, and during the North African campaign, the Sicilian campaign, and then against Allied forces in the fight for Italy itself, although by this time most of Italy's Fiat G.50s had been lost.

19. Ollie Grizzle to Oscar Allison, January 23, 1944, photocopy, in author's possession.

20. Harold Allison to Oscar, February 4, 1944, photocopy, in author's possession.

21. Turner, "War Diary," entry for January 23 notes, "There have been several bad gasoline fires. This evening one severely injured several men."

22. Pilot Bird was out of commission four days, until January 29, when the crew was back to flying combat missions. See 716th Bomb Squadron Official History, Air Force Historical Research Agency Archives, Maxwell Air Force Base, AL, hereafter cited as AFHRA.

23. Deane C. Manning, "The Night the Stove Caught Fire," in *And This Is Our Story*, compiled by Don Lapham, book II of *History of 449th Bomb Group, World War II* (Huntington Beach, CA: 449th Bomb Group Association, 1985), 18.

24. These belonged to the 416th Night Fighter Squadron of the Twelfth Air Force. "Grottaglie," American Air Museum in Britain, accessed September 12, 2020, http://www.americanairmuseum.com/place/167693.

25. Ollie to Ed and Annie Allison, January 23, 1944, in author's possession, provided by Georga Didlake Collins.

26. "American Women and World War II," *Khan Academy,* accessed April 23, 2022, https://www.khanacademy.org/humanities/us-history/rise-to-world-power/us-wwii/a/american-women-and-world-war-ii.

27. Winkler, *Home Front U.S.A.*, 57–63.

28. "American Women in World War II."

29. Oscar to Ollie and family, February 18, 1944, photocopy, in author's possession.

30. "Special Report," January and February 1944, 449th Official Records, AFHRA.

31. Turner, *Tucson to Grottaglie*, 15–16.

32. Bill Ganzel, "Food for War," *Wessels Living History Farm,* accessed April 25, 2022; https://livinghistoryfarm.org/farming-in-the-1940s/making-money/food-for-war/; Stephanie Mercier, "Agriculture during Wartime: The Ingenuity of American Farmers During World War II," *AGWEB,* accessed April 25, 2022, https://www.agweb.com/opinion/agriculture-during-wartime-ingenuity-american-farmers-during-world-war-II.

Notes for Chapter 7

1. Official Records, January–February 1944, 716th Bomb Squadron, Special Accounts, January, February, 1944, AFHRA.

2. Simpson, "Anzio," in Craven and Cate, *Army Air Forces*, III:343–44.

3. Simpson, "Anzio," in Craven and Cate, *Army Air Forces*, III:358–60.

4. Oscar Allison to Ollie Grizzle and family, February 19, 1944, photocopy, in author's possession.

5. War diary, February 1944, 716th, AFHRA.

6. The Italians were now on the side of the Allies, having made an armistice on the previous September 8. While some Italian soldiers continued to fight alongside the Germans, in most cases they simply deserted or joined the Italian Resistance. "End of the Regime," *Britannica*, accessed April 26, 2022, https://www.britannica.com/place/Italy/End-of-the-regime.

7. Damon A. Turner, "War Diary: 449th Bombardment Group," 449th Bomb Group (WWII), accessed September 6, 2020, https://449th.com/diaries/.

8. Josip Broz Tito at this time was the supreme commander of the Yugoslav partisans who fought the Nazis in Yugoslavia. He became president in 1953 and remained so until his death in 1980. He was the first Communist leader to defy Soviet Russia. "Josep Broz Tito," *Britannica*, accessed August 16, 2023, https://www.britannica.com/biography/Josip-Broz-Tito.

9. The story of Sophisticated Lady's demise was authored by Gilbert (Gil) F. Bradley, the pilot who flew this last mission: "The Crew of 'Pistol Packin' Mama' Lays That Pistol Down," *Journal of Arizona History* 36, no. 4 (Winter 1995): 351–66.

10. John F. Guilmartin, "BF-109," *Britannica,* accessed January 11, 2021, https://www.britannica.com/technology/Bf-109.

11. Arthur B. Ferguson, "The Big Week," in Craven and Cate, *Army Air Forces*, III:36–41.

12. Craven and Cate, "Foreword," in Craven and Cate, *Army Air Forces*, II:xi–xii; Thomas J. Maycock, "TORCH and the Twelfth Air Force," in Craven and Cate, *Army Air Forces*, II:43; Dr. Silvano Wueschner, "Operation Argument ('Big Week'): The Beginning of the End of the German Luftwaffe," *Maxwell Air Force Base*, February 11, 2019, https://www.maxwell.af.mil/News/Display/Article/1754049/operation-argument-big-week-the-beginning-of-the-end-of-the-german-luftwaffe/; Turner, *Tucson to Grottaglie*, 22; Walter J. Boyne, "Forceful Argument," *Air & Space Forces Magazine*, December 1, 2008, https://www.airforcemag.com/article/1208argument/. In bombers lost, Craven and Cate show 226, while Boyne shows 194–247.

13. Craven and Cate, "Foreword," in Craven and Cate, *Army Air Forces*, II:xi–xii; Wueschner, "Operation Argument"; Turner, *Tucson to Grottaglie*, 22; Boyne, "Forceful Argument."

14. Ferguson, "Big Week," in Craven and Cate, III:41, 46, 58.

15. The name for this B-24, Pistol Packin' Mama came from a popular honky-tonk tune released in 1943. Originally recorded by Al Dexter, it was also recorded by Frank Sinatra, Bing Crosby, and the Andrews Sisters. Aircrews evidently considered it a great name for their aircraft. There was another B-24 in the 449th Bomb Group who named their B-24 Pistol Packin' Mamma. Note the spelling difference. There also was a B-24 of the 389th Bomb Group, Eighth Air Force, named Pistol Packin' Mama. See "42-40768 Pistol Packin Mama," *American Air Museum in Britain*, accessed October 28, 2022, https://www.americanairmuseum.com/aircraft/19800.

16. That this mission was fouled up from the beginning was attested to by Don Lapham, a copilot in the 719th Bomb Squadron, flying a B-24, in "Everything Went Wrong," in Lapham, *This Is Our Story*, 3–4.

17. Bob Bird, "Our Final Mission," in Lapham, *This Is Our Story*, 22.

18. Both Bird's and Manning's account of the fight and shoot down are in Lapham, *This Is Our Story*, 17–22. Here we see a significant discrepancy between Oscar's story of the bailout and Deane's. Memory is certainly not reliable, especially over thirty years. Exactly what happened we will never know.

19. Lapham, "Everything Went Wrong," in Lapham, *This Is Our Story*, 3.

20. War Diary, 716th Bomb Squadron, February 1944, AFHRA.

21. War Diary, 716th Bomb Squadron, February 1944, AFHRA.

22. Pistol Packin' Mama had gone down about a mile southwest of the Austrian town of Koglhof, which was about 25 miles northeast of Graz. The straight-line distance between Graz and the Swiss border is about 350 miles. So it was indeed impractical. Christian Arzberger, email correspondence with author, December 30, 2021. Arzberger has researched and documented the air war over Austria for years. His research and investigation of crash sites has resulted in a productive effort to commemorate and memorialize bomber crews that crashed in his native region of Syria.

23. Yugoslavia was closer, about seventy-five miles south of Koglhof. But the northern part of Yugoslavia, closest to Austria, was dominated by the Nazis at this time, who were supported by the native Croats and Slovenians. Tito's

partisans were strongest in southern Yugoslavia, a much greater distance from Austria.

Notes for Chapter 8

1. "Stalag Luft IV," accessed August 19, 2023, https://www.c-lager.com/stalag-luft-iv.html#:~:text=This%20newly%20acquired%20facility%20was%20 intended%20to%20hold,largest%20stammlagers%20administered%20by%20 the%20German%20Air%20Force.

2. McManus, *Deadly Sky*, 223; Christian Arzberger, email to author, August 28, 2022.

3. Karl R. Stadler and Otto Leichter, "Austria: Anschluss and World War II," *Britannica*, accessed March 25, 2021, https://www.britannica.com/place/Austria/ Anschluss-and-World-War-II; "The Story of Austrian Catholic Resister Franz Jägerstätter," *National WWII Museum*, April 11, 2019, https://www.nationalww2 museum.org/war/articles/story-austrian-catholic-resister-franz-jagerstatter.

4. Bob Bird, "Forty Years Later: Meeting with Our Opponents," in Lapham, *This Is Our Story*, 49.

5. Dulag is short for German Durchgangslager. These were processing centers where prisoners were given the basic supplies and clothing before being sent to a more permanent Stalag. Barrett Tillman, "German POW Camps in World War Two," *History on the Net*, July 6, 2018, https://www.historyonthenet.com/ world-war-two-german-pow-camps.

6. Official POW German documents, from Fold 3 On-Line Military Archive, copies in author's possession.

7. This information comes from German processing documentation; Fold 3 On-Line Military Archive.

8. Bird, "Forty Years Later," in Lapham, *This Is Our Story*, 49; Bob and Ann Bird to friends, Christmas letter 1984, copy in author's possession; H. R. Hemmler (Das Bundesarchiv), email to author, December 18, 2020; Kracker Luftwaffe Archive, "Axis Powers Pilots and Crew," accessed December 20, 2020https://aircre-wremembered.com/KrackerDatabase/?q=beckmann&qand=&exc1=&exc2 =&search_only=&search_type=exact.

9. Hemmler, email to author; Kracker Luftwaffe Archive, "Axis Powers."

10. Kracker Luftwaffe Archive, "Axis Powers."

11. This information comes from German processing documentation from Fold 3 On-Line Military Archive.

12. Indeed, they were headed for Dulag Luft-Oberusel, which was a central processing center for Allied airmen who had been shot down and captured. Here the recently acquired POWs were mildly interrogated, completed processing, and were forwarded to a Stalag.

13. Ollie Grizzle to Ed and Annie Allison, April 9, 1944, in author's possession, provided by Georga Didlake Collins.

14. I could find no reference to this individual in the records of the 716th; he must have been with another squadron of the 449th Bomb Group.

15. There was not a shelling of San Francisco by a Japanese submarine, but in the wake of the Pearl Harbor attack, California citizens were on high alert as news reports of various Japanese threats—aircraft, ships, and submarines—came with alarming frequency. There were Japanese submarine attacks on American freighters and tanker ships along the California coast during this time. Also, there was a shelling of an oilfield and refinery near Santa Barbara by a Japanese submarine on February 23, 1942. It is no doubt that AAF units in California were ready to defend the United States in response to any of these threats. William A. Goss, "Air Defense of the Western Hemisphere," in Craven and Cate, *Army Air Forces*, I:278–80.

Notes for Chapter 9

1. "World War Two: The Geneva Convention," *History on the Net*, accessed November 18, 2021, https://www.historyonthenet.com/world-war-two-the-geneva-convention.
2. "WW2 American Prisoner of War Relief Packages," *WW2 American Medical Research Center*, accessed August 18, 2023; Kim Guise, "A POW Thanksgiving 1944 in Stalag Luft IV," *National WWII Museum*, November 27, 2019, https://www.nationalww2museum.org/war/articles/pow-thanksgiving-1944-stalag-luft-iv.
3. "WW2 American Prisoner of War Relief Packages."
4. "Red Cross Parcels for POWs," *Cloud Corridor*, accessed June 6, 2022, https://cloudcorridor.blogspot.com/2009/02/red-cross-parcels-for-pows.html.
5. Ollie Grizzle to Ed and Annie Allison, April 12, 1944, in author's possession.
6. Oscar Allison to Ollie, February 27, 1944, photocopy, in author's possession, provided by Sam Allison.
7. Ollie to Ed and Annie, May 2, 1944, in author's possession. Wiley Jr. had entered the AAF and was selected for fighter pilot training.
8. Ollie to Ed and Annie, June 4, 1944, in author's possession.
9. Stephanie Carpenter, *On the Farm Front: The Women's Land Army in World War II, Gender and War Since 1600*, (Evanston: Northern Illinois University Press, 2003), https://gwonline.unc.edu/node/965.
10. University of Nebraska–Lincoln, "Agriculture," *Great Plains during World War II*, accessed March 29, 2022, http://plainshumanities.unl.edu/homefront/agriculture.html.
11. "Poethig, Hans Rudoph and Schmid, Walter," oral history abstract, *New Mexico Farm and Ranch Heritage Museum*, September 9 and 16, 1999, https://oralhistory.frhm.org/detail.php?interview=192.
12. Heydekrug, now known as Šilutė, Lithuania, was the site of Stalag Luft VI. Stalag Lufts were built specifically for airmen.
13. Compiled and presented by Greg Hatton, "Stalag Luft 6 at Heydekrug," accessed March 16, 2021, https://b24.net/powStalag6.htm. This site provides a wealth of firsthand accounts of life and conditions at Heydekrug.
14. Hatton, "Stalag Luft 6."

15. Oscar to Ollie, March 7, 1944, copy in author's possession, provided by S. Allison.
16. Oscar to Ollie and family, April 17, 1944, photocopy in author's possession, provided by S. Allison.
17. Oscar to Ollie and family, April 26, 1944, photocopy in author's possession, provided by S. Allison.
18. T/Sgt. Linden Voight in Hatton, "Stalag Luft 6."
19. S/Sgt Don Kremper (Kingston, NY) in Hatton, "Stalag Luft 6."
20. Oscar to Ollie and family, June 6, 1944, copy in author's possession, provided by S. Allison.
21. Ollie to Harold and Jean Allison, July 28, 1944, copy in author's possession, provided by Georga Didlake Collins.
22. Bradley, "Crew of 'Pistol Packin' Mama'," 356; Gil Bradley, "Bradley Tells of Epic Battle," in Lapham, *This Is Our Story*, 124.
23. Bradley, "Crew of 'Pistol Packin' Mama," 356.
24. Bradley, "Crew of 'Pistol Packin' Mama," 351–66; Bradley, "Epic Battle," in Lapham, *This Is Our Story*, 124.
25. "Prices for Cotton Reach 16-Year High," *New York Times*, June 23, 1944, https://www.nytimes.com/1944/06/23/archives/prices-for-cotton-reach-16year-high-market-here-is-most-buoyant-in.html.

Notes for Chapter 10

1. "Operation Bagration; Soviet Offensive of 1944," *HistoryNet*, July 25, 2006, https://www.historynet.com/operation-bagration-soviet-offensive-of-1944/; "Soviet Re-Occupation of the Baltic States (1944)," *Wikipedia*, accessed June 3, 2022, https://en.wikipedia.org/wiki/Soviet_occupation_of_the_Baltic_states_(1944).
2. Here Oscar is implying a shepherding role over his men, the crewmen on his B-24.
3. Carter Lunsford in Greg Hatton, compiler, "Stalag Luft 6 Heydekrug POW Camp History WWII," accessed June 2, 2022, https://www.b24.net/powLuft6.htm.
4. Hy Hatton in G. Hatton "Stalag Luft 6."
5. "Stalag Luft 6 Details," POWvets.com, accessed March 29, 2021, http://powvets.com/camp-locations/stalags-luft-misc/stalag-luft-6-details/.
6. G. Hatton, "The Heydekrug Run," accessed June 6, 2022, https://www.b24.net/powLuft6.htm.
7. Lester Schrenk, "The Evacuation of Stalag Luft VI," accessed June 6, 2022, https://www.airmen.dk/pdfs/schrenkevac.pdf.
8. Hatton, "Heydekrug Run," "Stalag Luft 6."; "Stalag Luft IV Details," accessed June 6, 2022, http://powvets.com/camp-locations/stalags-luft-misc/stalag-luft-iv-details/; Jenni Waugh, "Evacuation of Stalag Luft VI," *WW2 People's War*, accessed June 6, 2022, https://www.bbc.co.uk/history/ww2peopleswar/stories/10/a8252110.shtml; Schrenk, "Evacuation of Stalag Luft VI."
9. Schrenk, "Evacuation of Stalag Luft VI."

10. Mr. Biner, "Report of the International Committee of the Red Cross, Visit of Oct. 5 & 6, 1944, Stalag Luft IV," accessed June 6, 2022, https://www.b24. net/powStalag4.htm; "Stalag Luft 4 POW Camp Gross Tychow, Germany," accessed June 6, 2022.

11. Kim Guise, "A POW Thanksgiving 1944, Stalag Luft IV," *National WW2 Museum*, accessed June 8, 2022, https://www.nationalww2museum.org/war/ articles/pow-thanksgiving-1944-stalag-luft-iv.

12. Oscar Allison to Ollie Grizzle, photocopy, August 6, 1944, provided by Sam Allison.

13. Oscar to Ollie, photocopy, September 6, 1944, provided by S. Allison.

14. Oscar to Ollie, undated, provided by S. Allison.

15. The author is not sure of the meaning of "hot rocks." Since Harold and Junior were both officers and pilots, or soon to be in Junior's case, it might mean an officer's and pilot's uniform with the appropriate insignia displayed.

16. "The German Officers and Guards of Stalag Luft I," *World War II Prisoners of War*, accessed November 19, 2021, http://www.merkki.com/the_guards. htm.

17. For details on this European "death march," see G. Hatton, "The Death March," and Gary Turbak, "The Death March Across Germany," https:// www.b24.net/powMarch.htm; "Stalag Luft IV Details," POWVETS, accessed June 7, 2022, http://powvets.com/camp-locations/stalags-luft-misc/ stalag-luft-iv-details/.

18. Susan Rieger, Gerhard Jochem, "A Brief History of Nuremberg POW Camps," accessed June 4, 2022, https://www.b24.net/powNurembergCamps.htm, accessed 4 June 2022.

19. Another internee, Lt. Chauncey Rowan, a fighter pilot, recalled that they left Nuremberg on April 3 and arrived at Moosburg on April 20. See Graham E. Cross, *Jonah's Feet Are Dry* (Netherhall: Thunderbolt, 2002), 328.

20. Cross, *Jonah's Feet Are Dry*, 328.

21. Borrowed from one of the final scenes of the movie *Saving Private Ryan*, directed by Steven Spielberg (Hollywood, CA: Amblin Entertainment and Mutual Film, 1998).

Notes for Chapter 11

1. Cameron, *Training to Fly*, 402.

2. Wiley Grizzle Jr. to Ollie Grizzle, postmarked March 15, 1944, provided by Georga Didlake Collins.

3. Wiley Jr. to Ollie, postmarked April 18, 1944, provided by Collins.

4. Wiley Jr. to Ollie, April 22, 1944, provided by Cindy Grizzle Pennington.

5. Wiley Jr. to Ollie, postmarked May 13, 1944, provided by Collins.

6. Cameron, *Training to Fly*, 319. Flight officers were winged pilots, but they were more or less restricted to flying and could not be commanders of any size unit.

7. Wiley Jr. to Ollie, postmarked May 20, 1944, provided by Collins.

8. Robert Guttman, "Curtis P-40 Warhawk: One of WWII's Most Famous Fighters," *HistoryNet*, accessed January 25, 2023, *https://www.historynet.com/ curtiss-p-40-warhawk-one-of-ww-iis-most-famous-fighters/.*
9. Wiley Jr. to Ollie, undated, provided by Collins.
10. Wiley Jr. to Ollie, postmarked June 15, 1944, provided by Collins.
11. Wiley Jr. to Ollie, undated, provided by Pennington.
12. This is actually a blend of two letters. Wiley Jr. to Ollie, both in an envelope postmarked July 17, 1944, provided by Collins.
13. The M was a type of a Farmall tractor.
14. Wiley Jr. to Ollie, postmarked August 3, 1944, provided by Collins.
15. Wiley Jr. to Ollie, postmarked September 3,1944, provided by Pennington.
16. Jay A. Stout, *The Men Who Killed the Luftwaffe* (Guilford: Stackpole Books, 2010), 218.
17. "Flying the Beam," *National Air and Space Museum, Smithsonian Institution*, accessed June 14, 2021, https://timeandnavigation.si.edu/multimedia-asset/ flying-the-beam.
18. All of Wiley Jr.'s training information and details comes from his USAAF official personnel and training files, in author's possession; hereafter cited as Wiley Jr. files.
19. Wiley Jr. to Jim Grizzle, postmarked November 3, 1944, provided by Pennington.

Notes for Chapter 12

1. Ollie Grizzle to Harold and Jean Allison, April 12, 1944, provided by Georga Didlake Collins.
2. Wiley Grizzle to Harold and Jean, May 12, 1944, provided by Collins.
3. *Agricultural Statistics 1949*, US Department of Agriculture (Washington: U.S. Government Printing Office, 1949), 7, accessed June 9, 2022, https:// downloads.usda.library.cornell.edu/usda-esmis/files/j3860694x/7m01bp438/ n296x195z/Agstat-04-23-1949.pdf.
4. Ollie to Harold and Jean, July 28, 1944.
5. "Farmall M," *Tractor Data*, accessed January 28, 2023, http://tractordata.com/ farm-tractors/000/2/9/291-farmall-m.html.
6. Gerald Allison to Harold and Jean, July 28, 1944, provided by Collins.
7. *Agricultural Statistics 1949*.
8. "The History of Anti-Freeze," accessed June 19, 2022, https://ethylene-glycol. weebly.com/history.html.
9. Ethel Allison to Harold and Jean, July 28, 1944.
10. Allison, *Love Lifted Me*, 92.
11. "Doolittle Raid," *Naval History and Heritage Command*, accessed June 30, 2021, https://www.history.navy.mil/browse-by-topic/wars-conflicts-and-operations/world-war-ii/1942/halsey-doolittle-raid.html.
12. Cameron, *Training to Fly*, 412.
13. "B-25 Mitchell Bomber," *Boeing*, accessed June 2, 2022, https://www.boeing. com/history/products/b-25-mitchell.page; Goldberg, "AAF Aircraft of World War II," in Craven and Cate, *Army Air Forces*, VI:197.

14. *Pilot Training Manual for the B-25 Mitchell Bomber*, Headquarters, U.S. Army Air Forces Office of Flying Safety, accessed June 30, 2021, https://archive.org/details/PilotTrainingManualForTheMitchellBomber/page/n1/mode/2up; McManus, *Deadly Sky*, 33.

15. His B-25 crew was composed of: pilot, 2nd Lt. Thomas E. Roche; navigator, 2nd Lt. Charles L. Habgood; engineer/gunner, Cpl. James H. Archer; rear gunner, Cpl. Thomas J. Looby Jr.; gunner, Richard L. McMillan. Harold Allison, AAF files.

16. H. Allison, AAF files.

17. Allison, *Love Lifted Me*, 113–14.

18. H. Allison, AAF Files.

19. Stout, *Men Who Killed the Luftwaffe*, 216.

Notes for Chapter 13

1. Cross, *Jonah's Feet Are Dry*, xix.

2. Wiley Grizzle Jr. to family, undated, provided by Georga Didlake Collins.

3. Wiley Jr. to Ollie Grizzle, V-mail dated December 20, 1944, provided by Collins. His first flight in the P-51 occurred on Christmas Day. The Saturday he mentions was the twenty-third. The two-day delay might have been because of his cold or for any number of other reasons.

4. Graham Cross, email to author, March 6, 2022.

5. Cross, *Jonah's Feet Are Dry*, 98, 246.

6. Cross, *Jonah's Feet Are Dry*, 98, 247.

7. Cross, *Jonah's Feet Are Dry*, 157–58, 252.

8. Cross, *Jonah's Feet Are Dry*, 256–58.

9. Cross, email to author, March 6, 2021; Cross, *Jonah's Feet Are Dry*, 94–95.

10. Wiley Grizzle Jr., AAF files.

11. Larry Dwyer, "Republic P-47 Thunderbolt," *Aviation History Online Museum*, accessed January 28, 2023, http://www.aviation-history.com/republiOnc/p47.html; John F. Guilmartin, "P-51 Aircraft," *Brittanica*, accessed January 28, 2023, https://www.britannica.com/technology/P-51.

12. Freeman, *Mighty Eighth*, 235; Stout, *Men Who Killed the Luftwaffe*, 183.

13. Freeman, *Mighty Eighth*, 217; Curtis Fowles, "The P-51K Mustang," accessed June 12, 2021, http://www.mustangsmustangs.com/p-51/variants/p51k; Cross, *Jonah's Feet Are Dry*, 289.

14. Cross, *Jonah's Feet Are Dry*, 95, 117.

15. Why Wiley named his fighter G-Nat is, unfortunately, not known.

16. Cross, *Jonah's Feet Are Dry*, 125–26, 130.

17. Cross, *Jonah's Feet Are Dry*, 111.

18. Cross, *Jonah's Feet Are Dry*, 111–15; William Lyons, "A Mustang Pilot's Mission: A Day in the Life," *HistoryNet*, accessed June 16, 2021, https://www.historynet.com/p-51-pilot-a-day-in-the-life.htm.

19. Cross, *Jonah's Feet Are Dry*, 111–13.

20. The life preserver was nicknamed after Mae West, a famous movie star of the time who had a generous bust. The name was first used by British flyers early

in the war. The inflatable bladders of the life preserver lay over the chest, thus giving the wearer a "generous bust." "How a Life Jacket Came to be Named After Mae West," *Word Histories,* accessed August 21, 2023, https://wordhistories.net/2018/03/09/mae-west-life-jacket/.

21. Gs, meaning gravity, is the force felt on one's body when turning, diving, or climbing in a sharp manner. Fighter pilots might experience a force of up to six times the force of gravity during combat, meaning their body weighed six times more than what it normally weighed.

22. This is a newspaper clipping that was obtained from family and the name of the newspaper and its date is not included with the clipping, author's files; Cross, *Jonah's Feet Are Dry*, 277.

23. Cross, *Jonah's Feet Are Dry*, 113–14.

24. Cross, *Jonah's Feet Are Dry*, 114; Lyons, "Mustang Pilot's Mission."

25. Wiley Grizzle Jr., AAF files.

26. Cross, *Jonah's Feet Are Dry*, 65–67.

27. Cross, *Jonah's Feet Are Dry*, 149.

28. Cross, *Jonah's Feet Are Dry*, 289; Wayne K. Blickenstaff, *Ace in a Day* (Philadelphia: Casemate, 2022), 210.

29. Fagg, John E., "The Climax of Strategic Operations," in Craven and Cate, *Army Air Forces*, III:725–26.

30. Blickenstaff, *Ace in a Day*, 221.

31. Wiley Jr. to Ollie, February 1, 1945.

32. Wiley Grizzle Jr., AAF files.

33. Cross, *Jonah's Feet Are Dry*, 105.

34. Fagg, "Climax of Strategic Operations," in Craven and Cate, *Army Air Forces*, III:732.

35. Cross, *Jonah's Feet Are Dry*, 589.

Notes for Chapter 14

1. Cross, *Jonah's Feet Are Dry*, 339-340; Stout, *Men Who Killed the Luftwaffe*, 232; Fagg, "Climax of Strategic Operations," in Craven and Cate, *Army Air Forces*, III:732–33.

2. Blickenstaff, *Ace in a Day*, 218–19.

3. Cross, *Jonah's Feet Are Dry*, 589.

4. Cross, *Jonah's Feet Are Dry*, 340–41; Fagg, "Climax of Strategic Operations," in Craven and Cate, *Army Air Forces*, III:734. The P-51 was especially vulnerable to small-arms fire because the Merlin inline engine, as good as it otherwise was, had one significant flaw: it was liquid cooled. Other fighters prominent in World War II, the P-47 Thunderbolt, the Marine Corps' F4U Corsair, or the Navy's F6F Hellcat, had air-cooled radial engines. A bullet hit to a radial engine, in most cases, did little harm. Hitting a coolant line in the P-51, however, would cause a leak of coolant and a pilot only had minutes of powered flight left.

5. "Douglas A-26 Invader," *Aviation History Online Museum*, accessed January 30, 2023, http://www.aviation-history.com/douglas/a26.html. The Douglas A-26 Invader was a twin-engine light bomber and attack aircraft. It was introduced

later in the war. The earliest combat deployment was September 1943 in the Pacific theater. The A-26 did not go to the European theater until a year later.

6. Harold L. Allison to Wiley Grizzle Jr., February 16, 1945, provided by Georga Didlake Collins.

7. This comes from a newspaper clipping, unidentified newspaper and date, provided by the children of Mary Andreas (née Grizzle), the youngest daughter of Ollie and Wiley Grizzle.

8. Fagg, "Climax of Strategic Operations," in Craven and Cate, *Army Air Forces*, III:737–38.

9. Cross, *Jonah's Feet Are Dry*, 341. From Major Walter Boone's, strike leader, testimony about this mission.

10. Cross, *Jonah's Feet Are Dry*, 341, 591–92.

11. Cross, *Jonah's Feet Are Dry*, 591.

12. Cross, *Jonah's Feet Are Dry*, 667.

13. Cross, *Jonah's Feet Are Dry*, 341.

14. 350th Fighter Squad Encounter Reports for February 27, 1945, author's files, courtesy of G. E. Cross; Cross, *Jonah's Feet Are Dry*, 592.

15. Cross, *Jonah's Feet Are Dry*, 341–42.

16. Wiley Jr. to Mary Grizzle, February 28, 1945, provided by Collins.

17. In the European theater the AAF allowed pilots to officially count enemy aircraft parked at an airfield as "kills." This was not allowed in the Pacific theater. Pilots knew the difference.

18. Wiley Jr. to Ollie, March 1, 1945, V-letter, provided by Collins.

19. Harold to Wiley Jr., March 5, 1945, provided by Collins.

20. Fagg, "Climax of Strategic Operations," in Craven and Cate, *Army Air Forces*, III:739, 745.

21. Fagg, "Climax of Strategic Operations," in Craven and Cate, *Army Air Forces*, III:746.

22. Blickenstaff, *Ace in a Day*, 227.

23. March 1945 and June 1944 tie as suffering the most losses, twenty during the month, either killed in combat or an accident, taken as prisoner of war, shot down but evading capture, or rescued. Cross, *Jonah's Feet Are Dry*, 669–70.

24. Wiley Grizzle Jr., AAF files.

25. Fagg, "Climax of Strategic Operations," in Craven and Cate, *Army Air Forces*, III:744.

26. Fagg, "Climax of Strategic Operations," in Craven and Cate, *Army Air Forces*, III:746. Operation Varsity was the largest airborne assault ever in one place on the same day: sixteen thousand troops, American and British, were dropped into Germany by parachute or were glider borne.

27. Fagg, "Climax of Strategic Operations," in Craven and Cate, *Army Air Forces*, III:747.

28. Cross, *Jonah's Feet Are Dry*, 350–51.

29. Freeman, *Mighty Eighth*, 222; Cross, *Jonah's Feet Are Dry*, 350–52.

30. "Sattenhausen," accessed October 12, 2022, http://wiki-goettingen.de/index.php/Sattenhausen; Cross, *Jonah's Feet Are Dry*, 351–52.

31. Aces in a day refers to shooting down five enemy aircraft in one day.
32. Cross, *Jonah's Feet Are Dry*, 351–52.
33. Cross, *Jonah's Feet Are Dry*, 352.
34. Cross, email to author, August 15, 2012. This email provides an excerpt of an interview that Cross did with Second Lieutenant Onkey in 1991, hereafter cited as Onkey interview. This account is also in Cross, *Jonah's Feet Are Dry*, 606.

    When the crash site was located later, there was hardly anything by which to identify the aircraft or the pilot. The aircraft might have exploded in flight, then smashed into the ground at a high speed and burned. Sattenhausen was a village of less than five hundred people about forty miles northeast of Kassel. Individual Deceased Personnel File (IDPF) in author's possession, hereafter cited as IDPF.
35. Onkey interview.
36. To pickle fuel tanks meant to drop them. This was done to allow the aircraft to better maneuver without fuel tanks hung on the wings.
37. Stout, *Men Who Killed the Luftwaffe*, 260–62; Cross, *Jonah's Feet Are Dry*, 605–6
38. Cross, email to author, August 15, 2012.
39. Ollie to Wiley Jr., March 8, 1945, provided by Collins.
40. J. A. Ulio, Major General, Adjutant General, War Department, to Ollie, April 12, 1945.
41. "Sattenhausen," *Wikipedia*, April 21, 2020, https://en.wikipedia.org/wiki/Sattenhausen.
42. Ollie to Wiley Jr., June 10, 1945, V-Mail letter, provided by Cindy Grizzle Pennington.

Notes for Chapter 15

1. "POW Camp Stalag VII-A," accessed March 24, 2021, https://www.moosburg.org/info/stalag/indeng.html. Moosburg, or Stalag VII-A, in southern Bavaria was Germany's largest POW camp.
2. Frank Murphy, "The Liberation of Moosburg," *Splasher Six*, 33, no. 2 (Summer 2002), ed. Cindy Goodman, https://100thbg.com/index.php?option=com_content&view=article&id=509:the-liberation-of-moosburg&catid=8&Itemid=120. Murphy provides a detailed description of Stalag VII-A as it was when Oscar was there.
3. Coincidentally, as Oscar's column moved south from Nuremberg toward Moosburg, they were within about thirty-five miles of Regensburg and thus the area where he had been shot down and captured.
4. The battle for Moosburg was, as Oscar says, fairly short, but it was deadly. Efforts to negotiate a surrender had failed and the fight was on. The 14th Armored Division liberated the camp, and a wild celebration ensued. It was pandemonium as the POWs exploded with emotion. An American air corps lieutenant kissed a tank.

"God damn, do I love the ground forces," he said. "This is the happiest day of my life!" "You were a long time coming, but now you are here!" Murphy, "Liberation of Moosburg."

5. Patton toured the Stalag on May 1, 1945: "He was dressed in a crisp, neat, fresh uniform and wearing his legendary wide black leather belt with a huge silver buckle to which were attached his famous paired set of ivory-handled six-guns. Maj. Gen. James A. Van Fleet, III Corps Commander, and Maj. Gen. Albert C. Smith, commander of the 14th Armored Infantry Division, accompanied General Patton. As he walked briskly through the camp General Patton occasionally stopped and exchanged a few brief words with small groups of American prisoners. When he came upon my group the General paused, looked at us, shook his head in disgust at the sight of the thin, unkempt scarecrows standing before him and said in a low voice, 'I'm going to kill these sons of bitches for this.'" Murphy, "Liberation of Moosburg."

6. Murphy, "Liberation of Moosburg."

7. "Camp Lucky Strike: Ramp Camp No. 1," accessed March 26, 2021, https://www.nationalww2museum.org/war/articles/camp-lucky-strike.

8. "Camp Lucky Strike."

9. "Camp Lucky Strike."

10. The USS *Lejeune* (named after the Marine Corps general John A. Lejeune) started life as a German cargo liner, having been built in Germany and completed in 1936. When World War II broke out, to flee the Royal Navy the *Lejeune*—its German name was *TS Windhuk*—sailed to Brazil in 1939. When Brazil broke ties with Germany and interned the ship, the German crew did extensive damage to it, to prevent its use by the Allies. The US government bought the *Windhuk* and repaired it to a seaworthy condition. By June 11, 1944, it was in service as a troopship, much needed at the time. Decommissioned in 1948, it was cut up for scrap in 1966. Only its bell survived, and it was eventually displayed at the Carolina Museum of the Marine. Here it is rung each morning in memory and honor of all Marines who made the ultimate sacrifice for Corps and Country. "The Lejeune Bell," *Carolina Museum of the Marine, Al Gray Civic Institute*, accessed December 6, 2020, https://www.museumofthemarine.org/stories/the-lejeune-bell/.

11. Camp Kilmer was an army base that was the largest processing point for troops going to war in Europe and returning from Europe.

12. Ollie Grizzle to Annie and Ed Allison, July 8, 1945, provided by Georga Didlake Collins.

13. Larry Allison, email to author, October 27, 2022.

14. Ivo de Jong, *Mission 376: Battle over the Reich, May 28, 1944* (Mechanicsburg, PA: Stackpole Books, 2012), 246–47; Aubrey Hewatt official AAF records, provided by Mack Allison; comments, Mack Allison.

15. Allison, *Love Lifted Me*, 129–31.

16. Susan Black, interview by author, May 15, 2022.

17. John P. Onkey to Ollie, postmarked March 11, 1946, provided by Cindy Grizzle Pennington

18. Onkey interview. He says in this interview that he had holes in his canopy and wing root. This type of damage would be characteristic of machine-gun fire from another aircraft, not antiaircraft fire. See also pg. 238, nn. 33 and 35.
19. Maj. Gen. Edward F. Witsell to Ollie, March 13, 1946, provided by Collins.
20. Onkey to Ollie. This letter was in the same envelope as the letter from Onkey noted above, postmarked March 11, 1946. The letter itself is not dated. Provided by Pennington.
21. Ollie to Major General Witsell, April 24, 1946, IDPF.
22. Major General Witsell to Ollie, May 7, 1946, IDPF.
23. First Lieutenant Reid to Ollie, May 17, 1946, IDPF, provided by Collins.
24. August Seebode, IDPF.
25. Heinrich Buermann, IDPF.
26. Paul Krope IDPF.
27. "Checklist of Unknowns," IDPF.
28. These three Christmas cards are all undated, except for the year noted by Ollie, and were in the same envelope (unaddressed.
29. Colin Colbourn, email to author, June 5, 2017.
30. Larry Allison, email to author, October 27, 2022.

Epilogue

1. The following account is referenced by Ann and Bob Bird to Friends, December 1984; Christopher Hammer, "World War II Flyer Returns To Scene of Capture In Austria," *Assabet Valley Beacon*, undated, copy in author's possession; Bird, "Forty Years Later," in Lapham, *This Is Our Story*, 49.
2. Bird, "Our Final Mission," in Lapham, *This Is Our Story*, 22.
3. Ann and Bob Bird to Friends, December 1984.
4. Bird, "Forty Years Later," in Lapham, *This Is Our Story*, 49; Bob and Ann Bird to Friends, Christmas letter 1984.
5. Bird, "Forty Years Later," in Lapham, *This Is Our Story*, 49
6. Fred Allison, "Monument Man," *Aviation History*, Spring 2023, 9.
7. Larry Allison, email to author, October 27, 2022.

Bibliography

Documents

350th Fighter Squadron. Encounter Report, February 27 1945. Official records, World War II. Air Force Historical Research Agency Archives. Maxwell Air Force Base, AL.

449th Bombardment Group (Heavy). Official records, World War II. Air Force Historical Research Agency Archives. Maxwell AFB, AL.

716th Bombardment Squadron Official History. Air Force Historical Research Agency Archives. Maxwell AFB, AL.

Allison, Fred H. "Majors Field and Greenville, Texas in World War II." MA thesis. Texas A&M University–Commerce, 1995.

Allison, Oscar I. "Memories of World War II, 1973. Unpublished manuscript.

Army Air Forces. Harold L. Allison Official Personnel and Training Files, 1943–1945.

Army Air Forces. Wiley Jr. Grizzle Official Personnel and Training Files, 1943–1945.

Hewatt, Aubrey E. Copies of selected documents from operation records.

Turner, Damon A. "War Diary: 449th Bombardment Group." 449th Bomb Group (WWII). Accessed September 6, 2020. https://449th.com/diaries/.

Articles

Allison, Fred H. "Monument Man." *Aviation History*, Spring 2023.

Baker, Rodney. "The Man Who Founded Frontier Airlines." *FARPA* Newsletter. 2009. https://fal-1.tripod.com/Ray_WilsonArt09-08FARPA.pdf.

Boyne, Walter J. Boyne. "Forceful Argument." *Air & Space Forces Magazine*, December 1, 2008. https://www.airforcemag.com/article/1208argument/.

Bradley, Gilbert F. "The Crew of 'Pistol Packin' Mama' Lays That Pistol Down." *Journal of Arizona History* 36, no. 4 (Winter 1995): 351–66.

Correll, John T. "But What About the Air Force?" *Air Force Magazine*. July 2009. https://www.airforcemag.com/PDF/MagazineArchive/Documents/2009/July%20 2009/07 09Corps.pdf.

Fleischman, John. "The Barnstormer."_Smithsonian. August 2021. https://www. smithsonianmag.com/air-space-magazine/barnstormer-1-180978267/.

Hammer, Christopher. "World War II Flyer Returns To Scene of Capture in Austria." *Assabet Valley Beacon*, undated.

Murphy, Frank. "The Liberation of Moosburg." *Splasher Six*, 33, no. 2 (Summer 2002), ed. Cindy Goodman. https://100thbg.com/index.php?option=com_content&view= article&id=509:the-liberation-of-moosburg&catid=8&Itemid=120.

New York Times. "Prices for Cotton Reach 16-Year High." June 23, 1944. https:// www.nytimes.com/1944/06/23/archives/prices-for-cotton-reach-16year-high- market-here-is-most-buoyant-in.html.

Phillips, Edward. "Wichita Builds the B-29." *KingAir Magazine*. July 29, 2016. http:// kingairmagazine.com/article/wichita-builds-the-b-29/.

Smith, Kiona N. "The Correction Heard Round the World: When the *New York Times* Apologized to Robert Goddard." *Forbes*. July 19, 2018. https://www.forbes.com/ sites/kionasmith/2018/07/19/the-correction-heard-round-the-world-when-the- new-york-times-apologized-to-robert-goddard/?sh=70d42c124543.

Wills, Matthew. "Robert H. Goddard: The Forgotten Father of Modern Rock-etry." *JSTOR Daily*. Accessed August 30, 2023. https://daily.jstor.org/robert-h-goddard-the-forgotten-father-of-rocketry/.

Books

Allison, Veta Jean. *Love Lifted Me*. San Antonio: Litho Press, 2012.

Ashcroft, Bruce A. *We Wanted Wings: A History of the Aviation Cadet Program*. Randolph Air Force Base, TX: HQ, AETC/HO, 2005.

Bird, Bob. "Forty Years Later: Meeting with Our Opponents." In Lapham, *This Is Our Story*, 49.

Bird, Bob. "Our Final Mission." In Lapham, *This Is Our Story*, 22.

Blickenstaff, Wayne K. *Ace in a Day*. Philadelphia: Casemate, 2022.

Bradley, Gil. "Bradley Tells of Epic Battle." In Lapham, *This Is Our Story*, 124.

Cameron, Rebecca H. *Training to Fly: Military Flight Training, 1907–1945*. Washington, DC: Air Force History and Museum Program, 1999.

Carpenter, Stephanie. *On the Farm Front: The Women's Land Army in World War II, Gender and War Since 1600*. Evanston: Northern Illinois University Press, 2003. https://gwonline.unc.edu/node/965.

Craven, Frank W., and James Lea Cate, eds. *The Army Air Forces in World War II*. 7 vols. Washington, DC: Office of Air Force History, 1983.

Craven, Frank W., and James Lea Cate. "Foreword." In Craven and Cate, *Army Air Forces*, II:v–xiv.

Craven, Frank W., and James Lea Cate. "Foreword." In Craven and Cate, *Army Air Forces*, VI:v–xliv.

Cross, G. E. *Jonah's Feet Are Dry: The Experience of the 353rd Fighter Group in World War II*. Netherhall: Thunderbolt, 2002.

Cross, G. E. *Slybirds: A Photographic Odyssey of the 353rd Fighter Group During the Second World War*. Fighting High, 2017.

Curry, Helen. "The Beginning." In Farrington, *Meeting the Train*, 15–23.

de Jong, Ivo. *Mission 376: Battle over the Reich, May 28, 1944*. Mechanicsburg, PA: Stackpole Books, 2012.

Fagg, John E. "The Aviation Engineers in Africa and Europe." In Craven and Cate, *Army Air Forces*, VII:239–75.

Fagg, John E. "The Climax of Strategic Operations." In Craven and Cate, *Army Air Forces*, III:715–55.

Farrington, William, ed. *Meeting the Train: Hagerman, New Mexico and Its Pioneers*. Compiled by the Hagerman Historical Society. Santa Fe: Sleeping Fox Enterprises, 1975.

Faulkner, Tom. *Flying with the 15th Air Force: A B-24 Pilot's Missions from Italy during World War II*. Denton: University of North Texas Press, 2018.

Ferguson, Arthur B. "The Big Week." In Craven and Cate, *Army Air Forces*, III:30–66.

Freeman, Roger A. *The Mighty Eighth: A History of the US Eighth Army Air Force*. Garden City, NY: Doubleday, 1978.

Futrell, Frank. "The Development of Base Facilities." In Craven and Cate, *Army Air Forces*, VI:119–68.

Goldberg, Alfred. "AAF Aircraft of World War II." In Craven and Cate, *Army Air Forces*, VI:193–227.

Goldberg, Alfred. "Allocation and Distribution of Aircraft." In Craven and Cate, *Army Air Forces*, VI:398–424.

Goss, William A. "Air Defense of the Western Hemisphere." In Craven and Cate, *Army Air Forces*, I:271–309.

Greer, Thomas H. "Individual Training of Flying Personnel." In Craven and Cate, *Army Air Forces*, VI:557–99.

Kooker, Arthur R. "Basic Military Training and Classification of Personnel." In Craven and Cate, *Army Air Forces*, VI:527–56.

Kooker, Arthur R. "Broadening the Basis of Procurement." In Craven and Cate, *Army Air Forces*, VI:427–53.

Lapham, Don, comp. *And This Is Our Story*. Book II of *History of 449th Bomb Group, World War II*. Huntington Beach, CA: 449th Bomb Group Association, 1985.

Lapham, Don. "Everything Went Wrong." In Lapham, *This Is Our Story*, 3–4.

Lapham, Don, comp. *Grottaglie and Home*. Book III of *History of 449th Bomb Group, World War II*. Huntington Beach, CA: 449th Bomb Group Association, 1989.

Lindbergh, Charles A. *The Wartime Journals of Charles A. Lindbergh*. New York: Harcourt, Brace, Jovanovich, 1970.

Manning, Deane C. "The Night the Stove Caught Fire." In Lapham, *This Is Our Story*, 18.

Maycock, Thomas J. "TORCH and the Twelfth Air Force." In Craven and Cate, *Army Air Forces*, II:41–66.

McManus, John C. *Deadly Sky: The American Combat Airmen in World War II*. New York: NAL Caliber, 2016.

Simpson, Albert F. "Anzio." In Craven and Cate, *Army Air Forces*, III:325–70.

Stout, Jay A. *The Men Who Killed the Luftwaffe*. Guilford: Stackpole Books, 2010.

Tillman, Barrett. *The Forgotten Fifteenth: The Daring Airmen Who Crippled Hitler's War Machine*. Washington, DC: Regnery History, 2014.

Turner, Damon A. *Tucson to Grottaglie*. Book I of *History of 449th Bomb Group, World War II*. Huntington Beach, CA: 449th Bomb Group Association, 1985.

Winkler, Allan M. *Home Front U.S.A.: Americans during World War II*. Wheeling, IL: Harlan Davidson, 2000.

Movies

Saving Private Ryan. Directed by Steven Spielberg. Hollywood, CA: Amblin Entertainment and Mutual Film, 1998.

Index